'Carpani makes an important contribution to contemporary psychosocial theory from a Jungian perspective. It will be of wider interest to clinicians, activists and theorists as they continue the debate about how the world makes us.'

Susie Orbach, *Psychoanalyst, Writer and Social Critic, UK*

'By opening a dialogue between Jung's psychological notion of individuation and Ulrich Beck's sociological notion of individualization, Stefano Carpani has created a foundational bridge that will bear fruitful insights for generations to come. Carpani has single-handedly established an I–thou relationship between the work of Jung and Beck that is a major breakthrough and achievement for both traditions in the notion of "relational psychosocial studies".'

Thomas Singer, *Psychiatrist and Jungian Psychoanalyst, USA*

'In this much-needed commentary on individuation and individualism, Stefano Carpani has clarified the theoretical and clinical issues surrounding Jung's and Jungians' use of individuation as the ideal goal of human development. By blending sociological and psychoanalytic perspectives into a nuanced and precise relational model, Carpani helps us understand the demands on human identity in our second-late-modern era. As a result, psychoanalytic clinicians and theorists can distinguish between the suffering of identity pathologies from ordinary existential stresses of late-modern identity development. I strongly recommend this very useful treatise.'

Polly Young-Eisendrath, *Jungian Psychoanalyst and Zen Buddhist, USA*

'Carpani has emerged as a leading figure among a new generation of Jungian analysts and theoreticians. His *Absolute Freedom* stands as a singular contribution to the growing sense of Jung's significance in the 21st century. While the book focuses on the relationship between Jung's theory of individuation and Ulrich Beck's analysis of individualization in late modernity, Carpani's masterful command of the sociological literature, as well as the work of Jung and the post-Jungians, promises to move our understanding of depth psychology's place in the larger cultural and political world in new and creative directions. With implications that reach well beyond analytical psychology, this book is highly recommended.'

George B. Hogenson, *Jungian Psychoanalyst, former vice-president IAAP, USA*

'With this work Stefano Carpani wants to build a bridge from sociology to psychoanalysis, from Beck with his principle of individualization as a main characteristic of our time to the individuation process of C.G. Jung, a lifelong process of transformation, involving conscious and unconscious influences, leading to a transitional identity: The merger of "I+I", how Stefano Carpani calls his theory. Does it bring us new insights? A relational psychosocial approach – to understand the developments of the narratives of self-identity today, leading to the "Absolute" freedom. Absolute freedom understood by Carpani as psychic and social freedom from the influences of authorities – in individuals psychologically understood as freedom from the constellated complexes. The main thesis of this book is an interesting and long-overdue consideration: It is self-evident that we all live in social relations, that society has an influence on us, and that there is a reciprocal effect between the social world and our psychic inner world. But these ideas have been given far too little attention in the relevant theories until now. It is the merit of this work of Carpani to change that. Interesting and thought-provoking is the direction of his thoughts: from today's current individuation as described by Beck back to the individuation of C.G. Jung. This basic idea of Carpani is broadly underpinned by the theories of Beck and Jung, by further diverse sociological and psychoanalytical theories. By presenting a clinical case Carpani shows himself as a clinician who builds a bridge from his work as a clinician to his theory "I+I". Lots of ideas, references and approaches in this book are stimulating, and above all they encourage further questions. An important field of mutual psychosocial influences is opened.'

Verena Kast, *Jungian Psychoanalyst and former president IAAP and the CGJIZ, CH*

Everything happens as it should happen; for if things should be different from what they are, they would be otherwise!

Sholem Aleichem

Absolute Freedom

Within this book, the fields of analytical psychology and sociology combine to examine and explore current social theory and the concept that the author has termed 'absolute freedom'.

This work serves as a vital contribution to contemporary social and psychoanalytic research, unveiling the intricacies of psychological and social dynamics in our current epoch. Stefano Carpani explores the intersection of psychology and sociology, providing a fresh perspective beyond conventional boundaries. It conducts a comparative analysis of C.G. Jung's individuation process and Ulrich Beck's individualization theory, presenting the groundbreaking 'I+I' merge. This latter concept acts as a linchpin in deciphering self-identity narratives in the 21st century's dynamic landscape, before the author introduces the concept of absolute freedom, contextualizing it within the multifaceted complexities of contemporary second-late-modern existence.

This compelling new book will be of great interest to academics, scholars and students in the fields of analytical psychology, sociology and psychosocial studies.

Stefano Carpani, Ph.D., is a psychoanalyst and sociologist (member and lecturer of the C.G. Jung Institute Zürich and post-graduate of the University of Cambridge). He initiated the YouTube series *Breakfast at Küsnacht, Lockdown Therapy* and *War as Reset*, co-created *Psychosocial Wednesdays* and currently chairs it. He also curates *Jungianeum: Initiatives for Contemporary Analytical Psychology and Neo-Jungian Studies*, the book series titled *Re-covered Classics in Analytical Psychology* and *Neo-Jungian Studies* and the *JUNGIANEUM/Yearbook*. For the Italian magazine *Doppiozero*, he hosts a column titled 'Cultivating the Soul in the SuperSociety'. He serves as a scientific consultant to Pacifica Graduate Institute (USA). Among his edited books are *Breakfast at Küsnacht* (Chiron, 2020 – IAJS Best Edited Book nominee) and *Anthology of Contemporary Classics in Analytical Psychology: The New Ancestors* (Routledge, 2022 – GRADIVA Best Edited Book nominee).

Absolute Freedom

Individuation and Individualization in Second-Late-Modern Societies

Stefano Carpani

Routledge
Taylor & Francis Group

LONDON AND NEW YORK

Designed cover image: © Courtesy of Olivia Carpani Ruano

First published 2025
by Routledge
4 Park Square, Milton Park, Abingdon, Oxon, OX14 4RN

and by Routledge
605 Third Avenue, New York, NY 10158

Routledge is an imprint of the Taylor & Francis Group, an informa business

© 2025 Stefano Carpani

The right of Stefano Carpani to be identified as author of this
work has been asserted in accordance with sections 77 and 78 of
the Copyright, Designs and Patents Act 1988.

British Library Cataloguing-in-Publication Data
A catalogue record for this book is available from the British Library

Library of Congress Cataloging-in-Publication Data
A catalog record has been requested for this book

ISBN: 978-1-032-48785-4 (hbk)
ISBN: 978-1-032-48784-7 (pbk)
ISBN: 978-1-003-39077-0 (ebk)

DOI: 10.4324/9781003390770

Typeset in Times New Roman
by codeMantra

For Andrew Samuels

Contents

Acknowledgements

I am especially grateful to Andrew Samuels, who, in 2016, not only acknowledged the significance of my research topic but also generously offered his support by becoming my supervisor. Since our initial meeting, Andrew has evolved into more than just a mentor; he has become a cherished friend and, in his own words, a mentoree. This work is dedicated to him.

I extend my gratitude to the teachers I have encountered since commencing my training at the Carl Gustav Jung Institute in 2015. They are Alessandro Albizzati, Günter Langwieler, Ursula Brasch, Verena Kast, Wolfang Giegerich, Marianne Meister and John Beebe.

Foreword

Introduced near the dawn of the 20th century, the practice of psychoanalysis was 75 years old before the cinema auteur Jean Luc Godard was able to reduce it to a visual wisecrack that announced to the world that psychoanalysis had laid an egg. At the beginning of a film of his that I saw in 1968, the year I began psychiatric residency, 'Weekend', the yoke of that egg dripping down her back was a recent memory, recalled by a patient trying to interest her analyst in its fate – a sociological absurdity that Durkheim would have loved. What could possibly come of such an exercise was the question my generation of future analysts was often led to ask. I was glad that at least I had opted for training in Jungian psychoanalysis. Five decades later, the author of this book has provided it with a whole New Wave of answers to that question. Stefano Carpani's mind pulses with particles of present-day psychosocial theory, and reading his book has recovered for me some of the energy that propelled me, along with many of my own generation of analysts, to buck the tide that told us not to waste our time. Instead, we have spent a lifetime making sense of what an analytic relationship can offer. What we didn't see when we started, but this book shows with commendable realism, is that while we were individualizing ourselves to become Jungians in a Freudian world, the world beyond us was just as busy individualizing itself. Soon enough, the 'Freudians' were even more relational than we were. All we Jungians had managed to do, sociologically speaking, was to keep pace with the momentum of a cultural moment.

But that was indeed something, given that the moment was so confusing. Already by 1970, Paul Goodman, whose *Growing up Absurd* had a decade earlier been calling for it, was describing the global counterculture that by then had emerged 'a farrago of misunderstood styles'.[1] He was talking about the hippies, whom he would not survive, but among the alt-styles that the hippies encouraged, and that he would have cynically disparaged, was the move from Freudian psychoanalysis to Jungian analysis. Those of us who did just that, and in Zurich style faithfully recorded and listened to our dreams for decades, discovered that a new social consciousness was being hatched in our sleeping selves. Andrew Samuels, in 1993, called this 'the political development of the person', the year before I had called it 'integrity in depth' and in 2000, an American presidential election year, Thomas Singer called it 'the vision thing'.

These catchphrases and the books that embedded them represented our individuation out of merely using analysis to individualize ourselves.

It is gratifying therefore to see that Dr. Carpani, someone about the age my colleagues and I were when we became aware that were birthing a form of Jungian analysis that was as relational as it was individual, has been able to make what we had to reach even to understand the basis of a new Jungian formula for the release of creative psychosocial energy. It's the agency permitted by that energy that Dr. Carpani calls absolute freedom. The recipe he has come up with is one that he no doubt developed himself in the course of becoming an analyst, but it seems to me to have been informed by noting what we elders had found contradictory about trying so hard to redeem our individuality. The deeply social vision of integrity he has distilled in this book is singularly his own, a novel notion of freedom that he is not afraid to describe as 'absolute'. I would call it having the option to choose how to regulate one's uniqueness in a socially constructive way without having to sacrifice any of the creativity that inheres in profoundly needing to be oneself. If I read his formula, "I+I" = absolute freedom, right, what comes of having two kinds of self is two I's, which I prefer to read as a pair of eyes. That's what Stefano Carpani has absolutely freed up, for those of us whose psychological minds have too long been caught up in trying to decide which eye belongs to self and which to the Self (a quandary that hasn't helped our discernment): the reality that we can use both of these I's to see with. Should it surprise us that such a simple insight also delivers the world to the psyche, disclosing to the latter its sociological context?

—John Beebe, Psychiatrist and Jungian Psychoanalyst, USA

Note

1   Goodman, Paul. Notes of a neolithic conservative. *New York Review of Books*, March 26, 1970, issue, online https://www.nybooks.com/articles/1970/03/26/notes-of-a-neolithic-conservative/.

Introduction

This book, with its publication, brings a stage of my life to an end. One might think that this work of mine began in 2016, when I sent my PhD proposal to Andrew Samuels at the Centre for Psychoanalytic Studies (now the Department of Psychosocial and Psychoanalytic Studies) at the University of Essex. Yet, the truth is that this book (whose fundaments can be found in my doctoral work at Essex) is a continuation of the work I started already in Manchester and Cambridge when I was an M.A. and M.Phil. student in their respective sociology departments.

It was in that biennium (2002/2003 and 2003/2004) and in that context that I became familiar with the work of Ulrich Beck and his *individualization process*. So, with this publication, I complete a work that has lasted 20 years. It is a work that I suspended after graduating from Cambridge University (2004) and that I resumed in 2016, in parallel with the beginning of my training at the Carl Gustav Jung Institute in Zurich in 2015.

What have I been doing since 2002 and especially since I started my doctoral research at Essex? I tried to look at the interaction between the social and the psychic perspective, and in doing so I drew on my academic and personal experience.

After Cambridge, I had to leave the academy partly because I was faced with personal difficulties but even more because I was faced with a theoretical dilemma: I could not fully answer the question that my research had posed: *what is the nature of the development of narratives of Self-identity at the beginning of the 21st century?* This is because the approach proposed by traditional sociology was not *good/convincing enough* for me. I realized, in 2015, that what it lacked (or to better phrase it: what I was missing) was the perspective brought about by depth psychology, and in particular, by analytical psychology.

So, I had to wait more than ten years to realize – thanks to the contamination proposed by analytical psychology and psychosocial studies – that the social is influenced by the psychic and vice versa. Therefore, I found in the context of analytical psychology and psychosocial studies a frame of reference suitable for my purpose and for continuing my research.

In essence, in this work, I propose that in current 21st-century second-late-modern societies, there is a renewed need for individuation. Therefore, this book provides an in-depth look at the concepts of individualization, individuation and freedom.

DOI: 10.4324/9781003390770-1

Here, I attempt a comparative study of Carl Gustav Jung's individuation process and Ulrich Beck's individualization theory, leading to a proposed merger of the two into a new third. The intention in creating this third, which I term 'I+I' (from individuation and individualization), is not to engender a brand-new perfect theory, particularly as it will lie within the spectrum of two theories and theorists who are, in the scheme of things, relatively minor; nevertheless, this merging of 'I+I' may serve in some measure to support current social theory and psychoanalytic research as well as to reinforce the discourse undertaken by psychosocial studies since the 1990s and by relational psychoanalysis since the 1980s.

Therefore, this comparison will serve to introduce a new configuration of *Jungian relational psychosocial studies*, wherein Jung is used to consider the psychic and Beck the social aspects. I will also propose that by employing such an approach the ways in which psychic experience and social life are fundamentally entangled can be examined.

To this end, I will suggest that the 'missing unconscious in sociology' is a fact and that traditional sociology has failed to take the unconscious into account. I will also claim that it is not sufficient merely to adopt a Freudian sociology (as in classical drive theory) or a post-Freudian sociology (and psychosocial studies)[1] and that Jung's immense contribution must also be considered, without, however, claiming that a Jungian approach is sufficient on its own – this too would be a mistake. Instead, I propose that Jung and the post-Jungians be studied alongside Freud and the post-Freudians (as well as alongside all the major contributors in this field), as is the case in relational psychoanalysis.

When looking at sociology, I will underline that it knows very much about Freud and very little of Jung, and when it does, it is inclined to trivialize Jung and even associate him with New Age thinking (see Bauman and Giddens) or National-Socialism (see Benjamin).

I argue that a relational approach to sociology, psychoanalysis and psychosocial studies (hence to *relational psychosocial studies*) is necessary for a number of different reasons: First, a relational psychosocial approach would be pluralistic, or in the words of Jungian analyst Andrew Samuels (1989, p.XII), it would be 'an approach to conflict that tries to reconcile differences without imposing false synthesis on them and, above all, without losing sight of the particular value and truth of each element in the conflict'. Second, as claimed by psychoanalyst Susie Orbach (2014, p.16), similarly to psychosocial studies, relational psychoanalysis:

> starts from the premise that the individual is born into a set of social and psychological circumstances. The human infant is a set of possibilities – not id based, not instinctually driven – but in order to become recognised as a human, will need to attach.[2]

Third, a new approach and even a new attitude of inclusion (to replace the split and separation typical of the history of psychoanalysis) would be beneficial, thereby avoiding the use of approaches that are school-driven or limiting. Relational psychoanalysis would allow for a cross-school approach with relationality set at the centre of the discussion.

In attempting to show the validity and usefulness of this new approach, in this study, I will answer the following research questions: What is the best tool to understand the nature of development of narratives of Self-identity at the beginning of the 21st century?

I will answer this question underlining that, to better understand the current world as it is (and also to provide a response to Beck's latest work *The Metamorphosis of the World* (2016)), there is imminent necessity to build a bridge from sociology towards psychoanalysis, or from Beck's individualization to Jung's individuation (and not vice versa), and in so doing, to leave behind traditional sociology in order to open the door to the unconscious with a relational psychosocial approach. Doing so may help to answer my research question, and thereby to understand the nature of the development of narratives of Self-identity at the beginning of the 21st century. This, in turn, leads to a second question: Are we really free in a second-late-modern society?

To answer these questions and to frame this research, it is also important to address the concepts of modernity and second modernity. As I have argued elsewhere (2004):

> Modernity is the term used to refer to the ways of living, or social organizations, which appeared in Europe around the 17th century and extended their influence to most of the world. [...] an essential element of modernity is the notion of change and progress.

As underlined by historians Maiken Umbach and Bernd Huppauf (2005, p.8), modernity is 'a matter of movement, of flux, of change, of unpredictability' rather than something static. Modernity is the period that corresponds to the beginning of modern society. According to sociologist Anthony Giddens (1998, p.94), modernity 'is associated with a certain set of attitudes toward the world, the idea of the world as open to transformation by human invention'. Modernity evolves into what Beck and Beck-Gernsheim (2002) call 'reflexive modernization' or 'second modernity', what Giddens (1990) calls 'high' or 'late' modernity and what sociologist Zygmunt Bauman (2000) calls 'liquid' modernity. This is characterized by the intensification and speeding up of aspects such as reflexivity (Beck, Giddens, and Lash, 1994) and the reduction of space and time separation (Giddens, 1990).

Furthermore, it is not easy to accurately define when second modernity began, and researchers' opinions vary in this respect. For clarity, I will adopt Beck's view that second modernity is the epoch that began concomitant with the collapse of the Berlin Wall and the Soviet empire. Thus, it was an epochal shift that changed 'the social and political landscape' forever (Beck, 2002, p.XX), a time that heralded the end of a world divided and separated into two poles, and the start of a globalized world. We can say for sure that the roots of second modernity lie in the revolutionary movements of 1968, in 1970s' neoliberalism, in *perestroika* and in other factors such as the end of the industrial model which characterized the late 19th and early 20th centuries. Second modernity, therefore, is a time of transformation from a society based on gender and class certainty into a post-gender, post-class society (Beck, 2002).

Giddens (1990) argues that late modernity diminishes the distinction between space and time. I contend that second-late modernity further intensifies this blurring of boundaries. Also, Umbach's and Huppauf's (2005, p.8) concepts of flux, change and unpredictability become accelerated. This period, in the radicalization of Marcuse's definition of modernity as 'advanced industrial society' (Marcuse, 1986 [1964], p.XV), can also be named 'advanced electronic society' or 'accelerated electronic society'.

In this work, amongst the wide range of possible definitions, I prefer to refer to the present epoch as a 'second-late modernity' or 'second-late individualized society', as I consider the current era to have followed the previous without a break. The start of this epoch can be traced back to the launch of the first iPhone in 2007, because the incorporation of this technology in our daily lives changed it radically in terms of how and when we relate to others and the world.[3]

Research structure

The process of establishing this new approach will be conducted in several steps. Chapters 1 and 2 will focus on a literature review of Jung and Beck (respectively) regarding whom, to my knowledge, there have been no previous comparative studies, a gap that this book will thus address.

In Chapter 1, I will include an explanation of Jung's theory of individuation. According to Jung, 'Individuation is the process in which the patient becomes what he really is' (CW16, par.11). It is the development of one's psyche towards wholeness. As beautifully clarified by Jung's pupils and psychoanalysts Marie-Louise von Franz and Jolande Jacoby, individuation is 'a process by which man lives out his innate human nature' (von Franz, 1964, pp.163–164).

> [It is a] spontaneous, natural process within the psyche; it is potentially present in every man, although most men are unaware of it. [...] it is a process of maturation and unfolding. [...] under certain circumstances, in practical psychotherapy for example, it can in one way or another be stimulated, intensified, made conscious, consciously experienced, and elaborated. The individual can thus be helped to 'complete' or 'round out' his personality.
>
> (Jacoby, 1973, p.107)

In examining Jung's concept of individuation, I will claim that it evolved throughout his lifetime, as did several of his key concepts – particularly the Self. I will parallel Jung's *Collected Works* with summaries thereof written by Marie-Louise von Franz and Jolande Jacoby, and by the post-Jungians James Hillman, Tom Singer and Samuel L. Kimbles, Andrew Samuels and Mary Watkins. In so doing, I will point out that Jung should be considered a pioneer of psychosocial studies and relational psychoanalysis.

Following on from this, I will stress that, according to Jung, both the group and the individual are influenced by multiple factors such as family, society, politics, the concept of the world they live in and religion, and I will link this with the concept of psychosocial studies. I will do so employing the work of two psychosocial theorists, Stephen Frosh and Michael Rustin (amongst others), and claim that psychosocial studies consider the psychological, the social and the cultural as means to study the relationship between individuals and their social situation.

This also applies to relational psychoanalysis, and here, I will employ the work of Jungian (relational) psychoanalyst Andrew Samuels,[4] to investigate the role of Jung as a founding father of relational psychoanalysis, while psychoanalysts Lewis Aron, Jessica Benjamin and Susie Orbach (amongst others) will be used to frame a definition of relational psychoanalysis.

Having looked at Jung, society and sociology, and on the post-Jungian tradition, I will then move on to consider Beck's individualization (as well as Anthony Giddens' and Zygmunt Bauman's views on the reflexivity of the self).

In contrast to individuation, individualization cannot be stimulated: One simply finds oneself in the midst of it, because it is not a spontaneous process of the psyche. Rather, it is a social process that is related solely to second-modern societies. According to Beck (2002, p.5), when individualizing, people become *homo-optionis* where 'life, death, gender, corporeality, identity, religion, marriage, parenthood, social ties – all are becoming decidable down to the small print'. When individualizing, therefore, 'everything must be decided' (Beck, 2002, p.5).

Beck and Beck-Gernsheim (1995, p.8) claim that individualization 'occurs in the wealthy western industrialized countries as a side effect of the modernization process designed to be long term' and that everyone born after 1950 has to be considered individualized.

In *The Normal Chaos of Love*, Beck (1995, p.6) notes that:

individualization means that men and women [are] released from the gender roles prescribed by industrial society for a life in the nuclear family. At the same time, and this aggravates the situation, they find themselves forced, under pain of material disadvantage, to build up a life of their own by way of the labour market, training and mobility, and if need be to pursue this life at the cost of their commitments to family, relations and friends.

In examining Beck, I will underline the importance of his approach within the context of current sociological thinking.[5] I will claim that the copyright of individualization theory (renamed 'The reflexivity of the self' by sociologist and 'Third Way' theorist Anthony Giddens) is more properly owned by Beck than Giddens. In so doing, I will take a closer look at the Polity Press Circle (particularly those that theorized high/ late (Giddens, 1990) and liquid (Bauman, 2000) modernity, while sociologists David Held, Scott Lash, John B. Thompson and John Urry will not be mentioned).

This will also lead me – in Chapter 3 – to address the influence of psychoanalysis on traditional sociology. I will examine whether Beck was influenced by and/ or whether he draws from Freud (or any other psychoanalytical school). This then begs the question: Has traditional sociology grasped the essence of Freud's theory of the unconscious? I am aware that Freud has been used (or misused) by those conceptualizing second modernity (as also happened with many other authors, including the Frankfurt School in particular), and for this reason, I will also examine Theodor Adorno, Max Horkheimer and Herbert Marcuse,[6] trying to assess their point of view on psychoanalysis – and conclude that a sociological investigation is appropriate only when paralleled by a relational (non-dogmatic) psychoanalytic approach. My aim is to demonstrate that traditional sociology is not equipped to take into account the unconscious (not even when it misuses Freud's work, and especially looking at Marcuse's *Eros and Civilization* and Beck (and the Polity Press Circle) due to two factors. First, traditional sociology exclusively takes into account classical drive theory; second, because of an ontological bias that is related to the genesis of sociology itself: that is, it is the study of society that contemplates mere rational and cognitive aspects of human behaviour (and the fact that traditional sociology is not interested in the individual but in the collective).

Throughout this work, I will contrast the above-mentioned views with those of Erich Fromm, Jessica Benjamin, Lynne Layton, Chiara Giaccardi and Mauro Magatti (proposing that we need a psychosocial approach instead of a sociological one).

Having introduced Jung's and Beck's theories in Chapters 1 and 2 and having shown the lack of extant comparative analysis between the two, in Chapter 4, I will address this research gap by conducting a critical comparison of their theories to ascertain the commonalities and differences between them (even making a checklist of what makes a person individuated and/or individualized).

I will also investigate whether, upon deeper examination, one presents a mere sociological model and the other a mere psychological one, whether Jung's individuation should be considered an a-temporal process and whether Beck's individualization can be linked solely to late modernity and the West.

In this chapter, it will be shown that while Beck (2002, p.X) recognizes the depth-psychological use of the term individuation, he does not expand the topic[7] and therefore fails to acknowledge the importance of the unconscious (collective or individual).

Additionally, this investigation and comparison of Beck and Jung arises from the fact that Beck's term 'individualization' is almost identical to Jung's 'individuation'. However, it seems that Beck paid little attention to Jung's work (not even as a critical reversion of such[8]), and the question then arises: Why did Beck use the term individualization? Is there a nexus between individuation and individualization, and if so, where does it lie? While Beck does discuss the difference between individualization and individualism, his neglect of the concept of individuation is a serious one. Perhaps Beck simply rejected Jung's oeuvre and understanding of the unconscious, drawing – as the Frankfurt School tended to do – from an orthodox and dogmatic approach to Freud. It is unclear whether Beck was aware of the potential relevance of the unconscious, and if so, to what extent.

A second question then arises: How do people, according to Beck and Jung, respectively, make decisions and what is the role of the conscious and unconscious in people's decision-making processes? This is an important question because it will help to illuminate the differences and similarities (particularly in relation to the unconscious) between Jung and Beck, which will be necessary to create a merger of their ideas. Furthermore, the above-mentioned checklist of what makes a person individuated and/or individualized might help to answer this question. I will, therefore, challenge Beck, emphasizing the importance of studying 'the individual' (the psyche) in relation to social issues.

I will claim that Jung's individuation theory is a possible frame (albeit not the only) within which to ascertain the deficits in Beck's theory of individualization (and therefore traditional sociology in general) and will underline that while individualization is a given in second-modern societies, on its own, it does not lead to freedom, not even to the freedom to dictate one's own biography of self.

Having conducted a comparative analysis of Jung and Beck's individuation and individualization theories respectively, in the second half of Chapter 4, I will introduce the 'I+I' concept, meaning individuation in a late-modern individualized society (which enables absolute freedom). The 'I+I' takes Beck's individualization process to be a valid picture of second modernity and merges it with Jung's individuation process. It is an attempt to claim that in order to attain freedom in second modernity, and thus to fulfil one's destiny, people need to individuate once they are individualized.

By introducing the 'I+I', my aim is to create a third concept, that results from a merger, and not a synthesis, hybrid or integration, of Beck's and Jung's respective concepts. I prefer to employ the concept of a merger because it implies something relational, while the other three terms do not. Additionally, according to the *Cambridge Dictionary*, to merge[9] means to 'to combine or join together'. According to the *Oxford Dictionary*, it means to create a single entity or to blend so that what is combined together becomes indistinguishable and this reflects my precise intention when examining Jung's and Beck's theories. Therefore, a merger can only happen by mutual agreement. It is not forced and transformed into something new: a third.

A merger is also not a synthesis[10] which, according to the *Oxford Dictionary*, means to place together and, in Hegelian philosophy, it denotes the conclusive phase in the dialectical reasoning process, where a novel concept resolves the conflict between the thesis and antithesis. Here, however, there is no thesis or antithesis. There are merely two valid theses (Beck's and Jung's), which I wish to merge to create a third: The 'I+I'.

A merger is also not a hybrid,[11] which, again according to the *Cambridge Dictionary*, is aimed to 'to get better characteristics' like when 'a plant or animal that has been produced from two different types of plant or animal'. While a hybrid could work theoretically, since my working idea is to merge psychoanalysis and sociology and thus to create a third, nevertheless, to pursue the definition of the hybrid as set out in the *Oxford Dictionary*, 'crossing a donkey with a horse: what you get is strong but it's completely sterile'.

Finally, integration,[12] according to the *Oxford Dictionary*, usually means integrating something into something else. However, this may also entail segregation and forced adaptation and thus I prefer a pluralistic approach as suggested by Samuels (1989) and indeed by relational psychoanalysis in general since the 1980s.

In merging the two theories (which is, according to the *Cambridge Dictionary*,[13] to '(cause to) combine or join: e.g. The sea and sky appear to merge at the horizon' or 'to change gradually into something else: e.g. Summer slowly merged into autumn'), I wish to employ the method used by philosopher Paul Ricoeur (1977, p.59) when studying Freud. This means not giving 'an interpretation on a single level but rather a series of readings each of which is both completed and corrected by the following one'. My intention is to follow Ricoeur's method in considering Jung and Beck as two readings that, when merged, will help to shed light on the nature of the development of narratives of Self-identity in late modernity. These two readings will bring me to propose a third (the 'I+I') that completes and corrects the previous two and that will also be corrected and completed (or disputed) by a following one.

The way to clarify my analytic generalization (leading to the creation of an ideal type) is to employ a clinical case. Thus, in Chapter 5, I will examine the biography of a patient of mine, Carla, from three different perspectives – individuation (Jung), individualization (Beck) and 'I+I' – to ascertain whether these two could be considered individuated, individualized or 'I+I'.

Carla emerged as a patient with a nuanced sociological perspective, skillfully navigating the complexities of an individualized society. On one hand, she boldly confronted the established norms of modern life, challenging societal constructs such as the order of the nation-state, class distinctions, gender roles, ethnic boundaries and the conventional family structure. Her pursuit was centred on self-fulfilment and achievement. However, concurrently, albeit subconsciously, she found herself ensnared in the existential impasse eloquently articulated by Bauman. In our initial session, Carla articulated a pervasive sense of emptiness, a feeling of being immobilized and a recurring pattern of impermanence in her romantic relationships.

Employing this method will demonstrate the need to merge the first two theories into a third and to prove that the merging of psychoanalysis and sociology into relational psychosocial studies is the correct move to understand current society and the individual. It will also demonstrate that the 'I+I' is an alternative and competent way to examine the current development of narratives of Self-development at the edge of psychoanalysis and sociology and thereby, to frame and contextualize my analytic generalization within the 21st-century context.

Finally, in the concluding chapter, I will recapitulate my findings. I will reiterate that Beck's research is fundamental to portraying and understanding second modernity and how people make decisions in shaping their own lives. I will claim that a renewed look at Jung's individuation process is fundamental in any attempt to examine our current epoch, particularly if we wish to understand how people duel within a psychological and social context (agency and structure), which is always a conscious/unconscious process. I will claim that a merge between individualization and individuation, or 'I+I', is key to understanding the nature of development of narratives of Self-identity at the beginning of the 21st century. I will stress the need to view Jung as a pioneer who examined the psyche as a whole, including its rational and irrational aspects (including synchronicity and meaningful incidences that are connected to the psyche such as the meaning of diseases, etc.).

Therefore, I will also underline that, when conceptualizing 'I+I', it may be beneficial to employ relational psychoanalysis and psychosocial studies for current investigation and thus to move to a relational psychosocial approach. Only once the 'I+I' has been introduced will I be able to discuss what I call *absolute freedom*.

Research methods

From a research methods point of view, I have divided my work into two parts. One comprises a theoretical presentation and assessment of my analytical generalization, employing Beck and Jung. The other part is intended to confirm my analytical generalization (leading to the creation of an ideal type), by investigating the biography of a patient of mine. The method employed in the second part will use data taken from individual colloquia with the patient, including the following: (i) notes from my sessions with this patient; (ii) the use of materials, such as dreams, as well as active imagination.

This material will be used to illustrate the 'I+I' concept and the fact that the Jungian relational psychosocial model could serve to support individuals to individuate in an individualized society.

Notes

1 In the *Introductory Lectures on Psychoanalysis* (1991, p.216), Freud claimed that 'Sociology [...], dealing as it does with the nature of people in society, cannot be anything other than applied psychology'. I will also emphasize that it is not sufficient to have a 'Freudian philosophy' such as the Frankfurt School, for example, because such is one sided.
2 This quote will appear many times from now. This is to reiterate Orbach's concept.
3 What I call second-late-modernity, Giaccardi and Magatti (2022, pp.80–81) term *supersociety*. This is: (1) constituted, first of all, by the intensity, density and extension of technical mediation in the relationship with reality; (2) with the supersociety, the framework of interdependencies is such that it is unrealistic to think separately about social organization and the planetary ecosystem; (3) the supersociety is qualified by the level reached in the human's capacity for self-production. [...] What is new is that supersociety tends to incorporate the entire human organism, in all its biological and cognitive dimensions, within its own dynamics. Translated from Italian by the author.
4 Private conversation (2017).
5 Looking in particular at *Risk Society* (1992), *The Normal Chaos of Love* (1995), *Individualization* (2002).
6 Initially, I wanted to also look at contemporary sociologists Eva Illouz and Byung-Chul Han. Lately, I decided to not do so to concentrate on Beck, Bauman and Giddens.
7 'There is a lot of misunderstanding about this concept of individualization. It does not mean individualism. It does not mean individuation – a term used by depth psychologists

to describe the process of becoming an autonomous individual [...]. Nor, lastly, does it mean emancipation as Jurgen Habermas describes it' (Beck, 2002, p.X).

8 After looking into Beck's work, I can state that there is no evidence of his interest in Jung's work, although he underlined (Beck, 2002) that the term *individuation* had been employed by depth psychologists. Of course, one can assume, because of his universal knowledge, that he was aware of the concept of individuation and even of Jung. But there is no evidence of his in-depth knowledge about both. I looked into the opportunity to interview his widow (and co-author) Elisabeth Beck-*Gernsheim*, to uncover the reasons for ignoring Jung's work, but I did get no answer from her.

9 See: https://dictionary.cambridge.org/dictionary/english/merge?q=to+merge.

10 See: https://en.oxforddictionaries.com/thesaurus/synthesis.

11 See: https://dictionary.cambridge.org/dictionary/english/hybrid.

12 See: https://en.oxforddictionaries.com/thesaurus/integration.

13 See: http://dictionary.cambridge.org/dictionary/english/merge.

Chapter 1

Individuation

C.G. Jung and the post-Jungians

The aim of Chapters 1 and 2 is to engage in a literature review of Jung[1] and Beck.[2] No previous studies have compared the works of these authors (a gap that this research seeks to address) and although Beck (2002, p.X) recognizes the use of the term 'individuation' by depth psychologists, he does not elaborate.

My intention here is to introduce Jung's individuation[3] process by employing Jung's own texts as a magnifying lens to show how individuation links to society and early sociology. I will also examine those authors who have furthered analytical psychology, taking Jung as an inspiration. To this end, I will examine selected post-Jungians – Progoff, Hillman, Samuels, Singer and Kimbles and Watkins – and claim that – following Samuels[4] – the post-Jungians rectified Jung's approach but have omitted serious consideration of sociological perspectives from their investigation. Consequently, I will expand my remit to take in both sociological and psychosocial points of view. Subsequently, returning to the field of depth psychology, I will turn to psychosocial studies and relational psychoanalysis and claim that Jung must be considered a pioneer of both, therefore, a pioneer of psychosocial studies.

C.G. Jung and the process of individuation

Like several of his key concepts, Jung's process of 'individuation' evolved over time.[5] As noted by M. Stein (2005), it is in *Septem Sermones ad Mortuos* (1916a) that Jung first introduced the term, referring to it as *principium individuationis*,[6] although it can already be traced in *Symbols of Transformation* (CW5).[7] It could be argued, however, that all of his writings are, in fact, steeped in the process, concluding with *Mysterium Coniunctionis* (CW14).

It is important to underline that while Jung was not the first to introduce such a concept, he was the first psychoanalyst to do so. Before it was picked up by psychoanalysis in the early 20th century, the *principium individuationis* had remained exclusively in the domain of philosophy and indeed can be said to have shaped the whole history of philosophy in different epochs, from its first traces in Plato's *Symposium* and Aristotle's *Metaphysics*, to Saint Thomas Aquinas' *Summa Theologiae* and Liebniz's *Über das Individuationsprinzip* (Jarrett, 1981). More recently, Schopenhauer (*The World as Will and Representation*) and Nietzsche (*The Birth of*

DOI: 10.4324/9781003390770-2

Tragedy) furthered the discussion, and both greatly influenced Jung's own thought, as did Kant, Freud, William James (Jarrett, 1981) and Hegel (McFarland Solomon, 2007). However, Jung's work was also heavily influenced by the early French sociology of Durkheim and Comte (Progoff, 1955), not just by 18th-century philosophy or his psychiatric masters in Zürich and Paris.

What then is the individuation process, according to Jung?[8] It is one's own 'identification with the totality of the personality, with the Self' (Jung, 1990, p.138) and a process 'of differentiation, having for its goal the development of the individual personality' (Jung, CW6, para.757). Thus, individuation is a time when the individual is 'a point of intersection or a dividing line, neither conscious nor unconscious, but a bit of both' (Jung, CW7, para.507).

von Franz (1964, pp.163–164) describes individuation as 'a process by which man lives out his innate human nature', adding that it is more than a simple acceptance of one's 'inborn germ of wholeness and external fate' but is rather 'as if something is looking at me [...] – perhaps that Great Man in the heart, who tells me his opinions about me by means of dreams'.

According to Jung (CW7, para.501), the aim of analysis is to empower the patient with 'adequate knowledge of the methods by which he can maintain contact with the unconscious, and has acquired a psychological understanding sufficient for him to discern the direction of his life-line at the moment'. Thus, analysis helps to identify the lifeline which, as Stein (2005, p.10) notes, 'looks ahead, not backward'. For Jung, analysis means (alchemical) transformation, development and differentiation from the collective, and thus becoming oneself, while therapy, on the other hand, means curing from an illness.

In this regard, Casement (2001, p.147) claims that in addition to becoming 'wholly and indivisibly oneself', individuation also means 'gathering the world to oneself in order to fulfil collective qualities more completely and satisfactorily'. Thus, individuation is intended to be intrinsically antithetical to any individualism or narcissism that a given person may harbour. This definition will later help us to contextualize the work of Beck and my own 'I+I' (see Chapters 3 and 4).

C.G. Jung's transcendent function

What Jung termed the 'transcendent function' (the union of conscious and unconscious contents) is key to analytical psychology and also fundamental to the claim that, when examining the individual and society, we cannot avoid examining the interaction between unconscious and conscious aspects. This is crucial to the innate transformational (even healing) aspect of humans and to some extent also of society, since Jung (CW7, p.186) claims that 'the transcendent function [...] leads to the revelation of the essential man', adding that it is a natural process 'which may [...] pursue its course without the knowledge or assistance of the individual'. Ultimately, he underlines that 'the meaning and purpose of the process is the realization, in all its aspects, of the personality originally hidden away in the embryonic germ-plasm; the production and unfolding of the original, potential wholeness'.

Therefore, the transcendent function is a process that enables the unfolding of something hidden, something that we are but do not know we are and that lies at the interface of conscious and unconscious, of the individual and collective. I would argue that this process is key to making sense of the world in which we live today and should be considered the basis for the 'I+I' and its consequent absolute freedom (see Chapter 4 and Conclusions).

C.G. Jung, society and sociology

While Jung´s roots in philosophy,[9] anthropology and ethnology[10] have been well documented, my aim here is to show that the concept of society (and early 19th-century sociology) is crucial to both Jung´s thinking and 'the process of individuation'.[11] It is also my opinion – following Progoff – that Jung built his theory on early French sociology (especially Durkheim and Comte, to whom Lévy-Bruhl is related).

Attempting to justify my reference to Progoff, it is important to underline that he was the first to link Jung with sociology and society and has influenced later writers. However, he does not justify his choice of Durkheim[12] and seems not to understand the question of structure *versus* agency in sociological theory.[13]

Progoff (1955, p.61) underlined Jung´s avoidance of the tendency, common amongst psychologists, 'to regard society as merely the plural of the individual'. Rather, notes Progoff, Jung sees man's social quality as inherent to human nature, and thus 'the individual must be understood in terms of the social situation in which he lives' (1955, p.167).[14] Progoff also claimed that since the individual comes before society, they cannot live without society, or indeed culture (Progoff, 1955, p.161).

Progoff then suggests that Jung's concept of the collective unconscious was inspired by Durkheim's collective representations or 'basic beliefs and assumptions about the nature of things' that are common to members of a given group and passed down or indeed imposed through the generations (1955, pp.167–168). I would argue that these assumptions emphasize the importance of society and sociological ideas in Jung's individual development as a psychoanalist.

Furthermore, 'in understanding the individual as a derivate of society, [Jung] is following his more fundamental idea that "consciousness comes from the unconscious"' (Progoff, 1955, pp.163–164). In other words, just as 'the process of bringing psychic contents to consciousness involves a sharpening and clarifying of the ambiguities of the unconscious, so the individual emerges out of society by a process of differentiation and individualization' (Progoff, 1955, pp.163–164). Here, again, we may find a link with the transcendent function.

What Jung called the social (a mix of traits from a specific society and culture) comprises the cradle within which an individual is born. It comprises not only the unconscious – hence the deeper layers of the collective unconscious – but is also linked to the concept of mother.[15] A good example is the noun *mother-tongue* (rather than father-tongue or native-tongue), which demonstrates the strong interconnectedness between the other (mother and society/culture) and the baby. Examined biologically, historically, anthropologically and psychologically, the mother spends the most time with the baby at the beginning of life, and her language and culture/society comprise the first input to an individual's identity.

That being the case, perhaps the social should be considered the mother itself (where we come from), from which we must separate (as from the biological mother) to become adults. Indeed, analytical psychology[16] underlines the need to separate from the personal (mother) and the collective (society/culture) to understand one's place in the world and role within society/culture and thereby to establish an adult dialectical relation with both, rather than being undifferentiated, like the baby with the mother.

This leads us to another sociological term, *participation mystique*, and to the influence of Lévy-Bruhl's laws of participation on Jung. Progoff (1955, p.171) underlines that Lévy-Bruhl's participation mystique is linked to Comte's gradation of consciousness and that the former means 'to fuse [...] with an object in such a way that all distinctions are obliterated' (Progoff, 1955, p.168). To this, I would link Jung's concept of *participation mystique* between mother and because there is a fusion, or as I frame it 'a merger', with the fact that 'our individual conscious psychology develops out of an original state of unconsciousness or, in other words, a non-differentiated condition' (Jung, CW7, para.225). In this context, it is interesting to extend the concept of *participation mystique* to the relation between the individual and society (or social context) and hence to the fact that participation 'involves a fusion between subject and object, a failure to differentiate' (Progoff, 1955, p.170). From this concept, Jung theorized that when an individual is under the spell of collective representations, fusing with the collectivity, 'the images of the group dominate his unconscious'. In this state, says Progoff, 'he can hardly be said to be individualized' (1955, p.171).

In sum, the social (society/culture) embraces the individual like a mother providing contents relative to the given society and culture. Additionally, as Progoff (1955, p.X) notes, Jung believes that 'all analysis must start from the primary fact of the social nature of man', to which I would add that this includes the unconscious, the mother and the environment.

It is also important, however, at a time when sociology speaks of detraditionalization, disembedding and globalization, to look at and beyond the society/culture in which an individual is born. This will help to position my claim in relation to cultural complexes.

Therefore, Jung, with the help of Durkheim and Lévy-Bruhl, was seeking a structure to 'handle the relation of the unconscious to consciousness' (Progoff, 1955, p.173). Thanks to the early sociological masters, Jung sought a formula that would enable individuals to separate from the social, thus from both the early container (mother) and the later collective one (society/culture).

Other traces of Jung's interest in sociology can be found again in Durkheim's work. Following Lukes' (1982, p.7) introduction to Durkheim's *The Rules of Sociological Method*, we understand that Durkheim sought to demarcate sociology from psychology, claiming sociology to be a 'special psychology, having its own subject matter and a distinctive method' (Durkheim, 1982, p.253), whereas psychology is 'the science of the individual mind' whose object or domain is as follows (Durkheim, 1982, p.40):

1 states of individual consciousness;
2 explanation in terms of 'organico-psychic' factors, pre-social features of the individual organism, given at birth and independent of social influences;
3 explanation in terms of particular or 'individual' as opposed to general or 'social' conditions (focusing, say, on an individual's intentions or their particular circumstances);
4 explanation in terms of individual mental states or dispositions.

These four points can be linked respectively to Jung's concepts of (1) the personal unconscious, (2) archetypes and the collective unconscious, (3) the persona and (4) Jung's theory of neurosis and psychodynamics.

Again, we find a link between Durkheim and Jung. Lukes (1982, p.8) underlines Durkheim's frequent use of terms such as 'collective forces' and 'social currents', as well as his exploration of the analogy of thermodynamics and electricity. Thus, Lukes specifically emphasized Durkheim's *Suicide* (2006, p.299 and pp.309–310, making the claim for 'a collective force of a determinate amount of energy, impelling men to self-destruction' and that the strength of this force can be measured just like an electric current. This may have inspired Jung's work on psychic energy and the collective unconscious, as well as Spielrein's 1912 intuition that 'destruction as the Cause of Coming into Being' (1994), which, according to various authors, inspired Freud's 'Death Drive' theory (Aldridge, 2014).

In his paper titled 'Marxism and Sociology', Durkheim (1982, p.171) claims that 'social life must be explained not by the conception of it formed by those who participate in it, but by the profound causes which escape their consciousness'. Why then has sociology overlooked the unconscious causes in the formation of society? In the positivistic and enlightenment-oriented fashion of sociology, Durkheim did not investigate this further.[17] However, he may have influenced the scientific arena within which the founders of psychoanalysis (particularly Jung) would tread. My impression is that Durkheim abhorred psychology but would have greatly appreciated the turn taken by psychoanalysis after his death, as well as a social science rather than a medical science or therapy. Furthermore, according to Durkheim (1982, pp.236–237), 'the sociologist offers the ultimate promise of penetrating the inmost depths of individuals, in order to relate to their psychological condition', while 'psychologists make the mistake of studying "general traits of our mentality"', which are 'too abstract and indeterminate to be capable of explaining any particular social form'. This is because, according to Durkheim, it is 'society which informs our mind and wills, attuning them to the institutions which express that society'. Hence, sociology offers the ultimate promise of a 'more concrete and complex' psychology.

Here, it is important to examine the merger of sociology and psychology as offered by psychosocial studies and to critique the possible attractiveness of certain psychological approaches. Psychoanalysis erupted at the beginning of the 20th century, linking the individual with society, as a critique of society and in relation to the repressive element of society and patriarchy. Here, we may recall – among others – Freud's *Civilization and Its Discontents* (2002), Adler's work on inferiority, compensation and the impact of the environment, Gross' work on society and anarchy (2009) and, needless to say, Jung's work (2014) on the role of the individual within society and the need to individuate.

Therefore, psychoanalysis has, from its beginnings, merged the psychological and sociological. However, the two have been separated for too long and it is now time to examine them jointly, more than 120 years since Durkheim claimed that 'the sociologist will not have completely accomplished his mission so long as he has not penetrated the inmost depths of individuals, in order to relate to their psychological condition, the institutions of which he gives an account' (1982, p.236).

Here, I agree with Durkheim's claim that when psychology does not work *in depth* it might instead give a general account of the facts. Conversely, in depth analysis,[18] it is possible to examine both conscious and unconscious aspects in depth and thus to make better sense of the world. Thus, sociology,[19] which was born out of 19th-century positivism, concentrates on tangible facts and has interpreted facts (and therefore society) following this positivistic approach. However, I claim – in antithesis to this and following Nietzsche's (1969, p.267) critique of positivism – that facts do not exist; only interpretations exist. But what does this mean in relation to Jung (and considering Jung's own claim that 'it all depends on how we look at things, and not how they are in themselves' (Rimbach, 2011))? It means, I propose, that a fact is a symbol that conceals archetypal content; thus, a fact is numinous, and its contents can only be fully discovered by bridging the fact itself (conscious) and its meaning (unconscious). In this respect, I see Jung's work on synchronicity as fundamental (see his paradigmatic example of synchronicity and the scarab beetle event) (CW8).

In conclusion, Progoff (1955, p.160) underlines that Jung's 'study of society is a necessary consequence of his main research into the problems of personality' and 'is carried out altogether with the purpose of answering psychological questions'. But, says Progoff, the nature of his study, which comprised analysing the psychic processes that underlie the workings of history led him to discover 'the inner dynamic of social change' and perhaps even 'a theory of history' (Progoff, 1955, p.160).

Progoff's structure/Durkheimian approach and agency theory: a comparison

It is timely, because Beck could be clustered into the action theory and agency/structure theory traditions, to present an in-depth discussion connecting Jung to both theories. This will help to set against and (possibly) balance Progoff's structure/Durkheimian approach. Again, it is useful to not only look at agency theory but also action theory.

When considering the aforementioned description of what action theory is – namely 'the analysis of action starting with the individual actor' (Abercrombie, Hill, and Turner, 2000, p.2) – it could be argued that there is a link between action theory and Jung (and not vice versa). The same could be said also when considering Weber, who defined action in terms of 'meaningfulness' and that 'sociological analysis must proceed by identifying the meaning that actions have for actors' (Abercrombie, Hill, and Turner, 2000, p.3). Hence, this could be confirmed by the fact that both – although with great distinctions – as Abercrombie, Hill and Turner (2000, p.3) remind us, 'acting and meaning are inextricably linked'. It could be said that Weber's concept of *ideal types* (social action can be distinguished and generalized into ideal types) has something in common with Jung's concept of archetypes. Even Weber's work on disenchantment can be helpful when looking at Jung.

The truth is that Jung did not read Weber (at least to my knowledge) and there is no mention of Weber in the *Collected Works*'s index. Hence, to put it in Giegerich's[20] words:

> there is no indication that Jung took note of Max Weber's work. And I would say that Jung's work would hardly have benefited from his having acquainted himself with Weber's topics. They may not be really incompatible, but certainly do not touch, perhaps one could say they bypass each other.

Or to put it with Roderick Main (2022, p.5) 'Jung does not appear to have been more than casually aware of Weber'.

Also, when looking at Schutz, it could be argued that there is a link with Jung, considering that he believed 'each experience has no meaning in itself but can be given meaning by reflection on it as it recedes into the past' [...] and that 'this form of reflection is crucial, for action is the product of intention and reflection. It is that which is determined by a project or plan' (Abercrombie, Hill, and Turner, 2000, p.3).

Guy Rocher (1989, pp.303–304) states that 'the starting point of Parsons' analysis is action, any possible human conduct, individual or collective, conscious or unconscious' and that 'the terms action and human conduct must here be understood in their broadest sense, including not only outwardly observable behaviour, but also thoughts, feelings, aspirations, desires, etc. Now, action always and simultaneously takes place in four 'contexts':

1 the biological context, that of the neurophysiological organism with its needs and demands[21];
2 the psychic context, that of the personality studied by psychology;
3 the social context, that of interactions between people and groups, studied above all by sociology[22];
4 the cultural context, that of norms, models, values, ideologies and knowledge, studied in particular by anthropology'.[23]

Woodman (2009, p.7) – employing Robert van Krieken's work (2002), who sees the beginning of the agency and structure dichotomy in the early work of Parsons and also Giddens (amongst others) – claims that 'Parsons was interested in opening a space for a sociological answer to the question of what holds the social together', and that 'Parsons sees in subjectivity and the irrational, the residual categories of other approaches, the possibility for an alternative, sociological, approach to the question of action'. As such, Woodman (2009, p.8) underlines that 'the structure/agency problematic is central to Parsons' efforts to develop a sociological theory of action, and to provide an alternative answer to the problem of social order'.

Therefore, Parsons' work can be traced to Jung (again, not vice versa) because Jung brings into the sociological discourse the interaction between an individual and his/her ability to act alone and choose. This means his/her ability to decide independently, although, within a determined structure (of social relationships and institutions) that shape and constrain one's behaviour. But he also was among the first to look at and study – from a sociological point of view – how *thoughts, feelings, aspirations,* and *desires* shape and constrain one's behaviour. As just underlined, Parsons understood that subjectivity and the irrational are to be linked when studying the relation between agency and structure.

Yet proposing a connection between Weber, Parsons and Jung seems a forced exercise. Employing Rocher (1989, p.304) – who underlines that, according to action theory, 'every concrete action is always global, "molar", insofar as it is inscribed in all four contexts together and is always the result of an interaction of forces or influences deriving from each of them' and that 'only on an analytical or theoretical level is it possible to establish a distinction between these four contexts' – I propose that the wish to establish a link between action theory and Jung is nothing but *the wish to establishing distinctions that are only possible on an analytical or theoretical level.*

If anything, following this line of reasoning, one could say – as Durkheim's work was influenced by Simmel's (Crespi, Jedlowski, and Rauty, 2000, p.154) – that Jung's work was also influenced by Simmel's. The latter, as Del Lago maintained,

> had no 'messages or prophecies to deliver', did not dispense certainties and urged an ambivalent reading of all the phenomena he dealt with, so as not to provide in any way the formation of a school of thought organised around a defined position.
>
> (Del Lago, 1994, in Crespi, Jedlowski, and Rauty, 2000, p.154)

This description, to my reckoning, fits Jung like a glove.

Therefore, in my opinion, attention should be paid to Simmel's work in relation to Jung, instead of the works of Weber, Parsons (not only because in recent years Parsons' work has been overshadowed while Simmels' work has gained new visibility) and Beck, who is considered by many as an agency theorist.

Also the following fits like a glove to Jung's work, when considering Simmel's *The Problems of the Philosophy of History: An Epistemological Essay* (1997), and his emphasis that:

- 'Forms are an a priori of the understanding' – Could this refer to Jung's archetypes?
- 'The forms of the understanding change with time' – Could this refer to Jung's stages of life?
- 'Life is fixed in certain symbolic determinations through which it is understood' – Could this refer to Jung's theory of Complex?
- 'The flow of life itself always involves the dissolution of each determination and its transformation into different determinations' – Could this refer to Jung's work on alchemy?

It must be clarified that the above principles by Simmel have deep roots in the thought of Kant, Nietzsche and Schopenhauer (Crespi, Jedlowski, and Rauty, 2000, p.156), who are the three philosophers who most influenced Jung. Therefore – if there 'must be' a link – this is with Simmel, not Weber.

In conclusion, a discussion relating Jung to action theory and agency/structure theory, and (to set against and balance Progoff's structure/Durkheimian approach) is a specious (superficially plausible, but actually wrong) and misleading argument. This is because, I do not consider Beck an agency theorist, and because structure and agency theories deal with any kind of psychoanalysis differently, but Beck does not. Beck is not interested in psychoanalysis and does not employ it in his work.

Woodman (2009, p.9) also helps to shed light on why I do not consider Beck to be an agency theorist. He does so by employing van Krieken (2002), who distinguished a sociological niche opposed to Parsons' work. Woodman states that Beck's work 'starts from a tension between human intentionality and, a largely unintentional, social order'. This sociological *lineage*, as Woodman prefers to call it, can be found – following van Krieken – in 'relatively marginalized aspects of Durkheim and Weber, on to Elias and Bourdieu among others'. In this regard, Woodman proposes that 'Beck's work fits more closely with the second line of sociological theory' as 'he is primarily interested in unintended consequences' of first modernity 'than structure and agency, which is at best a secondary concern' (2009, p.9). Woodman continues:

> The characterization, and I believe caricature, of Beck as overemphasizing choice or agency arises in large part from conceptualizing his work within a structure/ agency framework and focusing on only one part of an ambiguity that is the key to his attempt to conceptualize contemporary modernity. Fitting with van Krieken's minor lineage, Beck's major contribution is to argue that new frames are needed for sociology and that attempting to conceptualize the current moment with the dominant sociological concepts of the twentieth century is unhelpful.
>
> (2009, p.9)

Therefore, I argue, in agreement with Woodman (2009, pp.243–256) that Beck, although widely recognized (*de-jure*) as an agency theorist because of the afore-mentioned idea (Beck, 1992, p.137), *de facto* is not.

Woodman (2009, pp.243–256) proposes 'that the relationship and balance between structure and agency is of little interest to Beck and aim to discourage forcing his work into this frame'. He, therefore, adds:

> Instead of focusing on a shift towards agency, and proposing the concept of choice biographies to understand the shift, Beck is making the more complicated claim that at the very moment, and through the same processes, that some of the constraints placed on people are breaking down, the predictability and security that would allow these new options to function as deliberate choices also weaken'.
>
> Woodman concludes that 'more importantly, Beck asks the question of whether the concepts developed by twentieth-century sociology are up to the task of theorizing the contemporary world'.

Another important reason why Beck cannot be considered an agency theorist is that agency theories (and theorists) deal with any kind of psychoanalysis, though differently. Beck, as I will underline below, does not deal with psychoanalysis at all. He is a sociological sociologist. One that employed psychoanalysis widely is Giddens. Another is Bauman. I will focus on both in Chapter 2.

Hillman and archetypal psychology

If Jung somehow managed to de-pathologize psychoanalysis and make of it 'a system of education and spiritual guidance' (Jacoby, 1973, p.60), Hillman furthered this, making psychoanalysis a poetical matter and claiming the need to move away from the consulting room and to understand archetypes as 'the primary forms that govern the psyche'. Thus, 'archetypal psychology's first links are with culture and imagination rather than with medical and empirical psychologies' (Hillman, 1997a, p.9). This is because, according to Hillman, 'at the most basic level of reality are fantasy images', which are 'the primary activity of consciousness' (1975, p.174). Hence, it could be said that images precede language, that they are 'the first and only reality we apprehend directly' (1975, p.174). But what does this mean and how does it link to this theme, to Jung, and to the social?

For Hillman (1997a, p.11), there is a need to move radically away from the 'biochemical, socio-historical, and personal-behavioristic bases of human nature and toward the imaginative' or *the poetic basis of mind*, which is evident in the cultural patterns of mythology, religion, art, architecture, etc. If, for Jung, the social was constituted by both society and culture, for Hillman, it is culture that is fundamental. Furthermore, the soul is 'a perspective rather than a substance' (Hillman, 1975, p.X), 'constituted by images' and therefore 'primarily an imagining activity'. This is seen in, for example, dreams, 'where the dreamer is in the image rather than the image is in the dreamer' (Hillman, 1997a, p.14). For archetypal psychology, the dilemma between *vera imaginatio* (Paracelsus) and false (Coleridge) is resolved when one responds to and works the image (Hillman, 1997a, p.16); thus, 'fantasy' and 'reality' exchange places and values and are no longer opposed. While fantasy 'is always being enacted and embodies' (Hillman, 1997a, p.31), 'whatever is physically or literally "real" is always also a fantasy image' (Hillman, 1997a, p.32). Thus, analytical psychology follows Jung's claim that 'the psyche creates reality every day', which Jung terms 'fantasy' (CW6, para.18).

Hillman also claims that the image has no 'referent beyond itself' (1997a, p.14), so that, contrary to Jung, the image is not 'the result of a sensation and perception', nor is it 'a mental construct that represents in symbolic form certain ideas and feelings which it expresses' (1997a, p.14). The image is merely the image, nothing else. As primary data, images are irreducible and pure, 'neither good nor bad, true nor false, demonic nor angelic' (Hillman, 1983, p.8), even if they are always evoking 'a precisely qualified context, mood and scene' (Hillman, 1983, p.62).

Lopez-Pedraza (2018) – following Jung – suggests that one should 'stick to the image' (CW16, para.320), 'rather than associate or amplify into non-imaginistic symbolism, personal opinions, and interpretations' (Hillman, 1997a, pp.17–18). This sticking to the image is 'the golden rule of archetypal psychology' (Hillman, 1997a, p.18), by which means 'reductionism' is defeated. Thus, the innovation of archetypal psychology is that 'an archetypal image is psychologically "universal" because its effect amplifies and de-personalizes. [...] resonates with collective trans-empirical importance' (Hillman, 1997a, pp.19–29). Furthermore, the universal quality of the image lifts 'the soul beyond its egocentric confines' (Hillman, 1997a, p.29), and 'in presenting a claim – moral, erotic, intellectual, aesthetic, every image demands an affective response' (Hillman, 1997a, p.22).

Thus, Hillman claims that the poetic sense of images frees them from the need to be narrative, linear, sequential or causal, from their constraint as egocentric first-person reports of 'a personalistic subject'. Thus, in its rejection of the image as narrative, archetypal psychology turns away from the 'egocentric, epic narrations' of traditional psychologies (Hillman, 1997a, p.24). Hillman also notes that 'psychology cannot be limited to being one field among others since psyche permeates all fields and things' (Hillman, 1997a, p.27). While I fundamentally agree with this claim, I would add that archetypal psychology has failed to fruitfully link theory with the dayworld claims of individuals, to support individuals practically, not just theoretically.

Archetypal psychology has moved from a curative/transformative method towards a philosophy, thus distancing itself from the claims of depth psychology. This is reflected in Hillman's own discontinuation of his therapy practice to dedicate himself to theory and writing. Although it is due to archetypal psychology (and particularly to Hillman's work) that analytical psychology has survived 'the death of the master' and his ostracism,[24] and has found a way to 'move from Bollingen' to the wider world, there is – I feel – a need to restore analytical psychology to the heart of depth psychology and mainstream intellectual discussion and to link theory with action.[25] This is what sociology has done for a century and why it has succeeded in entering the policy room, where analytical psychology has not.

To redress this, I feel, analytical psychology must become extroverted and follow sociology (see Samuels below)[26] in placing our knowledge at the service of the collective, both in the consulting room (for patients) and outside the consulting room (for groups, policy makers, public and private institutions, corporations, etc.). However, in leaving the consulting room, analytical psychology must change language to ensure comprehensibility to lay people. This action may help psychoanalysis regain the initial revolutionary *quid* so dear to its founders. While within the therapeutic room, there is a need to follow the first commandment of psychoanalysis – 'the problem has to heal itself'[27] – and rely 'on literary and poetic devices to expound its vision' (Hillman, 1997a, p.19), if attempting this outside the consulting room, analytical psychology would continuously fail to support those who do not speak the language and who cannot or will not wait, as Giegerich suggests, for Self-knowledge 'to correct its attitude by itself'.[28]

By becoming more accessible, we may also repair the accusation that Jung and analytical psychology are mystical, esoteric, ascientific, elitist (to name but a few) and detached from the dayworld claims of individuals. According to Hillman, analytical psychology is moving 'towards mythical accounts as a psychological language' and thus 'grounds itself in a fantasy that cannot be taken historically, physically, literally'. This is a fundamental problem of language (impossible communication) and approach (methodological inconsistency). It is only in the consulting room that myths can be 'understood as metaphors', and thus 'open the questions of life to transpersonal and culturally imaginative reflection' (Hillman, 1997a, p.29).

Instead, Jungians must become aware of our limitations and elitism and strive to remain grounded if we are to support various collectivities and individuals. This perspective is bolstered by Hillman's statement:

> the soul's metaphorical nature has a suicidal necessity (Hillman 1964), an underworld affiliation (Hillman 1979), a morbism (Ziegler 1980), a destiny – different from dayworld claims – which makes the psyche fundamentally unable to submit to the *hubris of an egocentric notion of subjectivity as achievement (Leistung)*.
>
> (Hillman, 1997a, p.31)

In a nutshell, psychosocial studies, and my own 'I+I', should bridge the soul's metaphorical nature with dayworld claims.

To conclude, Hillman describes how Freud and Jung vied 'to discover the fundamental "mistake" in Western culture', a mistake that archetypal psychology would describe as 'loss of soul' (Hillman, 1997a, p.31) and that resulted in our loss of 'relation with death and the underworld' (Hillman, 1997a, p.31). Rather than speaking of decline, I claim that there is only circularity – an uroboric lifeline – where a phase of decline is followed by a phase of development and so on. Rather than pinpointing where the West went wrong, I propose that psychoanalysis should be – as suggested by Giegerich – 'a method to help people get out of their own traps'[29] so that they can live in balance between conscious and unconscious contents, between dayworld claims and the metaphors of the soul. Thus, psychoanalysis should use the images provided by the soul while remaining grounded in the dayworld claims and needs of individuals. Only then will it be possible to reduce the 'intensification of subjectivity', 'self-enclosed egocentricity', 'hyperactivism' and 'life-fanaticism' proposed by Hillman (1997a, p.31).

I would also add that, although Giegerich (2010, p.190) queries whether 'the loss of meaning in modern times is the ultimate reason for neurosis', I propose instead that the ultimate reason for this loss is the lack of love. When we lack love we seek meaning, and it is when we are unable to find meaning that we become neurotic. Therefore, meaning is not sufficient to become conscious; we require firm love to integrate and overcome our demons, to transform and become renewed as who we really are, to move from despair to ashes to rebirth to absolute freedom.

Singer's and Kimbles' cultural complex

Cultural complex theory builds on Jung's complex theory and seeks to examine complexes from a collective point of view, particularly since Jung, according to Singer and Kimbles (2004, p.4) 'tended to divorce the development of the individual from the individual's life in groups'. Thus, as Singer and Kimbles remind us, while 'personal complexes emerge out of the level of the personal unconscious in their interaction with deeper levels of the psyche and early parental/familial relationships' (2004, p.4), cultural complexes arise from the cultural unconscious in its interaction with 'both the archetypal and the personal realms of the psyche and the broader outer world' (2004, p.4). For this reason, they claim that 'cultural complexes can be thought of as forming the essential components of inner sociology' (2004, p.4) and help in providing 'a description of groups and classes of people as filtered through psyches of generations of ancestors' (2004, p.4).

Thus, cultural complexes, and the activity thereof, bridge the personal and archetypal levels of the psyche, and thereby provide a link between 'the individual, society, and the archetypal realm' (Singer and Kimbles, 2004, p.20).

The effort to shed light on the complex dynamics that occur between the individual and the group (or collective) is an admirable challenge and Singer and Kimbles' work is invaluable in this respect; however, they fail to take into consideration what society and sociology is in essence, and their approach is limited to the concept of modern society and does not apply to current society.

The approach of sociology in investigating society is, by its very nature, forward-looking; otherwise, it would be history. With this, I mean that it looks at the present (keeping in mind the past) to suggest tools and methods for possible future scenarios. In this regard, the work of Beck – on the *Risk Society* (1992), love (1995 and 2013), cosmopolitanism (2006), and *The Metamorphosis of the World* (2016) – is an excellent example.

Thus, I challenge Singer and Kimbles' use of the term 'sociology'. August Comte, who coined the term in 1824, described sociology as a science to 'produce knowledge of society based on scientific evidence' with the aim of understanding, predicting and controlling human behaviour (Giddens and Pierson, 1997, p.8). He also claimed that 'sociology would discover general laws of social change similar to those found in Newtonian physics and Darwinian biology' (Abercrombie, Hill and Turner, 2000, p.333). Thus, sociology aims to discover general laws of social change, and because we live – de facto – in a world that has changed increasingly rapidly since the Industrial Revolution of the late 19th century, it is no longer fitting to seek 'a description of groups and classes of people as filtered through the psyches of generations of ancestors'. Society no longer works like this; it is not (only) like a DNA spiral in which we can find traces of the past and so it is inappropriate to claim that cultural complexes contain 'all sorts of information and misinformation about the structures of society' (Singer and Kimbles, 2004, p.20). This would lead to gross generalization and thus into error.

Thus, I challenge the definition of cultural complexes as 'a truly, inner sociology' that bridges the individual, society and the archetypal realm (Singer and Kimbles, 2004, p.20). Rather than referring to an 'inner sociology' – and avoiding the temptation to call this an 'inner psychology' – I would instead refer to 'psychosocial data'. This is because, it is by merging conscious and unconscious contents both from the psychological and social realms that we can make sense of the world, and such contents are a bridge between the individual, the archetypal realm and society. This, then, leads us to further questions, which are not addressed by Singer and Kimbles: which society? Moreover: what is society? Should we refer to Western society, to the 'local society' in which one is born or to the larger region/nation or even continent? Instead of talking about society, I prefer to follow Jung and refer to the social (which, as I have previously claimed, is the unconscious – the deep layers of the collective unconscious – and the mother). Thus, it is the *summa* of what we are and where we come from.

Second, in my opinion, those who take into account the transformation of society and the interplay between structure and agency and consciousness and the unconscious propose a static, rather than dynamic, approach. I make this claim because, in a dynamic structure, we should refer to individuals living in a detraditionalized, disembedded and highly networked society that is connected globally (although the importance of local networks must also be taken into account), and above all, to a society that is increasingly multicultural and not bound to a specific local identity. This, in my view, is the shadow aspect of Singer and Kimbles' approach; therefore, this approach is fixed on a structure that could be considered 'modern', where the fundamental aspects of such a society are certain. We live today in a second-late-modern individualized society where concepts such as gender, class, race, religion and work have gone through a process of de-traditionalization (therefore are no longer certain) and are therefore negotiable.

This view is confirmed by Singer and Kimbles' (2004, p.7) emphasis that 'cultural complexes are based on repetitive, historical group experiences which have taken root in the cultural unconscious of the group'. This view may have been valid before globalization and when the borders between states were well defined but not so anymore. An example could be: what is the cultural complex of a person born in Germany by an Italian father and a Spanish mother, who moves to the United States to study and marries a Kenyan before making their home in China? Moreover, what is the cultural complex of their children? And how would this complex change if, for example, they were unable to conceive and used a surrogate mother? Multicultural identities are increasingly the norm today, and the effect of media and technology in shaping identities should be taken into consideration.

This being the case, is Jung's study of the individual, groups and the collective, sufficient? I claim that it is and as I have noted elsewhere (Carpani, 2004), we should look at the formation of Self-identities in terms of the interplay of different cultures, societies and traditions. I claim that following de-traditionalization, there is always re-traditionalization as in a uroboric circle. I also understand that Singer and Kimbles stressed that cultural complexes must not be confused with cultural identity or national character, and I agree that 'cultural complexes are lived out in group life and they are internalized in the psyche of individuals' (Singer and Kimbles, 2004, p.20); however, such complexes can be local and global as well glocal[30] and trans-cultural. My claim is that society is not bound to a specific place; wherever there is a group, there is the possibility of a complex.

I also challenge Singer's and Kimble's (2004, p.21) claim that 'the Jungian tradition has tended to emphasize the development of the individual out of his or her particular collective experience, but has not been particularly clear or helpful in differentiating individual from cultural complexes'. As claimed above in my discussion of Progoff, Jung 'realizes that the social quality of man is something inherent in human nature' and since society is the primary human datum, 'the individual must be understood in terms of the social situation in which he lives' (1955, p.167). Therefore, the individual must be understood more broadly than the categories of where s/he comes from or was born.

In conclusion, I sense that a traditional Jungian approach is sufficient to examine complexes because cultural complexes are part of the realm of the collective unconscious, and personal complexes are also, therefore, always cultural and in particular linked to the social.[31]

Samuels: plurality, politics and 'the individual'

In *Jung and the Post-Jungians*, Samuels (1985) claimed that there are three main post-Jungian traditions – the 'classical', 'developmental' and 'archetypal'. It may now be time for a fourth: the plural. This approach, encompassing eclecticism and integration, is rooted in Samuels' work and aims to restore and enhance Jung's work and analytical psychology at the core of depth psychology, by studying the psyche as plural and, therefore, as political.

As a writer who blends Jungian with relational psychoanalytic and humanistic approaches, Samuels is not a 'classical', a 'developmental' or an 'archetypal'

Jungian analyst and his work can be divided into two different but linked elements: 'the plural' and 'the political', underpinned by an interest in psychosocial studies.

Samuels' 'plural' period was solidified in the late 1980s with the publication of *The Plural Psyche* (1989), the first in a series, of which the second and third books, *The Political Psyche* (1993) and *Politics on the Couch* (2001), marked his 'political' period. These were followed in 2015 by *A New Therapy for Politics*.

According to Samuels, the plural psyche is a concept necessary to both analytical and depth psychology to 'hold unity and diversity in balance', because pluralism is an 'instrument to make sure that diversity need not be a basis for schismatic conflict' (Samuels, 1989, p.1). This is what makes Samuels a relational psychoanalyst *ante litteram*. He also examines the post-bipolar world (communism vs capitalism) from a merging perspective, in suggesting that the 'fostering of competitive bargaining between conflicting interests produces creative rather than destructive results' (Samuels, 1989, p.1).

Therefore, as the Cold War world (1989) was ending, Samuels suggested 'reconciling our many internal voices and images of ourselves with our wish and need to feel integrated and speak with one voice' (Samuels, 1989, p.2). This applies to both depth psychology and the socio-political sphere and Samuels emphasized that pluralism can serve as a political metaphor.

Samuels' political interest heightened, as Peay has underlined (2015, in Samuels), in the early 1990s when, during and after the Gulf War and Iraqi invasion, he noticed patients bringing war-inspired dreams into the analytic hour. He also realized that not only do psychotherapists 'have little time for politics' but that, in turn, many politicians 'scorn introspection and psychological reflection as a waste of time' (Samuels, 2001, p.3).

Examining the plural and political psyche thus enabled him to work both within and outside of the consulting room, as a successful consultant for politicians, organizations, activist groups, etc. In contrast to Hillman, Samuels actively demonstrated 'how useful and effective perspectives derived from psychotherapy might be in the formation of policy, in new ways of thinking about the political process and in the resolution of conflict' (Samuels, 2001, p.XI) and claimed that 'our inner worlds and our private lives reel from the impact of policy decisions and the existing political culture'. In considering why policy committees do not include psychotherapists, Samuels notes that 'you would expect to find therapists having views to offer on social issues that involve personal relations' (Samuels, 2001, p.2). This is Samuels' most innovative aspect: to see psychoanalysts (as well as individuals) as activists, with a fundamental role to play within society.

Samuels suggests that within both the microcosm of an individual and the macrocosm of the global village, 'we are flooded by psychological themes' and that 'politics embodies the psyche of a people' (Samuels, 2001, p.5). Thus, he reminds us that 'the founders [of psychoanalysis] felt themselves to be social critics as much as personal therapists' (Samuels, 2001, p.6) and, in this respect, he recalls Freud, Jung, Maslow, Rogers, Perls, the Frankfurt School, Reich and Fromm. He also notes that in the 1990s, psychoanalysts such as Orbach, Kulkarni and Frosh began to consider society once more, but notes that although 'the project of linking therapy and the world is clearly not a new one [...] very little progress seems to have been made'. Thus, he stresses that today 'more therapists than ever want psychotherapy to realize the social and political potential that its founders perceived in it' but is aware of the 'large gap between wish and actuality' (Samuels, 2001, p.7). I argue that psychosocial studies might fill this gap.[32]

In 2014 (p.100), Samuels opened the discussion on the role of the 'individual in contemporary progressive and radical political discourse', engaging with Giddens, Beck and Beck-Gernsheim, who are also key to my work.[33] In his paper,[34] Samuels – concurring with Jung – underlines that 'individuals are socially constructed, even when they believe themselves to be autonomous and inner directed entities' (Samuels, 2014, p.100). Therefore, referring to Giddens, Beck and Beck-Gernsheim on the so-called 'self-invented identity,[35] cut off from traditional context' (Samuels, 2014, p.100), he claims that although challenging and useful, these authors offer only an 'experience distant' perspective (Samuels, 2014, p.100) and adds – quoting Layton (2013, in Samuels, 2014, p.100) – that 'sociologists today [...] have reached the conclusion that individuals need to be better theorised, though this is usually in order to make a deeper and more fecund contribution to their own discipline of sociology'.

This is reminiscent of Durkheim's dispute between what constitutes psychology and sociology, and I also sense that Samuels here is attempting to 'repair' Hillman's error in leaving the consulting room in order to theorize, without considering societal development and the claim of individuals. Instead, for Samuels, the psychosocial turn is imperative for its ability to approach the *individual* from a psychological and social standpoint. Examining the individual through this lens, Samuels sought to recover the aim of the founders of psychoanalysis: to examine the individual within the social environment and the complexities arising from this relation. Therefore, he has worked to regain the revolutionary *quid* of psychoanalysis and to remind us – as alchemy suggests, and in contrast to Hillman – that *our Art* comprises both theory and practice.

Samuels comments that 'the sociological individual of the past twenty-five years' is 'interested mainly in her or his life issues, and not in the life of the times and its issues' (Samuels, 2014, p.100). I see this interest 'mainly in her or his life issues' – or what Beck and Beck-Gernsheim called individualization – as a fantasy[36] exercise (or in Freudian *jargon* wish fulfilment!), the fantasy of fulfilling one's own fantasies. Once such a fantasy has developed, however, it must be grounded in reality to avoid neurosis. In this regard, Freud is key, since he theorized that the cause and symptoms of neuroses are rooted in wishes (not memories), which have an impellent and (partly) unconscious need to be satisfied (Wollheim, 1971, p.19).

Perhaps individualization, as a fantasy of fulfilling one's own fantasies,[37] comprises nothing more than an inflated mind and as such borders the *folie a deux*, a narcissistic and megalomaniac set of fantasies; which align with the idea of a neoliberal society (based on the fantasy of infinite growth).

Hence, the difference between a second or late-modern society, or today's second-late-modern individualized society and the previous advanced industrial society (Marcuse, 1986, p.XV) is that, today, everyone can fantasize about developing, as Beck puts it, 'your-do-it-yourself biography', unchained from tradition, gender or class certainty. This is possible due to the changes that came about in the Western society since the fall of the Berlin Wall. However, this is where sociology can fail, since this so-called de-traditionalization cannot eradicate emotion *tout court*. Thus, Samuels refers to this as 'self-invented identity, cut off from traditional context' (Samuels, 2014, p.100). In this regard, an example could help. Let's examine the case of a young couple meeting their couple counsellor for the first time. She is 35 years old, a mother and wife, as well as a manager in a multinational company (although dissatisfied with her well-paid job). She is anxious and upset about her husband's job situation and feels guilty (and angry) each morning when her husband brings their kids to school while she goes to work. He is 33 years old, has been unemployed for a year because his company relocated elsewhere and he has decided to undertake postgraduate training in a field he has always dreamt of. He is happy with his studies but also feels guilty for not contributing a good enough salary (as he used to). Does sociology consider this from an emotional point of view (also taking into account the hints given by the unconscious), and if so, what proposals would it make? According to my research – further developed in Chapter 2 – on the below authors, it does not. Giddens (1992), Beck and Beck-Gernsheim (1995) as well as Bauman (2003) wrote extensively about it, but these authors claim that everything in our current society must be negotiated and that nothing is certain. In my view, this couple cannot yet negotiate because they are trapped in their own emotions, projections and complexes towards the other, as well as in the need to transition between a society based on sociological certainties and a post-certainty one. They are also dealing with the fact that everything today is a wonder, and that there are (currently) no good-enough role models. With the help of counsellors, they could examine both societal demands and their current emotional state (Asper, 1993, p.61) and work towards developing 'a positive, loving relationship with oneself and a more tolerant attitude toward others'. This also means 'a "coming to light" of possibilities that were previously inhibited and overshadowed' (Asper, 1993, p.66) This, in my opinion, is what psychosocial studies aim at – the merging of aspects of societal development with individuals' emotions.

I argue that in societies based on 'self-invented identity', not only are individuals neurotic – since the myth of limitless material growth or becoming 'someone' is false – but it is also a suicidal society because external growth (if not paralleled by inner growth and grounding) leads to sterility, apathy and depression. In this regard, the fairy tales of 'the cricket and the ant' and 'the naked king' are useful reminders of the need to balance the inner and outer realms.

Paraphrasing Layton (2013, p.139), Samuels notes that 'individualization is not just about the expansion of autonomy to an ever-widening portion of the population, but rather has been about the creation and extension of a certain version of subjectivity and autonomy'. He adds that 'the sociologically perceived narcissism and plasticity of that kind of individual actually potentiate her or him as far as political activism is concerned' (Samuels, 2014, p.100). I agree and also claim that, in Jungian terms, individualization is a compensation and therefore stems from centuries of patriarchy, traditions, gender and class certainty.

Thus, I propose examining individualization from a psychosocial approach because – following Samuels – I also believe that individuals 'are embedded and constructed by and in social relationships, communal networks, task-oriented groups and ecosystems' and 'if Jungian psychology could refashion its approach to the individual, then it could become a sort of support and inspiration to embattled citizens whose experience of their battles is often that they are in it on their own' (Samuels, 2014, p.101). I will investigate this in Chapter 3 together with Jung's remark that individuation is 'for the few' (Shamdasani, 2003, p.307).

Watkins and the concept of liberation

In her discussion of ancient Hebraic tradition, Mary Watkins (2003, p.2) noted that it is the capacity for dialogue, not reason, that distinguishes humankind from other living creatures. Such dialogue takes place with oneself, with one's neighbour and with God (Niebuhr, 1955, cited in Watkins, 2003, p.2), and 'the capacity for dialogue is a necessary precondition for human liberation' (2003, p.87), particularly 'from rigid, stereotypic, and unidimensional narrowness' (2003, p.88).

As one of the few psychoanalysts[38] to have worked on the concept of liberation, Watkins is undoubtedly useful to this research and her work is fundamental (when considering psychoanalysis as a political tool) to examining current society and the social. Furthermore, her work will help to conceptualize the concept of absolute freedom (see conclusions), proposed here as a consequence of the 'I+I'. But in the words of Magatti and Giaccardi (2014), if, in Western society, we have already liberated ourselves, 'what other *liberation* must we therefore seek?' Watkins claims that liberation opens one 'to the polyphony of thought, comprised of multiple voices and perspectives, best mediated by dialogue' (2003, p.2).[39] In this view, liberation is based 'on a paradigm of interdependence, where the liberation of one is intimately tied to the liberation of the other' (2003, p.4). In this sense, 'the other' may comprise 'economic, political, sociocultural, spiritual, and psychological' entities (2003, p.4).

Watkins also claimed that '"the other" – be it part of oneSelf, be it one's neighbour or enemy, nature – can be silenced, used, abused, destroyed' (2003, p.4). Without liberation, there can be no development, and this is fundamental when viewing psychoanalysis as a 'relational dialogue' between two (or more) individuals, in the process of becoming oneSelf. As addressed in the introduction, freedom always occurs in relation to the other and is concerned with relationality; thus, a person is always in relation to (i) another person (or persons), (ii) something else (object/symbol), or (iii) oneSelf, and this relation is made up of both conscious and unconscious elements.

Watkins (2003, p.6) queries, however, whether it is possible to 'achieve inner liberation while part of an oppressive cultural system' and whether 'liberation in one's daily context supports liberation of thought'. This question may be linked first to Magatti and Giaccardi, but also to Mandela (1995, p.751), who claimed that 'to be free is not merely to cast off one's chain, but to live in a way that respects and enhances the freedom of others'. Therefore, Watkins and Mandela agree that 'the other' is key to liberation; Marcuse (1957, p.13) claims that 'freedom is always in relation to domination and the authority'[40]; and Arendt affirms that 'the existential conflict of modern times is not between different economical systems or classes, but between freedom and authorities' (2009, p.22). I will attempt to contextualize these views in the concluding chapter, when discussing my own concept of 'absolute freedom' while adding that freedom is always related to the numinous.

Now, it suffices, however, to note Watkins' (2003, p.5) claim that 'in the most private of the dialogues in our dreams and fantasies, in the most intimate portions of our conversations with ourselves, we come upon the metabolization of culture, economics, and politics', which allows us 'to transcend culture' and become liberated. From this, it could be argued that Watkins – following Hillman – views liberation mystically, therefore cutting it off from the dayworld claims of ordinary people. I would, however, refute this notion: Watkins develops from Hillman's perspective in claiming that our thought process, our inner critic, is a mélange of voices from our past – mother, father, teacher, etc. – as well as the structural resonance of school and workplaces. Thus, she says (2003, p.6) of the interior, the imaginal:

> It is a distillation of history, culture, religion, and nature. If we can hear how the intimate, so called interior, dialogues of thought and dream body forth the public, the cultural and the economic, then can we continue to believe that these dialogues can deeply transform without attention to interpersonal, cultural, ecological, and economic life?

This quote relates to my aim of examining Jung and society in relation to 'absolute freedom' (see concluding chapter). In particular, it helps to clarify my critique of Hillman and the need to link the poetic basis of the mind and the dayworld claim of individuals (see previous section).

In conclusion, Watkins (2003, p.6) asks, 'Is it likely for one to be able to achieve inner liberation while part of an oppressive cultural system? Does not liberation in one's daily context support liberation of thought?' The answer she provides is that one must 'maintain one's own voice amidst the fray of relationship' (Watkins, 2003, p.23), since dialogue ultimately requires both 'the capacity to deeply receive the other and the capacity to receive oneself' (Watkins, 2003, p.26). Dialogue is both a fact of our givenness and a deep potentiality of our being. From our very beginning, we are 'thrown' into a multiplicity – ancestors, family, trees, rivers, earth, animals, neighbours. In the words of Jung (1946, p.477), 'the Self comprises infinitely more than the mere ego, as symbols have shown since time immemorial. It is just as much another or others as it is the ego. Individuation does not exclude the world but includes it'. Thus, we are always selves-in-relation or selves-in-dialogue. What is at stake is the kind of relationship we are in, and the paths from it to a manner of dialogical relationship that liberates being (Watkins, 2003, pp.10–11). This brings us to relational psychoanalysis.

Relational psychoanalysis: an overview

In this section, I will employ the work of psychoanalysts Lewis Aron, Jessica Benjamin, Del Loewenthal and Susie Orbach to frame a definition of relational psychoanalysis and why this tradition is important in the context of a comparative study of Jung and Beck. To investigate Jung's role as a founder of relational psychoanalysis, I will employ two (relational) psychoanalysts, Andrew Samuels and Susie Orbach.

As noted by Aron (Aron and Mitchell, 1999, p.XXI), relational psychoanalysis emerged in the context of early 1980s' American psychoanalysis and now 'operates as a shared subculture' that 'has stuck deep, common, chords among current clinical practitioners and theorists'. Relational psychoanalysis developed thanks to the pioneering effort of psychoanalyst Stephan Mitchell, supported by Robert Stolorow, Jay Greenberg and Aron himself (Aron, 1999, p.X). The contributing factors to its development were (Aron, 1999, p.X): (a) the influence of the interpersonal psychoanalysis of Harry Stack Sullivan, Erich Fromm and Clara Thompson from the 1930/1940s; (b) object relations theory and the works of Fairbairn, Winnicott and Bowlby from the 1970s; (c) Kohut's 'self-psychology' of the late 1970s; and (d) American psychoanalytic feminism and feminist psychoanalysis, including the work of Jessica Benjamin and social criticism of the late 1970s and early 1980s.

It was in this landscape that, as Aron (1999, pp.XI–XII) noted, Greenberg and Mitchell coined the term 'relational' in 1983 to bridge the various strands of psychoanalysis current at that time, which included interpersonal *relations*, object *relations*, self-psychology, social constructivism, psychoanalytic hermeneutics and gender theorizing.[41] From these standpoints, Greenberg and Mitchell worked on a model (Aron, 1999, pp.XIII–XV) that would:

1 Provide an alternative understanding (to classical drive theory).
2 Generate a new understanding of precisely the phenomena that drive theorists have traditionally regarded as foundational: the body, sexuality, pleasure, aggression, constructionality, the patient's free association.
3 Argue that mind occurs in 'me-you patterns' (see Sullivan) and that the analyst is merely a 'participant-observer [...] embedded in the transference-countertransference matrix' (Aron, 1999, p.XV).
4 Build on Winnicott's (1960: 39n, cited in Aron, 1999, p.XI) statement that 'there is no such a thing as an infant – only the infant-mother unit'.
5 'The purpose of "two-person psychology" is to emphasize the emergence of what Ogden calls "the intersubjective Analytic-third"' (Aron, 1999, p.XV).

Del Loewenthal (2014, p.4) recently highlighted the 'widespread realization that the therapy relationship runs in both directions, is mutual, and involves the whole person of the practitioner', adding that 'the "relational" is most apparent in [...] Freud, Klein and object relations theories as well as Jung'. Thus, he (2014, pp.4–5) reminds us of the mounting research evidence that the analytic relationship is the crucial factor in successful psychological therapy, and in asking why this is the case, he refers to Hargaden and Schwartz's (2007) description of relational psychoanalysis:

6 Emphasize the centrality of the relationship.
7 Emphasize that therapy involves a bi-directional process.
8 Emphasize that therapy involves both the vulnerability of the therapist and the client.
9 Emphasize the use of countertransference in thoughtful disclosure and collaborative dialogue.
10 Emphasize the co-construction and multiplicity of meaning.

Meanwhile, in the late 1970s and early 1980s, Susie Orbach and Luise Eichenbaum repositioned 'both the mother and the psychotherapists not solely as the "failing" and fixed object of the analysand but also as subjects in the process of becoming' (2014, p.13). Therefore, Orbach criticizes Mitchell's failure to recognize that 'social movements such as feminism, the New Left and [...] radical therapy' greatly influenced developments, adding that it was thanks to these critical movements of the late 1970s and early 1980s that the relevance to radically oriented therapy of 'structures such as the Oedipus complex, penis envy and separation-individuation' was considered. She adds (2014, p.13) that these movements served to 'contextualise the intrapsychic life of the individual as an outcome of relationship' within the individual's social milieu.

Thus, Orbach (2014, p.13) claims that these various streams merged to form relational psychoanalysis, with its 'democratic, co-created view of the therapeutic relationship', whereby the patient is not the sole object of the therapeutic gaze; rather, the therapeutic dyad together brings their subjectivity to the relationship (2014, pp.13–14). Orbach (2014, p.14) also claims that in relational psychoanalysis, 'the therapist's subjectivity is always present' and 'the patient's behaviour and affects are not pre-described or interpretable according to a formula'.

Jung, the relational

Having defined relational psychoanalysis, I will here outline why Jung should be considered a pioneer in the field. In so doing, I will compare Samuels' unpublished paper (2012) titled 'The analyst is as much "in the analysis" as the patient (1929): Jung as a pioneer of relational psychoanalysis' with the traits of relational psychoanalysis described above as well as Benjamin's and Orbach's contributions.

As noted by Samuels (2012), Jung asserted that analysis was 'dialectical', involved mutual transformation through the therapeutic relationship, and that the 'emotionally charged interactions' between therapist and patient are two-way, thus rendering them equals. This, to my understanding, matches Ogden's view (point 5 above) as well as Jung's idea that 'the soul is the very essence of the relationship' (point 6 above) (Jung, CW16, para.504). In this regard, Jessica Benjamin (1995, p.3) has suggested that the relational perspective comprises an 'inquiry into questions of common concern' that emerge from the two-person model. Thus, notes Orbach (2014, p.17), the analyst is drawn into and actively participates in the relational field, for which reason, s/he cannot avoid being affected. Thus, Orbach (2014, p.18) claims that, in the therapeutic dyad, the analyst must be available to 'absorb' the material, both that which is said and that which is not. It is through the process of self-reflection this entails, she notes, that 'we study ourselves and our analysands'.

Secondly, Samuels (2012) notes that analysis, according to Jung, is 'an encounter… between two psychic wholes in which knowledge is used only as a tool' (points 3 and 4 above). Therefore, with Sullivan's idea 'that mind always emerges and develops contextually, in the interpersonal field' (Aron, 1999, p.XV) and with Greenberg and Mitchell's assertion that 'There is not such a thing as either the patient or the analyst – only the patient-analyst unit' (Aron, 1999, p.XV), this matches points 7 and 8 (above) as well as with Orbach's view that the therapist's subjectivity and patient's behaviour are mutually affecting.

To reiterate and to show that analysis can only work when a relation exists, Jung (1929, p.49, cited in Samuels, 2012) stated that 'you can exert no influence if you are not susceptible to influence'. Thus, Samuels shows that, according to Jung, the patient–analyst relation comprises a 'possibility of mutual "contamination" that goes with mutual transformation' (2012). In this regard, Jung emphasized that 'the meeting of the two personalities is like the contact of two chemical substances: if there is any reaction, both of them are transformed' (1929, p.49). Samuels also introduced two statements by Jung: 'the living mystery of life is always hidden between Two' (in Jaffe, 1979, p.347) and 'the soul is the very essence of relationship' (Jung, 1946, p.504). This highlights the need for Jung and the 'relationals' to distance from drive theory (points 1 and 2) and the concept of transference and countertransference (point 9) because, following Jung:

> the patient, by bringing an activated unconscious content to bear upon the doctor, constellates the corresponding unconscious material in him, owing to the inductive effect which always emanates from projections in a greater or lesser sense. Doctor and patient thus find themselves in a relationship founded on mutual unconsciousness.
>
> (CW16, para.364)

Also, of note is Jung's desire to sit in front of (not behind) the patient and to merge with the patient in a sort of participation mystique. Orbach claims that in the process of discovering what we feel, 'relational psychoanalysis goes beyond an understanding of the countertransference as exclusively a diagnostic tool' to also involve 'a personal response that is an expression of our own subjectivity' (2014, p.18).

Additional reasons why Jung should be considered a relational analyst *ante litteram* (points 1 and 2; see also the discussion of Orbach above) is that Jung (together with Adler) realized the need to move beyond Freud's drive theory and sought an alternative in which Freud's drive theory and sexuality, Adler's inferiority and compensation and Jung's symbolic life and spirituality could coexist. Such an approach would, as Aron underlines, examine 'issues of sex and gender' (Aron, 1999, p.XI), which, in drive theory, with its fixed attitudes towards sexuality and aggression, are obscured with regard to how they take in meaning in the relational context (Aron, 1999, p.XVI).

A final point that makes Jung a relational analyst *ante litteram* (point 10 above) is his appreciation for the possible co-construction and multiplicity of meaning (the opposite of drive). This matches Orbach's claim that relational psychoanalysis employs an 'off the shelfs'[42] understanding of what is happening in the consulting room, and with Jung's (CW8, para.213) claim that 'Freud's theory is a faithful account of his actual experience during the investigation of complexes'. However, it is fundamental to remember that 'such an investigation is always a dialogue between two people' and therefore 'in building up the theory one has to consider not only the complexes of the one partner, but also those of the other'. Moreover, Jung claimed that:

> complexes are very much a part of the psychic constitution, which is the most absolutely prejudiced thing in every individual. His constitution will therefore inexorably decide what psychological view a given observer will have. Herein lies the unavoidable limitation of psychological observation: its validity is contingent upon the personal equation of the observer.
>
> (CW8, para.213)

Relational psychoanalysis and society: Jung and Beck

I want now to show that relational psychoanalysis is useful in light of my comparative study of Jung and Beck, and therefore, in connecting the psychic and the social. I will do so by underlining that Orbach's approach helped psychoanalysis to move beyond a patriarchal standpoint. First, however, I claim that, in my understanding, while the founders of relational psychoanalysis took their first steps in the early 1980s in Europe (before later formalizing their school at New York University), Orbach and Samuels (amongst others) trod a path similar to their US-based colleagues. Orbach did so (in association with L. Eichenbaum[43]) from a feminist perspective at the Women's Therapy Centre in the late 1970s and early 1980s, claiming space (and rightly so!) for feminist psychoanalysis. Samuels did so by developing his concept of plurality as well as examining the 'new' father and the father and mother 'of whatever sex'. I see their works as complementary and fundamental within contemporary psychoanalytical theory. Interestingly, they both later joined relational psychoanalysis as full members of the group.

The importance of Orbach's thinking is that she recognizes in the movement of the 1970s and 1980s an important factor in the development of relational psychoanalysis. I, in parallel, claim that this movement inspired the changes in contemporary society later described by Beck, Giddens and Bauman (but also what Samuels calls plurality or the plural psyche). As mentioned above, Orbach claims that such movements helped examine, decontextualize and reconceptualize traditional relationships (thus, Beck, Giddens and Bauman would argue, detraditionalizing them, and as I would claim, traditionalizing them in a new fashion). In this, I see the advent not only of a post-class, post-gender society but also a post-biblical society (that is a post-class and post-gender society *per se*) wherein biblical metaphors could no longer serve as guidance and people therefore sought new forms of guidance, leading to increased wealth and the current *golden calf syndrome*. This also brought up for reconsideration whether or not God is the 'ultimate authority' (in the search for a place in Paradise), as well as a post-biblical society wherein the 'truth' must be found outside of God, the Ten Commandments and the Bible. This helped to shed light on the shadow aspect of Catholicism and thus moved from God's (the Pope's and priests') infallibility, to the recognition of their human fallibility. This is confirmed by the fact that suicide is no longer viewed by the Catholic Church as a sin. That those who commit suicide can now receive a church funeral is important in signifying that the Church acknowledges the influence of the psyche in the act of suicide. Therefore, the above-mentioned movements helped to empower and 'free' certain categories from their traditional complexity.

To summarize, relational psychoanalysis – when scrutinized employing Jung's magnifying lenses – is helpful in linking psyche, society and the analyst–patient dyad and provides a pluralistic (Samuels, 1989), 'self-critical, non-dogmatic attitude of the therapist, and it means a permanent attention of the therapist for observations during psychotherapy which contradict his theoretical expectations' (Langwieler, 2018). As underlined above, Orbach notes that 'relational psychoanalysis starts from the premise that the individual is born into a set of social and psychological circumstances' and that 'the human infant is a set of possibilities' that 'in order to become recognised as human, will need to attach' (Orbach, 2014, p.16). Therefore, the role of the analyst is fundamental in repairing primary-failed attachment. Orbach (2014, p.16) adds that relational psychoanalysis 'proposes a conflict-relational model' in which 'the struggle to be an individual' involves 'an inevitable dialectic conflict between the wish to connect and to experience one's distinctiveness while understanding that one can only connect with another if one is distinct and one's distinctiveness has been recognized'. This, to me, has two levels: the attachment between two single individuals (mother, father, partner, etc. which I call the primary environment) and between the single individual and the collective, or society (which I call the extended environment). If the relation with and within the primary environment fails or is difficult, the relationship to the extended environment will also fail (see the development of a socio/psychopathic personality).

From the Jungian perspective, a conflict-relational model always starts by examining the complex in which the patient finds him/herself, followed by the recognition that while the complex remains unconscious, the patient will have no tools to address it. Jungian psychotherapist Günter Langwieler[44] claims, following Jung, that 'it is not possible to solve a complex. It is only possible to find ways to solve the conflict(s)', by, I would add, accepting the complex as it is.

To support the claim of a conflict-relational model and to link Jung's complex model with Langwieler's complex/conflict, Samuels' plurality and Orbach's feminist approach, I will here share a clinical case in which 'fat' and its psychosocial component were examined. A 25-year-old man came to see me because he had suddenly and inexplicably lost 60 kg in three months.[45] In working with him, I used the approach offered by Orbach in her book *Fat is a Feminist Issue* (1998) and recognized a complex and a conflict about which my patient was unaware. My own clinical 'Jungian-relational-psychosocial'[46] approach helped me to (a) establish a relation and (b) examine the psychosocial stressors that might be part of his symptomatology. Thus, by examining his symptoms to shed light on his complex(es) and trying to solve the conflict(s), my act of 'accompanying' (Watkins, 2013) him facilitated his 'liberation' (Watkins, 2003) and enabled an inner development in line with Jung's idea of individuation and the recognition that, although a complex cannot be solved, together we could examine and solve the conflict and create the opportunity for psychosocial development.

From this standpoint, Orbach also supports my hypothesis that 'being' involves a merging of conscious and unconscious elements. She claims that 'being is constituted out of the enactment and living of both conscious behaviour and behaviour of which we are unaware' (Orbach, 2014, p.17). This point is fundamental when examining Beck's individualization and my criticism of such and the missing unconscious (see Chapter 2). Orbach (2014, p.17) claims that 'our present stance in relationship involves a foisting onto the relationship a template about relationship (be it authoritarian, benign, push-pull, withholding, merged or more commonly a combination of different elements)'. This is fundamental when examining society and the relation between agent and structure. Thus, if we avoid the fact that the relation between these two 'encodes ways of being and experiencing which are less open than we might desire or think' or, put simply, if the relation needs to be brought to consciousness, we avoid fully grasping our 'being' (wholeness) in the present.

This links to another important point made by Orbach (2014, p.17), namely that 'longings and desires [...] are necessarily infused by the understandings and experiences we have imbibed in the course of development'. This is again fundamental when examining Beck, and his concept of *homo optionis* (2002, p.5), as well as traditional sociology which lacks a deep understanding of the unconscious. Therefore, if we do not carefully scrutinize our longings and desires, we might fool ourselves and hope for that which is *false* (in Winnicottian terms) rather than *true* or *authentic* (in Jungian terms).

Orbach (2014, p.17) confirmed this, claiming that these understandings 'may operate in a conflictual manner with our longings [...] And it is a version of those internalized relationships [...] that will precipitate and form a significant part of the experience of the therapy relationship'. Thus, therapy could be seen as a political (revolutionary) tool when Orbach (2014, pp.20–21) underlines that it 'tells unequivocally that we cannot relinquish the power and dominance of past relationships in our psychic functioning until we accept them as they were [...]' and adds that 'we endeavour to move towards acceptance [...] so that our present expresses our actual and potential power, rather than the victimized or angry stance of thwarted power'.

Psychosocial studies: an overview

Building on Orbach's (2014, p.17) claim that there are 'understandings' that 'may be out of conscious knowledge and may operate in a conflictual manner with our longings' and desires, I now wish to examine how psychosocial studies have successfully merged the psychic with the social. In doing so, and to frame a definition of what psychosocial studies is, I will employ the work of psychosocial theorist Stephen Frosh, who is recognized as the most prominent figure in this new field as well as one of its founders. Other founders include Peter Redman and Wendy Hollway. Once done, I will also claim Jung's role as a pioneer of psychosocial studies. I hope to convince Frosh that Jung is a pioneer of psychosocial studies without coming under such criticism as Frosh afforded to a work comparing Lacanian and psychosocial studies, in which he wrote, 'one author defended a manuscript on the grounds that the notion of 'extimacy' means that any Lacanian work is by very nature psychosocial', adding 'we want more than just the expression of a point of view that might be easily cast within another discipline' (Frosh, 2014, p.164).

Frosh recalls that the term psychosocial studies emerged 'in a small meeting of dissident Birkbeck psychologists in 2000' (2014, p.159), who were working in a department of predominant cognitive neuroscience. He also claims that psychosocial studies 'is a new terrain for interrogating the "social subject", at odds with both psychology and sociology and drowning in a range of deliberately "trans" spaces, such as postcolonial theory, queer theory, psychoanalysis, feminism and relational ethics' (2013, p.1). Frosh (2014, p.161) adds that one of the first definitions of psychosocial studies appeared on the Palgrave[47] website, authored by Redman, Holloway and Frosh. They claimed that:

1 Psychosocial studies seek to investigate the ways in which psychic and social processes demand to be understood as always implicated in each other, as mutually constitutive, coproduced, or abstracted levels of a single dialectical process.
2 As such, it can be understood as an interdisciplinary field in search of transdisciplinary objects of knowledge.
3 Psychosocial studies is also distinguished by its emphasis on affect, the irrational and unconscious process, often, but not necessarily, understood psychoanalytically.

Thus, Frosh (2014, p.163) underlines with this definition, that they intended to:

4 object to the idea of thinking separately about psychological and social processes and then examining the way they intersect with each other.

This last point explains in detail what I aim to do with my own 'I+I' and the merging of the psychic (Jung) and the social (Beck) in the 21st century.

Jung and the psychosocial

Having looked briefly at what psychosocial studies is, let us now turn to Jung. Frosh (2014, p.159) claims that psychosocial studies 'is still in a pre-disciplinary state, and maybe it is best it stays that way, as a "transdisciplinary space"'. I sense, therefore, that psychosocial studies could benefit from the learnings (even merging!) of relational psychoanalysis and also by examining Jung as a pioneer of this new discipline.

I am aware that, when examining Jung, it could be claimed that he did not discuss or write about society directly in his work, or that – with Giegerich[48] – Jung was not interested in society; rather, his interest lay in the collective unconscious. It is my opinion that, despite this, Jung's work is very helpful in framing both the psyche and the social, and that his work has inspired the work of people that later clearly connected to both. Amongst those, I recognize Progoff, Samuels and Watkins on the analytical psychology side and also non-Jungians such as Craib, Orbach and Layton. Others, in my opinion, are on the psychosocial side. For this reason, I claim that when examining the four points by Frosh above, a connection can be found between Jung's thinking and psychosocial studies. Thus, I wish to consider Jung as a pioneer of psychosocial studies.

In detail, in the above section titled 'C.G. Jung, society and sociology', I clarified the connection made by Jung between the psychic and the social, and the fact that the two cannot be understood separately. This corresponds to the first point from Frosh (2014, p.163) and the fact that psychosocial studies 'object to the idea of thinking separately about psychological or social processes'.

Above, employing Progoff (1955, p.161), I showed the first element that makes Jung a pioneer of psychosocial studies, and thereby the fact that Jung perceived that 'the human psyche cannot function without a culture, and no individual is possible without society'. Moreover, Jung 'makes it his principle that all analysis must start from the primary fact of the social nature of man'. To this, I link Redman's claim (2014 unpublished, cited in Frosh, 2014) that psychosocial studies:

> have [...] an equal concern for the depth and range of *social* processes that are in play and help constitute the context or phenomenon in question [...] this implies a concern for phenomena over and above those arising from social interaction to include those belonging to large groups and social system and structure.

Frosh (2014, p.163) also claims that in examining the ways in which the psychological and social are intermingled, psychosocial studies might 'rule out a lot of "traditional"' psychological and sociological approaches and terminology. Therefore, it questions tradition and dogma, which is what Jung did when distancing from Freud.

The second point stems from the fact that both Jung's approach and that of psychosocial studies are transdisciplinary and hence 'have no disciplinary location' (Frosh, 2014, p.164). Psychosocial studies, as underlined by Frosh

(2014, p.161), examines 'sociology, social and critical psychology, political science, postcolonial studies, feminist studies, queer studies, management and organization studies, cultural and media studies and psychoanalysis'. From a first look, it could be said that these areas have nothing to do with Jung or his approach. I sense that this first assumption is wrong because Jung tried to find a method – at the beginning of the 20th century – to help people better understand themselves, and ultimately found his own method that steered away from the pathologizing attitude of psychoanalysis (the same goes for psychosocial studies) and into archetypes, myths and the collective unconscious. I sense that psychosocial studies does the same in a post-biblical society where symbols have lost their traditional meaning and role in society. Therefore, psychosocial studies, like Jung's works, provides a method to understand the individual and society in the here and now (when the here and now is always linked to the past). Another link stems from the fact that both Jung's works and psychosocial studies are interested in criticizing (any) existing 'traditional' discipline or approach. This, Frosh underlines (2014, p.164), is 'a liberating idea' that 'allow[s] in studies that are rooted in an existing discipline but strive[s] to push away from it'. Jung had the same view. On Jung's side, we have alchemy (versus drive theory), while on the psychosocial studies side, we have feminism, queer theory and postcolonial studies (versus the traditional psychological and sociological traditions).

A third point, which clearly shows the link between Jung and psychosocial studies, is that both look with interest at how affect, emotions, the irrational and the unconscious condition people's lives. The fact that psychosocial studies do not examine this merely from a psychoanalytic point of view reminds me of Jung's wish to look beyond medicine, psychiatry and psychoanalytical drive theory into (to mention just two) the psychological implications of alchemy and synchronicity, which are not psychoanalytical concepts *per se*. This is despite Frosh's (2014, p.165) claims that the three founders agreed that although 'psychosocial studies is not *defined* as having a psychoanalytic basis, all three of us are heavily involved in using psychoanalysis in our work and see it as a particularly valuable way of advancing psychosocial concerns' and that

> the concern of Psychosocial Studies with the interplay between what are conventionally thought of as 'external' social and 'internal' psychic formations has resulted in a turn to psychoanalysis as the discipline that might offer convincing explorations of how the 'out-there' gets 'in-there' and vice versa, especially through concepts such as projection, internalization and identification.[49]

Additionally, following Jungian psychoanalyst Alfred Ribi (2020, p.204), it could be said that Jung was:

> the pioneer who discovered the psyche. [...] A 'pioneer' because Freud is usually taken as the pioneer who discovered the psyche, but he was still in the area

of enlightenment, so he missed the irrational side of the psyche, which Jung took into account. So, the whole of the psyche is, to my understanding, understood by Jung only, and of course then, this is his message to his followers – to integrate the rational side of the psyche and the irrational side. And, to my understanding, the irrational side, which is, for instance, synchronicity, meaningful incidences, and a lot of happenings which are connected to the psyche, for instance, the meaning of diseases.

Therefore, both Jung's works and psychosocial studies investigate and try to integrate the rational and irrational sides of the psyche.

On this basis, I claim that Jung's work is by its very nature psychosocial and vice versa. I claim so since Frosh (2014, p.161) – when underlining which books would be published by Palgrave's *Studies in the Psychosocial* – underlines that 'books in the series will generally pass beyond their points of origin to generate concepts, understanding and forms of investigation that are distinctively psychosocial in character' and that 'transdisciplinary objects of knowledge are continually invented in ways that demand the blurring of previously disciplinary boundaries' (Frosh, 2014, p.167). This is certainly Jung's approach: from medicine to psychiatry to occult phenomena (Ph.D. Thesis) to alchemy (beyond drive theory) to myth (collective unconscious) and physics (synchronicity).

This is also confirmed by Redman (cited by Frosh, 2014, p.166), who underlined that 'seeking to investigate how the social is implicated in the psychological, psychosocial studies necessarily pay close attention to psychosocial and emotional states and view these states as lively and consequential, for psychological and social life as well'.

Furthermore, Frosh underlines that psychosocial studies 'draws heavily on psychoanalytic studies, but also on various models of social and political theory'. In this attitude, I frame also Jungians such as Progoff, Samuels, Watkins and also non-Jungians such as Craib, Orbach and Layton. All these authors share a common characteristic of transdisciplinarity. Frosh developed his theory from the core premises of depth psychology, which he linked to different areas of investigation; sometimes giving the impression that his work was about religion or anthropology, ethnology, philosophy, etc. rather than psychology.

Interestingly, both psychosocial studies and Jung's method are concerned with what Freud suggested in 1926, although he only partially implemented it within his tradition: 'if – which may sound fantastic to-day – one had to found a college of psycho-analysis, much would have to be taught in it which is also taught by the medical faculty' alongside 'branches of knowledge which are remote from medicine [...] the history of civilization, mythology, the psychology of religion and the science of literature'. Therefore, if we add ethnology, anthropology and alchemy (among other of Jung's interests), we describe the usual curriculum of the C.G. Jung Institute in Zürich since 1948. I therefore claim that psychosocial studies and the C.G. Jung Institute in Zürich made Freud's fantasy possible, as well as helped to link psychology with sociology in a concrete way.

The Jungian relational-psychosocial model

To conclude this chapter, I would like to clarify the reasons why I think that the relational-psychosocial model is key to understanding the narratives of Self-development in the 21st century at the bridge of conscious and unconscious materials. In this chapter, I was able to introduce Jung's individuation process as well as examine Jung's perspective on society and the social. To that end, I also examined Hillman, the cultural complex, Samuels and Watkins, and examined Jung's role as a pioneer of relational psychoanalysis and psychosocial studies. This has allowed me to claim that a relational–psychosocial model, constituted by a relational approach (merely clinical) and a psychosocial one (merely theoretical), is necessary to look beyond traditional psychology, psychoanalysis and sociology in contemporary 21st-century advanced electronic society. I ought also to show that my own Jungian relational–psychosocial model is based on the following pillars:

1 It connects theory and clinical work (therefore helping to prove the accuracy and efficacy of analytical work with patients).
2 It is transdisciplinary.
3 It is pluralistic (Samuels, 1989) and demonstrates an attitude of inclusion (to replace the split and separation typical of the history of psychoanalysis).
4 It 'starts from the premise that the individual is born into a set of social and psychological circumstances' (Orbach, 2014, p.16).
5 It 'investigate[s] the ways in which psychic and social processes demand to be understood as always implicated in each other' (Frosh, 2014, p.161).
6 It has an 'emphasis on affect, the irrational and unconscious process, often, but not necessarily, understood psychoanalytically' (Frosh, 2014, p.161).
7 It offers a conflict-relational approach (Orbach, 2014) and stresses the need for continuous adaptation in the process of becoming who people authentically are.
8 Becoming (who people authentically are) is seen as a liberation (Watkins, 2003).
9 Analysis is framed as 'accompaniment' (Watkins, 2013) based on 'the co-construction and multiplicity of meaning' (Hargaden and Schwartz, 2007).

These premises (pillars) will be useful to examine Beck (Giddens and Bauman) and his work in the next chapter. In Chapter 3, these pillars will help the comparison between Jung and Beck by conducting a critical comparison of their theories to ascertain the commonalities and differences between them (even making a checklist of what makes a person individuated and/or individualized).

Notes

1 This chapter.
2 Next chapter.
3 In this examination of Jung's theory, I will not review the key concepts of analytical psychology (in this regard, see: Progoff (1956), von Franz (1964), Jacoby (1973), Campbell (1976), Samuels (1985), Dieckmann (1991), Stein (2005 and 2006), Tacey (2012)). Nor

is it my intention to compare Jung with Freud, Adler or any other author (in this regard, see: Progoff (1956), Frey-Rohn (1974) and Kaufmann (1980).

4 Private conversation (2017).

5 Particularly the concept of the Self.

6 Both Plato and Schopenhauer (amongst others) had already introduced this concept prior to Jung.

7 Jung then continued his investigation in *Psychological Types* (1921) and *A Study in the Process of Individuation* (1934).

8 I have decided to quote rather than paraphrase the authors selected for this critical review, to respect their work and give a fully accurate account.

9 Jarrett (1981); Nagy (1991); Bishop (1995, 2017); Dixon (1999); Huskinson (2004).

10 C.G. Jung's CW8 and CW10.

11 I have decided to employ Progoff as my main source. I am aware that there are some other prior studies of Jung in relation to sociology. These include: Richard Gray, *Archetypal Explorations: Towards an Archetypal Sociology* (1996); J. R. Staude, *From Depth Psychology to Depth Sociology: Freud, Jung, and Lévi-Strauss* (1976); and Walker, *Jung and Sociological Theory* (2017) and 'Sociological Theory and Jungian Psychology' (2012).

12 Having stated this here, I will not investigate this further as it would shift the focus of my thesis.

13 Gavin Walker (2017) – although I will not focus on this further – looked at Jung and sociology. Walker claims that: (a) 'the sociologists here have really only pointed to Jung as being sociologically coherent in terms of one or other theoretical tradition. There has been almost no argument as to why one tradition should be considered rather than another, nor debate between them. In short, there has been a lack of metatheoretical argument (Gray, [1996] is a partial exception). This is something I want to begin'; (b) 'Jung's psychology is quite different from Freud's; his sociological affinities may surely be different too. Apart from the theoretical potentials, this could also throw light onto the actual history of the adoption of psychodynamic theory into the sociological repertoire. I also previewed six elements that I thought the American anthropologists of the interwar years and the more recent sociologists had sought to get from Jung, pointing to some common factors and differences between them'.

14 Progoff (1955, p.161) also states that Freud's view was that the individual came first and only then society.

15 By 'mother' I mean – following Samuels (2001) – 'the mother of whatever sex'. Samuels meant by such locutions to break up parental essentialisms.

16 See my comments on Kast (1993) and Hillman (1997b) in Chapter 4.

17 In my view, this was because he wanted to differentiate sociology from psychology and was following Comte, who believed that sociology 'should contribute to the welfare of humanity by using science to understand and therefore to predict and control human behaviour' (Giddens, 1997, p.8).

18 Therefore, 'depth psychology'.

19 As Abercrombie, Hill, and Turner (2000, p.333) underlined 'would discover general laws of social change similar to those found in Newtonian physics and Darwinian biology'.

20 Private conversation (30.1.2023).

21 Here, the link to the aforementioned idea that Jung, 'in understanding the individual as a derivate of society, is following his more fundamental idea that "consciousness comes from the unconscious"' (Progoff, 2013 [1955], pp.163–164). Therefore, just as 'the process of bringing psychic contents to consciousness involves a sharpening and clarifying of the ambiguities of the unconscious, so the individual emerges out of society by a process of differentiation and individualization' (Progoff, 2013 [1955], pp.163–164).

22 Here, the link to the aforementioned idea that Jung believes that 'all analysis must start from the primary fact of the social nature of man' (Progoff, 2013 [1955], p.X), and that

Jung sees man's social quality as inherent to human nature, and thus 'the individual must be understood in terms of the social situation in which he lives' (2013 [1955], p.167).

23 Here, the link to the aforementioned Progoff's claim that since the individual comes before society, it cannot live without society, or indeed culture (Progoff, 2013 [1955], p.161).

24 Including the accusations that he was not scientific, mystical, esoteric and a Nazi.

25 See next paragraph.

26 Ibid.

27 Ibid.

28 Private conversation (2017).

29 Private conversation (2016).

30 Global as well as local.

31 I am aware of the criticisms of the theory of cultural complexes by colleagues (e.g., Kevin Lu), although, here, I did not include those discussions, as I consider mine a deep enough dive to get a general overview on what cultural complexes are, especially when I do not find this key to the development of my work.

32 See below for an overview of psychosocial studies.

33 See Chapter 2 for an overview of each author.

34 Which evolved into the publication of *A New Therapy for Politics?* (2015).

35 Thus, Giddens, Beck and Beck-Gernsheim, but I would also add Bauman's *Liquid Modernity* (2000).

36 Fantasy in the Jungian glossary is a creative exercise fundamental for development. Winnicott (1989, 1990, 1991) and Erickson (1995) also see fantasy as a fundamental stage in teenagers' development.

37 Which is fine if confined to the teenage years (Erickson, 1995).

38 As a post-Jungian and close to archetypal psychology.

39 She also suggests replacing the term 'development' with 'liberation', because 'with regard to economic and cultural progress, "development" of one group seems often to require an oppression of the other' (2003, pp.3–4). She adds that 'a dominant culture's idea of development is too often imposed on a culture, depriving it of undertaking its own path of development' (2003, p.3).

40 My translation from Italian.

41 It is also worth mentioning that relational psychoanalysis is linked to the rediscovery of Ferenczi´s work and mutual analysis, but it is important to underline that Jung was the first to open to mutual analysis (with Otto Gross in 1908), much earlier than Ferenczi. I therefore claim that Ferenczi built on Jung´s legacy. The same can be said of Rank and his work on individuation.

42 Orbach (2014, p.14) adds that, when a patient brings flowers to the analyst as a present, 'the entry point to the relational analyst would be to register how the analysts herself feels about the flowers'.

43 I am aware that Orbach's and Eichenbaum's work began in the United States and not in Europe; however, I have decided to frame Orbach within a European identity (albeit a British thinker).

44 Private conversation (2018).

45 He used to weight 140 kgs.

46 See below, what I mean with 'Jungian-relational-psychosocial' approach.

47 See: http://www.palgrave.com/page/detail/studies-in-the-psychosocial-peter-redman/?K=9780230308589.

48 Private conversation (2018).

49 This matches Orbach's (2014, p.16) view (see above) that 'relational psychoanalysis starts from the premise that the individual is born into a set of social and psychological circumstances'.

Chapter 2

Individualization
Ulrich Beck, Anthony Giddens and Zygmunt Bauman

In this chapter, I will examine Beck (and Beck-Gernsheim), Giddens and Bauman by employing their own texts as a magnifying lens to demonstrate how individualization must be linked to the psyche and the concepts of the conscious and unconscious.

In this chapter, I will claim that each of the above omitted from their investigations a serious consideration of the power of the unconscious (although Giddens and Bauman did consider the psychic processes and the nature of psychology/psychoanalysis).[1] This chapter helps to clarify that sociology knows very little of Jung (or does not want to employ him for political reasons – see Walter Benjamin below), and a lot about Freud. It also underlines that sociology has three kinds of attitude towards him (Jung): (a) ignoring the whole issue (found across the sociological spectrum); (b) heavy use of a 'pure' form of Freudian thought with a structured sociology (Frankfurt School, Lacan/Althusser; feminism, functionalism) and (c) use of an Adlerianized, neo-Freudian approach (Marcuse and Lacan condemn this as dilution).

Here, I will offer an overview of Beck's sociology, focusing on his general theory of second or reflexive modernity. Like Jung, Beck also worked on his Individualization theory (from 1986) throughout his life and it became his trademark, along with the concepts of *Risk Society* (1992), *The Normal Chaos of Love* (1995), *Cosmopolitan Vision* (2006), *Distant Love* (2013) and his final and posthumous work titled *The Metamorphosis of the World* (2016). It was in *Risk Society*, published in Germany in 1986, that Beck first mentioned individualization theory and the concept of second modernity. He subsequently worked with Elizabeth Beck-Gernsheim on a collection of essays dedicated to the Anglo-Saxon countries titled *Individualization* (2002).

In the same years,[2] the sociologist Anthony Giddens was working on similar topics in *Modernity and Self-Identity* (1991), referring to individualization as the 'reflexive project of the self'. A third very important player who investigated themes related to the development of narratives of self-identity is Zygmunt Bauman who published his work *Liquid Modernity* in 2000.

Thus, Beck and Beck-Gernsheim, Giddens and Bauman all considered individualization, the reflexivity of the self and liquidity as a modern process linked to the

DOI: 10.4324/9781003390770-3

'disembedding' of the ways of life of industrial society and the disintegration of previously existing social forms (i.e. class, social status, gender role, family, neighbourhood), without re-embedding, and linked to the detraditionalization of society. Additionally, Beck and Beck-Gernsheim, Giddens and Bauman all examined how love and intimacy were being transformed in second modernity, with Beck and Beck-Gernsheim publishing *The Normal Chaos of Love* in 1995, Giddens *The Transformation of Intimacy* in 1992 and Bauman *Liquid Love* in 2003.

In this chapter, I will frame what Beck and Beck-Gernsheim meant with their concept of individualization, followed by an examination of Giddens and Bauman.[3]

I will also investigate the possible influence of Freud (and other psychoanalytical schools) on Beck and Beck-Gernsheim (and also, superficially, on Bauman and Giddens) to consider whether traditional sociology has grasped the essence of Freud's theory of the unconscious, followed by an examination of the Frankfurt School (Adorno, Horkheimer and Marcuse).[4] The aim in so doing is to demonstrate that traditional sociology is not equipped to consider the unconscious – first because it relies exclusively on the classical drive theory, and second, due to its ontological bias towards the rational and cognitive aspects of human behaviour.

Consequently, I will expand my remit to take into consideration those authors who were able to adopt both sociological and psychosocial perspectives. I will examine the work of psychoanalyst and former *Frankfurter* Erich Fromm, feminist and intersubjective psychoanalyst Jessica Benjamin, sociologist and psychoanalyst Lynne Layton and sociologists Chiara Giaccardi and Mauro Magatti. I will propose a psychosocial approach that merges the conscious and unconscious and, in so doing, critique the Frankfurt School's *one-dimensional* point of view[5] in examining institutions without consideration of the individual and his/her emotions and affects.

Ulrich Beck: an overview

When looking at Ulrich Beck, it is important to remark on his avoidance of methodological debate and his eclecticism as regards classical and later traditions. This is what makes Beck an unusual and valuable action/agency theorist, with a clear focus on the reflective individual navigating a real and problematic social structure.

Beck's focus has always been on the following: 'How can social and political thought and action in the face of radical global change (environmental destruction, financial crisis, global warming, the crisis of democracy and the nation-state institutions) be intertwined in a new modernity?' (Beck, 2007, p.54) Therefore, Beck's work centred around the following concepts: modernity (*second modernity* and *reflexive modernization*), ecology (*risk society*), individualization, globalization and cosmopolitanism.

As emphasized in the introduction, the trajectory of modernity unfolds into what Beck and Beck-Gernsheim (2002) refer to as 'reflexive modernization' or 'second modernity', Giddens (1990) terms as 'high' or 'late' modernity and sociologist Zygmunt Bauman (2000) labels as 'liquid' modernity. This phase is marked by the heightened acceleration of factors such as reflexivity (Beck, Giddens, and Lash, 1994) and the diminishing separation of space and time (Giddens, 1990).

Pinpointing the precise onset of second modernity proves challenging, and researchers hold diverse views on this matter. For clarity, I will align with Beck's perspective, positing that second modernity commenced concurrently with the fall of the Berlin Wall and the collapse of the Soviet empire. This epochal shift irreversibly altered 'the social and political landscape' (Beck, 2002, p.XX), signifying the end of a divided world and the emergence of a globalized one. The roots of second modernity can be traced back to the revolutionary movements of 1968, the neoliberalism of the 1970s, *perestroika* and other factors, including the demise of the industrial model that characterized the late 19th and 20th centuries. Second modernity thus signifies a transformative era, transitioning from a society anchored in gender and class certainties to a post-gender, post-class society (Beck, 2002).

From industrial to risk society: From first to second modernity

Woodman's (2009, p.11) study of Beck is helpful to understand what first and second modernity are. The Australian author underlines that according to Beck and Lau (2005), societies of the West are still to be considered modern. Originating in this idea, Beck warns against an oversimplification of first modernity as well as an overemphasizing of second modernity as a new era.

Woodman (2009, p.12), based on Beck and Lau (2005), points out that boundaries were a key concept of first modernity, which they depict in the time between the 'mid 19th Century Europe to 1960s America'. This is a 'complex but highly ordered process of boundary making built on a social logic of increasing functional differentiation, and hence interdependency' seeking for 'collective progress and control over nature'. According to Beck, 'this is the "either/or" logic, which manifested itself in social institutions such as the nuclear family and "career" work', which contributed clear roles for people and their position in society' (2009, p.12).

Danish authors Mads P. Sørensen and Allan Christiansen (2013, p.23), in their monumental work on Beck, underline that the 'industrial society can be described as a gigantic and very effective cure against material need and poverty'. They (2009, pp.30–31), based on the work of Beck, Wolfgang Bonß and Christoph Lau (2003), name six features of first-modern societies:

1 Society as nation-state society
2 Programmatic individualization
3 Society as employment society or perhaps rather gainful employment society
4 Nature is perceived as being separate from society
5 Leaning on a scientifically defined concept of rationality
6 'First modern societies understand and manage their development according to the principle of functional differentiation'.

Sørensen and Christiansen remind us that according to Beck, in the advent of second modernity, 'the securities, wisdoms and core institutions of first modernity are, little by little, being dissolved' (2009, p.31). This especially applies to concepts such as nations, class, the nuclear family, gender divisions of labour and employment. Hence, Beck, Bonß and Lau (2003, pp.6–7) address second modernity to be the outcome of the below aspects:

1   a multidimensional globalization,
2   a radicalized/intensified individualization,
3   a global environmental crisis,
4   an all-out gender revolution and
5   a so-called 'third industrial revolution'.

Increasing prosperity and in general better living conditions were accompanied by a list of what – as mentioned before – can be termed *bads*. These 'new kinds of risks and man-made disasters and hazards' are what 'Beck calls unintended side effects, and they are the key to understanding his theory of the risk society' (Sørensen and Christiansen, 2013, p.23). Therefore, a process of transformation (opposed to destruction), Woodman (2009, p.12) claims, sets off second modernity, where the 'both/and' logic replaces the 'either/or' one of first modernity.

As underlined by Beck, Bonß and Lau (2003), second modernity corresponds to the self-reflexive activity of realizing that actions of mankind influence its surrounding, especially nature. This recognition goes hand in hand with a change in technology towards more ecological solutions that also foster economic growth.

In conclusion, 'the reflexivity of modernity back on itself weakens the relatively taken for granted boundaries and boundary definitions, like that of the family, that were provided by first modernity's institutional forms' (Woodman, 2009, pp.12–13).

Risk society: an overview

Beck and his student and collaborator Gabe Mythen (2020, pp.383–409), underline that in the West the years between the mid and late 1980s showed a turmoil in terms of 'social, economic and cultural' matters. The concept of 'the nuclear family, mass production, full employment, economic growth and political democracy', on which society was based upon during first modernity went through a process of questioning and de-traditionalization. Additionally, she underlines that events such as Chernobyl and Vila Parisi gave substance to Beck's discourse, who saw in them the fading of the industrial society and the advent of the risk society. Therefore, she adds 'while Beck's predecessors Marx and Weber were preoccupied with the need to establish a fair distribution of socially produced goods', Beck (1994) is the first sociologist that focuses on the *bads* of modernization.

The events of Chernobyl and Vila Parisi set the advent of what Beck termed *risk society*, which for him is a synonym for second modernity. In this context, the uncertainties of first modernity that we got rid of, 'by means of science and rationality to begin with' (Sørensen and Christiansen, 2013, p.9), return because of the completion of such modernization that technology and progress brought forward. Therefore, Beck underlines that with advanced technology 'humanity has once and for all emancipated itself from the bonds of nature' (Sørensen and Christiansen, 2013, p.10).

Sørensen and Christiansen note that – according to Beck – the risk society is not only about the acknowledgement of new risks, but it is very much about a public debate about those. Hence, 'we have, once and for all, entered the risk society' when 'we can no longer ignore the dangers of radioactive emission, global warming and all the other kinds of risks that have followed in the wake of our industrialized way of life' (Sørensen and Christiansen, 2013, p.10). They (2013, p.20), remind us that according to Beck, in risk societies 'consciousness determines being' (Beck, 1992). This means that 'the anticipation of catastrophe' (Beck, 2009) is the predominant feature of risk societies. But risk, I propose, as the *anticipation of catastrophe* cannot be seen only by its political and social implications it may have. It must be seen by its psychological (or psychosocial) implications. I will return to this later (Chapters 3 and 4) where I will devote attention to the Marx/Freud fusion (as proposed by the Frankfurters) and the merging of Beck and Jung (the I+I), as well as the problem of Jung's prioritization of individual development over collective life.

In conclusion, first modernity was about progress, wealth and prosperity, while second modernity is about recognizing and handling the risks brought about by first modernity (Sørensen and Christiansen, 2013, p.19). This means that 'faith and optimism about the future', emphasized by 'progressive and forward-looking thinkers such as Turgot, Adam Smith, Condorcet, Hegel and Marx' is fading in favour of the 'rival pessimistic' views of Nietzsche, Spengler, Horkheimer and Adorno, and that 'the global environmental crisis which has finally, once and for all, turned our notion of progress pessimistic and made pessimism a fundamental governing principle' (Sørensen and Christiansen, 2013, p.19).

Beyond the risk society

Beck and Elisabeth Beck-Gernsheim (2013) adventured themselves in the study 'toward sexual equality in the West on interpersonal relationships and family life', and they became pioneers in opening 'debates around the impacts of individualization on gender relations, familial structure and modern notions of love' (Mythen, 2020, pp.383–409).

In this regard, Woodman (2009, p.13) claims that such categories 'no longer provide the same strong, and taken for granted, social integration' typical for first modernity. The outcome of this is a 'structured relative plurality as people and institutions struggle to find compromises between two or more fundamentally contradictory positions, that of plurality and that of bounded singularity, into a single formula for action, or hierarchically structured pluralisms' (Woodman, 2009, p.13), which – as already described above – correspond to the 'both/and' logic of second modernity.

Below I will return to this and focus, specifically, on what Beck terms individualization, which – in brief – involves 'a relatively macro, but difficult to locate and far from total, sociological phenomenon, imposed on people by institutions, that has ambiguous and difficult to predict effects on attitudes' (Woodman, 2009, p.14 from Beck, 2007).

Ulrich Beck's theory of individualization

According to Beck, the concepts of risk, individualization and the transformation of love and intimacy are intrinsically related. As I have discussed elsewhere (2004), Beck asserts that individualization is becoming the source of the social structure of second modernity itself. Thus, he states that individualization is a concept that describes a structural sociological transformation of social institutions and the relationship of the individual to society.

Beck and Beck-Gernsheim (2002, p.XXII) refer to individualization as 'institutional individualism', which is no longer Parsons' idea of a linear, self-reproducing system but rather 'the paradox of an individualizing structure as a non-linear, open ended, highly ambivalent, ongoing process […] related to the decline of narratives of given sociability'. They (Beck-Gernsheim and Beck, 1995, p.8) also underline that individualization is not a new concept but one that Weber, Simmel, Foucault, Burckhardt and Elias have already investigated. However, they claim that the individualization of second modernity differs from that previously discussed since 'one of the most important aspects is its "mass character"', which 'occurs in the wealthy Western industrialized countries as a side effect of the modernization process designed to be long term'. They continue:

> While earlier generations often knew nothing but the daily struggle for survival, a monotonous cycle of poverty and hunger, broad sections of the population have now reached a standard of living which enables them to plan and organize their own lives.

Therefore, Beck-Gernsheim and Beck (1995, p.9) claim that the individualization process should be understood as 'the outcome of long-term developments which start earlier in some places and later in others' rather than being 'abrupt changes of direction suddenly affecting everybody'. This explains why such developments seem 'like news from a strange far-off country to some', while to others, they are merely a 'familiar account of their everyday lives'.

Beck and Beck-Gernsheim (2002, p.165) claim that we live 'in an age in which the social order of the nation state, class, ethnicity and the traditional family is in decline', in an age where

> the ethic of individual self-fulfillment and achievement is the most powerful current in modern society. The choosing, deciding, shaping human being who aspires to be the author of his or her own life, the creator of an individual identity, is the central character of our time.

From the outset of his research, Beck and Lau (2005, p.6) claimed that 'individualization means that men and women [are] released from the gender roles prescribed by industrial society for a life in the nuclear family'. Thus, he dealt with the fact that society was transforming and moving from class and gender certainties into a new phase – which I call post-biblical – in which those certainties are either detraditionalized (and in my opinion re-traditionalized in a new fashion) or lost (as a consequence of the 'loss of symbols' and the 'end of meaning' peculiar to second modernity). Such a change occurs because these certainties have not been transferred to the next generation or because the next generation rebels against tradition and extirpates them.[6]

Beck-Gernsheim and Beck (1995, pp.1–2) note that since the 1980s, there has been

> a collision of interests between love, family and personal freedom. The nuclear family, built around gender status, is falling apart on the issues of emancipation and equal rights, which no longer conveniently come to a halt outside our private lives. The result is the quite normal chaos of love.

They add that we must rethink the concept of a traditional 'nuclear family' to become familiar with such concepts as 'the negotiated family, the altering family, the multiple family, new arrangement after divorce, remarriage, divorce again, new assortments from your, my, our children, our past and present families'.

Thus, Beck-Gernsheim and Beck (1995, p.2) introduce the concept of individualization in second modernity, claiming that we 'compulsively [...] search for the right way to live, trying out cohabitation, divorce or contractual marriage, struggling to coordinate family and career, love and marriage, "new" motherhood and fatherhood, friendship and acquaintances'. Beck-Gernsheim and Beck (1995, p.4) then ask why

> there are so many millions of people in so many countries deciding individually as if in a collective trance to abandon what used to be marital bliss and exchange it for a new dream, living together in an 'open marriage' beyond the safety net and the security of the law, or choosing to bring up a child single-handed? Why do they prefer to live on their own, pursuing ideas like independence, diversity, variety, continually leafing over new pages of their egos, long after the dream has started to resemble a nightmare?

The answer, according to Beck and Beck-Gernsheim (2002), is that individualization corresponds to the need people feel, mostly in Western countries where the prospect of living one's own life is the force that moves inhabitants,[7] to create a so-called do-it-yourself biography; that is, the need to take control of their own lives. This, Beck and Beck-Gernsheim (2002) argue, is an experimental life, condemned to activity, where everything is a matter of self-responsibility.

Therefore, individualization, according to Beck and Beck-Gernsheim (2002, p.3), is the process through which

> the normal biography becomes the 'elective biography', the 'reflexive biography', the 'do-it-yourself biography'. This does not necessarily happen by choice, neither does it necessarily succeed. The do-it-yourself biography is always a 'risk-biography', indeed a 'tightrope biography', a state of permanent (partly overt, partly concealed) endangerment.

Beck adds (2002, p.133) that if one were to ask these individuals what they are doing and how they are struggling, they would probably say that they engage and fight for 'money, the work, the power, the love, God or anything else'. He adds that, for these individuals, 'money is their own money, space is their own space, even in the elementary sense of an assumption to live a life that can be defined'. So, Beck says, 'the daily struggle for a life has become the collective experience of the Western World' (Beck and Lau, 2005, p.133).

That being the case, Beck and Beck-Gernsheim claim, following Ley (1984, cited in Beck-Gernsheim and Beck, 1995, p.5) that 'standard biographies are transformed into "choice biography"' and that 'biographies are removed from the traditional perceptions and certainties. From external control and general moral laws, becoming open and dependent on decision-making, and are assigned as a task for each individual' (Beck and Beck-Gernsheim, 2002, p.5). They also claim that the concepts of family, marriage, parenthood, sexuality, and love are no longer fixed, but vary 'in substance, exceptions, norms and morality from individual to individual and from relationship to relationship'. Thus, they say, individuals must negotiate the meaning of these concepts, even if doing so 'might unleash the conflicts and devils that lie slumbering among the details'. Through this negotiation, we increasingly become the 'legislators' of our own lives, forming our own moral judgements and 'loosen[ing] the bonds' of our own past (Beck and Lau, 2005, p.5). Consequently, Beck-Gernsheim and Beck (1995, p.6) claim that individuals

> find themselves forced, under pain of material disadvantage, to build up a life of their own by way of the labour market, training and mobility, and if need be to pursue this life at the cost of their commitments to family, relations and friends.

In sum, Beck (2002, p.5) claims that individualization means that:

> the human being becomes (in the radicalization of Sartre's meaning) a choice among possibilities, *homo optionis*. Life, death, gender, corporeality, identity, religion, marriage, parenthood, social ties – all are becoming decidable down to the small print; once fragmented into options, everything must be decided.

Moreover, in the individualized society, people 'think, calculate, plan, adjust, negotiate, define, revoke (with everything constantly starting again from the beginning):

these are the imperatives of the "precarious freedoms" that are taking hold of life as modernity advances' (Beck, 2002, p.6). Responding to his critics, Beck said:

> It is sometimes claimed that individualization means autonomy, emancipation, the freedom and self-liberation of humanity. This calls to mind the proud subject postulated by the philosophy of the Enlightenment, who will acknowledge nothing but reason and its laws. But sometimes anomie rather than autonomy seems to prevail – a state unregulated to the point of lawlessness. […] Any generalization that seeks to understand individualized society only in terms of one extreme or the other – autonomy or anomie – abbreviates and distorts the questions that confront us here.
>
> (Beck, 2002, p.7)

Having investigated Beck's theory of individualization, I will now shift my focus to Giddens and Bauman. I will return to Beck later in this chapter to critically review his theory. I will do so by assessing why, while he noted that individuation is a term from depth psychology, he did not investigate further. I will also examine his final work (*The Metamorphosis of the World*, 2016) which I have avoided until now. In this book, he seeks to rescue himself from a major embarrassment while examining today's world, claiming that 'there was nothing – neither a concept nor a theory – capable of expressing the turmoil of this world in conceptual terms, as required by the German philosopher Hegel' (Beck, 2016, p.4). To this, I suggest examining Jung (instead of Hegel) and his individuation process as a valid theory to understand the world as it is (and thus opposing the idea that 'the world is unhinged' that 'the world is out of joint and it has gone mad' Beck, 2016, p.XI). I will also claim that Jung's individuation comprises a theory of metamorphosis of the individual and therefore of the world. Finally, I claim that anomie (as used by Beck, following Durkheim and Merton) might serve as a sociological synonym to what psychoanalysis has termed neurosis.

Biograph sociology

Before turning to look at Giddens and Bauman, it is fundamental to look at Beck's work and contextualize it within the wider sociological spectrum and traditions, as well as to recognize that Beck's intellectual work could be represented with different stages in his thinking. This helps to appreciate the evolution of his ideas over time.

According to Roy Boyne (2001, p.54) and Mythen (2020), Beck 'challenged social scientists to reflect on what we "know" about the world, how we go about acquiring such "knowledge" and what the effects of academic knowledge production might be'. They add that his '"methodological utopianism" was geared towards the development of projective social theory, rather than adherence to the strictures of assiduous empiricism', and this will help me to place him outside of the agency theorists' cluster.

In one of his early books, Beck underlined that individuals work to find 'biographic solutions to systemic contradictions' (1992, p.137). This, according to many, makes him a *de-jure* (although not *de-facto*) agency theorist. I will challenge the idea that Beck is an agency theorist later in this chapter. But before that, it is important to look – although briefly – at what action theory is and how it is linked to agency theory.

Action theory and agency/structure theory are related concepts. Both focus on individual behaviour and its relationship to social context. Action theory concentrates on individual agency and intentionality, while agency/structure theory considers the broader social structures and power relations that shape individual behaviour.

Sociologists Nicholas Abercrombie, Stephen Hill and Bryan S. Turner, state in *The Penguin Dictionary of Sociology* (2000, p.2) that agency theory focuses on the relationship between agents and institutions, while action theory focuses on the nature of human action and behaviour or how 'structure determine what individual do, how structures are created, and what the limits are, if any, on individuals' capacities to act independently of structural constrains'.

Abercrombie, Hill and Turner (2000, p.9) underline that action theory originates from the work of Weber and consists in 'the analysis of action starting with the individual actor'. They underline that action taken by an individual is related to a set of elements like their goals, expectations and values. Parsons, they add, calls this the *action frame of reference*.

Abercrombie, Hill and Turner (2000, p.3) name Parsons as the most distinguished positivist action theorist, who believes that 'norms and values are critical as they regulate and make predictable the behaviour of others' (Abercrombie, Hill and Turner, 2000, p.255).

They (2000, p.255) state that for Parsons:

> action is behaviour directed by the meanings attached by actors to things and people. Actors have goals and select appropriate means. Courses of action are constrained by the situation and guided by symbols and values. The most important category is interaction; that is, action oriented towards other actors.

Having briefly discussed action theory, I will now focus on the meaning of agency theory.

Again, employing the work of Abercrombie, Hill and Turner (2000, p.9), agency (and structure) theory can be described – in a nutshell – as 'the relationship between individuals and social structure'. They debate how an individual is embedded in a social environment that affects their actions. How the ability of individuals to act and make decisions is shaped by societal patterns that would even limit decision-making. They (2000, p.9) describe three perspectives on this:

1   'structures cannot be seen as determining and the emphasis should be placed on the way that individuals create the world around them';

2 'The contrary position is that sociology should be concerned only with social structures that determine the characteristics and actions of individuals, whose agency or special characteristics therefore become unimportant';

3 A compromise between (1) and (2), 'avoiding both the idea of a structure determining individuals and also that of individuals independently creating their world'.

Another position is the one developed by Giddens, who:

> attempted to overcome the division between agency and structure by means of the notion of 'duality of structure'. He argues that 'structure' is both the medium and the outcome of the actions which are recursively organized by structures. He emphasizes the 'knowledgeability' of actors, who depend on existing knowledge and strategy to achieve their ends.
>
> (Abercrombie, Hill, and Turner, 2000, p.9)

Anthony Giddens: modernity and the reflexivity of the self

Having investigated Beck's and Beck-Gernsheim's individualization process, it is necessary to examine Giddens for three main reasons: first, because he praised Beck's work (in life and in his obituary); second, because he was able to contextualize modernity as late or high modernity; and third, because – parallel to Beck – he investigated the development of the narrative of self-identity.

In January 2015,[8] Giddens wrote of Beck that he was 'the greatest sociologist of his generation', for which he gave several reasons. First, because Beck 'was one of the very first authors to discuss globalisation – at a time, in the 1980s [...] when in fact many disputed its essential validity'. Second, because *Risk Society*, which Beck published shortly before the Chernobyl disaster, was – as Giddens underlines – 'a remarkable anticipation of the future on his part', 'broke new ground in many ways', and 'influenced legions of researchers since the time at which it first appeared'. And finally, in *The Normal Chaos of Love* (1995) co-authored with Beck-Gernsheim, they examine the fact that 'love is "chaotic" because the world of "relationships" is one continually in flux. Love is rarely "for life" today any more than a job is' (Giddens, 2015).

Modernity is the term used to refer to the ways of living, or social organizations, which appeared in Europe around the 17th century and extended their influence to most of the world. In *The Painter of Modern Life*, Baudelaire (1995) was the first to introduce the concept of *modernité*, which is associated with the idea of *nouveauté*. An essential element of modernity is the notion of change and progress. Modernity, as underlined by Lash and Friedman (1992), is about movement, flux, change and unpredictability, rather than being static.

Giddens (1998, p.94) notes that modernity is the period that corresponds to the beginning of modern society and industrial civilization and is 'associated with a certain set of attitudes toward the world'. This world, according to Giddens, can be transformed by human intervention, comprises a complex of economic and political institutions, and differs from previous cultures by its emphasis on living 'in the future rather than in the past'.

Giddens (1990, p.36) claims that the idea of contrast with tradition is thus inherent and implicit in the idea of modernity, even if 'many combinations of the modern and the traditional are to be found in concrete social settings'. Giddens (1990, p.36) also defines reflexivity as:

> a defining characteristic of all human action. All human beings routinely 'keep in touch' with the grounds of what they do as an integral element of doing it. I have called this elsewhere the 'reflexive monitoring of action,' using the phrase to draw attention to the chronic character of the processes involved.

Giddens (1990, p.37) thus claims that traditional cultures honour the past and its attendant symbols because such symbols 'contain and perpetuate the experience of generations'. This honouring allows for all aspects of experience to be embedded 'within the continuity of past, present, and future', and for activities to be structured by recurrent social practices. However, traditions do not remain static but are reinvented by each subsequent generation. Thus, according to Giddens, 'tradition does not so much resist change as pertain to a context in which there are few separated temporal and spatial markers in terms of which change can have any meaningful form'.

However, according to Giddens (1990, p.38), in modernity, reflexivity has a different character 'such that thought and action are constantly refracted back upon one another'. As such, daily life becomes removed from its embeddedness in the past, unless the past 'coincide(s) with what can be defended in a principled way in the light of incoming knowledge'. Thus, in modernity, while tradition does not become obsolete, the significance of its role is greatly diminished.

Giddens also claims that:

> Reflexivity, an unavoidable and distinctive characteristic of all human actions, allows the link between tradition and modernity. Reflexivity, with the advent of modernity, allows thought and action to be constantly reflected back upon one another. [...] the reflectivity of modern social life consists in the fact that social practices are constantly examined and reformed in the light of incoming information about those very practices, thus constitutively altering their character.
>
> (1990, p.38)

Modernity then, according to Giddens, is based on knowledge reflexively applied together with four fundamental institutional dimensions – capitalism, industrialism, military power and surveillance – which together differentiate this era from others.

Modernity evolved into what Giddens called high or late modernity which is characterized by the intensification and speeding up of aspects like reflexivity (Beck, Giddens and Lash, 1994).

Giddens worked on a parallel path to Beck and termed what Beck calls individuation *self- reflexivity*. In *Modernity and Self-Identity* (1991, p.70), he claims that people ask themselves 'What to do? How to act? Who to be?', which 'are focal questions for everyone living in circumstances of late modernity – and ones which, on some level or another, all of us answer, either discursively or through day-to-day social behaviour'. He then adds that:

> A person's identity is not to be found in behaviour, nor – important though this is – in the reactions of others, but in the capacity to keep a particular narrative going. The individual's biography, if she is to maintain regular interaction with others in the day-to-day world, cannot be wholly fictive. It must continually integrate events which occur in the external world, and sort them into the ongoing 'story' about the self.
>
> (1991, p.54)

As I have underlined elsewhere (2004), in the setting of what Giddens calls 'high' or 'late' modernity, the self must be reflectively created, like the broader institutional context. Therefore, self-identity becomes a reflexively organized endeavour, wherein 'the reflective project of the self, which consists in the sustaining of coherent, yet continuously revised biographical narratives, takes place in the context of multiple choices, as filter through abstract systems' (Giddens, 1991, p.5).

The reflexivity of self-identity, according to Giddens, means that the self must be reflexively understood by the individual in terms of his or her biography. The reflective process of the self must be seen as the self-identity that is constituted by the reflexive ordering of self-narratives, where the self corresponds to the formation of a specific lifespan in the condition of modernity. By this means, self-development, as reflexively organized, tends to become internally referential.

In *Modernity and Self-Identity* (1991), Giddens investigated the concept of Self between ontological security, trust and existential anxiety by not only examining (amongst others) Garfinkel, Kierkegaard, Wittgenstein, Goffman and Foucault but also Freud, Erickson, Winnicott, Sullivan and other psychoanalysts. Giddens underlines that (1991, p.35) 'an account of self-identity has to be developed in terms of an overall picture of the psychological make-up of the individual' and added that 'such a picture should take the form of a stratification model'. Interestingly, this model links Wittgenstein to Winnicott, but unfortunately, Giddens does not investigate any psychoanalytical theorist after Winnicott, and therefore fails to recognize the most recent developments in this field, such as the relational and, in particular, intersubjective turns (this latter stressing the importance of mutuality rather than Freudian and post-Freudian duality and the tension of opposites arising therefrom, such as oneness and separateness and difference and sameness (Benjamin, 1988)). This model means that:

1   'We begin from the premise that to be a human being is to know, virtually all of the time, in terms of some description or another, both what one is doing and why one is doing it'.

2 'All human beings continuously monitor the circumstances of their activities as a feature of doing what they do, and such monitoring always has discursive features' (Giddens, 1991, p.35).

Therefore, Giddens (1991, p.35) claims that 'agents, are normally able, if asked, to provide discursive interpretations of the nature, and the reason for the behaviour in which they engage'. He then adds:

> the knowledgeability of human agents, however, is not confined to discursive consciousness of the conditions of their action. Many of the elements of being able to 'go on' are carried at the level of practical consciousness, incorporated within the continuity of everyday activities. Practical consciousness is integral to the reflexive monitoring of action, but it is 'non-conscious', rather than unconscious.
>
> (1991, pp.35–36)

I disagree with this approach and prefer, as noted in the previous chapter, to adopt Orbach's (2014, p.17) view that 'being is constituted out of the enactment and living of both conscious behaviour and behaviour of which we are unaware' [i.e., unconscious] and that agents mutually influence each other, as underlined by the intersubjective view (Benjamin, 1988), while structure and agency are also mutually influential.

Drawing from Winnicott, Giddens (1991, p.41) underlines that 'the establishing of basic trust is the condition of the elaboration of self-identity just as much as it is of the identity of other persons and objects'. He also claims (1991, p.42) that:

> *acquired routines*, and forms of mastery associated with them, in the early life of the human being, are much more than just modes of adjusting to a pre-given world of persons and objects. They are constitutive of an emotional acceptance of the reality of the 'external world' without which a secure human existence is impossible.

In this case, I also prefer to follow Orbach (2014, p.16) who says that 'the individual is born into a set of social and psychological circumstances. The human infant is a set of possibilities – not ID-based, not instinctually driven – but in order to become recognized as a human, will need to attach'.

Investigating the 'trajectory of the self', Giddens (1991, pp.70–108) draws from *Self-Therapy* (1989) by Janette Rainwater, a clinical psychologist and founding member of the emerging Gestalt Therapy Institute of Los Angeles. He selected ten features from this work that he believed to be distinctive of the search for self-identity in the late-modern age and investigated how to connect these features with the institutional transformations characteristic of the late-modern world. These are:

1   The self is seen as a reflexive project for which the individual is responsible.
2   The self forms a trajectory of development from the past to the anticipated future. The lifespan rather than external events is in the foreground, the latter are cast as either fortuitous or throwing up barriers that need to be overcome.
3   Reflexivity becomes continuous – the individual continuously asks the question 'What am I doing in this moment, and what can I do to change?'
4   The narrative of the self requires continual creative input.
5   Self-actualization implies the control of time.
6   The reflexivity of the self extends to the body. Awareness of the body is central to the grasping of the moment. The point here is to establish a differentiated self, not to dissolve the ego.
7   Self-actualization is understood as a balance between opportunity and risk.
8   Personal growth depends on conquering emotional blocks and tensions that prevent us from understanding ourselves – recover or repeat old habits is the mantra.
9   The life course is seen as a series of 'passages'. All such transitions involve loss.
10 The line of development of the self is *internally referential* – it is the creation of a personal belief system by which someone changes – one's first loyalty is to oneself.

Therefore, Giddens (1991, p.80) claimed that it seems:

> justified to assert that, partial, inadequate and idiosyncratic as the ideas just outlined may be, they signal something real about self and self-identity in the contemporary world – the world of late modernity. How that may be we can begin to see by connecting them up to the institutional transformation characteristics of that world.

In *The Transformation of Intimacy* (1992), Giddens attempted to rethink the relation between sexuality and power, examining Freud's assumptions and comparing them with the work of Michel Foucault, William Reich and Herbert Marcuse. Giddens used these authors to examine Freudian concepts and to draw his own conclusions.

In *Reflexive Modernization* (1994), Giddens examines Freud (as well as Lacan, thus proving the links with language) and uses Freud (or Lacan) to reach his objectives, and hence to prove his structuration theory. However, I argue that Giddens is not interested in the individual but merely in the relation between structure and agency. Thus, he seeks to understand how societies evolve within the context of reflexive modernity or the reflexivity of the self. In so doing, he looks at sociological concepts such as power, security and trust (which link with psychoanalytical concepts such as emotions of anxiety and fear as well as domination and differentiation) from a classical Hegelian and Freudian perspective where:

the hypothetical self presented by Hegel and Freud does not want to recognize the other, does not perceive him as a person just like himself. He gives up omnipotence only when he has no other choice. His need for the other – in Freud, physiological, in Hegel existential – seems to place him in the other's power, as if dependency were the equivalent of surrender.

(Benjamin, 1988, p.53)

Benjamin will also be useful when examining Beck's *Metamorphosis of the World* (2016) later in this chapter.

Giddens, therefore, examines the relation between structure and agency (and vice-versa) to offer insight for governance and policy. However, he fails to explore how people should navigate these difficult and changing times and when he does use psychoanalytical authors, he does not go into depth or into the most recent work (as just underlined with Benjamin and intersubjectivity, for example). Giddens argues that people are always knowledgeable about what they are doing, but, if that is the case, how do the conscious and unconscious come into play? How do the irrational, emotions and affects as well as fate and destiny come into play?

Moreover, Giddens, similarly to Beck, offers no solution to the conflicts arising from late-modern social transformations both at the collective and individual levels.

However, Giddens – contrary to Beck (2002) who, while noting that individuation is a term from depth psychology did not investigate further – draws extensively from psychoanalysis, and his interest in this field is clear. Nevertheless, I propose that he uses classic drive theory as a theoretical framework, as the critical theorists did with Freud, but fails to go beyond Freud's dogma. Another deficiency is that Giddens' interest in psychoanalysis is limited to Freud (and the post-Freudians), and only theoretical, not clinical.

In conclusion, Giddens' openness to and interest in psychoanalysis must be acknowledged, but it cannot be said that his work shows how affect, emotions, the irrational and the unconscious condition people's lives and society. Therefore, I propose, that his theory is too rigid. This is because he never adventured beyond Freudian/Post-Freudian drive theory. Second, it seems that he failed to fully grasp the essence of Freud's theory of the unconscious, falling under the same spell that trapped the Frankfurt School. That is to say, he failed to extend his view beyond Freud, as if psychoanalysis stopped there. This was the same mistake as was made by Marcuse (see next chapter), of which his disputes with Fromm are evidence. This also demonstrates that mainstream sociology has not been able to keep up to date with the times and new theoretical psychoanalytical developments. Nevertheless, it is interesting to see that Giddens was more open than Beck to examining the field of psychoanalysis.

Zygmunt Bauman: Marx, post-modernity and liquidity

It is timely at this point to investigate the work of Zygmunt Bauman. First, because his late work is written solely for the non-academic reader and therefore, compared to Beck's and Gidden's more academic and opaque style, his theories are intelligible. Second, Bauman's theory overlaps with those of Beck and Beck-Gernsheim and Giddens in claiming that, in second modernity, individuals become responsible for their own lives (*homo-optionis*). Third, Bauman made liquidity (which I will introduce in the next few pages) an existentialist matter (while for Beck it was a matter of options and for Giddens one of reflexivity). Therefore, Bauman acknowledges that liquidity (or the impasse incurred by liquid modernity) is linked to values such as free choice, inner strength, authenticity, personal responsibility, self-determination and individualism. It remains to be seen, however, whether Bauman's liquidity comprises a 21st-century existentialism in the line of Kierkegaard, Nietzsche, Camus, Sartre or R. D. Laing. Here, I will propose that liquidity stems from early existential theories (minus a *purpose* and *substance*) and that the more we turn to this 21st-century existentialism, the more we turn to anomie (anxiety, depression and suicide). Therefore, in this paragraph I will propose that Jung's individuation could be seen as a way out of anomie.

Bauman is well known for his theory of liquidity, as espoused in his works *Liquid Modernity* (2000), *Liquid Love* (2003), *Liquid Life* (2005), *Liquid Fears* (2006) and *Liquid Times* (2007). Previously, however, he was associated with Marxism and the concept of post-modernity which he claimed to comprise modernity 'minus its illusion' (Bauman, 2002, p.2).

As Giaccardi and Magatti (2022, p.17) underline, Bauman 'called "liquid" the society in which relationships had become open and functional, and therefore necessarily unstable and provisional, according to the model of the "pure relationship"', dear to the first modernity. In *Liquid Modernity* (2000, p.82), Bauman notes that what unites all forms of modern life 'is precisely their fragility, temporariness, vulnerability and inclination to constant change'. Thus, 'to "be modern" means to modernize – compulsively, obsessively [...] forever "becoming", avoiding completion, staying underdefined'. For Bauman, the modern person never reaches completion, but is, rather, embroiled in a never-ending series of new beginnings with 'each new structure' replacing the previous 'as soon as it is declared old-fashioned'. Thus, a *sine qua non* of modernity is being at all times 'post-something'. In liquid modernity, 'change is the only permanence, and uncertainty the only certainty'.

According to Bauman (2005, p.2), this 'liquid life' is precarious; 'the conditions [...] change faster than it takes the ways of acting to consolidate into habits and routines' (2005, p.1). This forces its members 'to forget, erase, leave and to replace' their relationships and work (2005, p.11). Bauman also cites Italo Calvino's *Invisible Cities* (1978) 'whose inhabitants, the day they "feel the grip of weariness" and can no longer bear their job, relatives, house and life, simply move to the next city and take up a new life' (2005, p.4). Thus, with its 'succession of new beginnings', liquid life is marked by 'swift and painless endings, without which new beginnings would be unthinkable' (2005, p.2). It is these endings that comprise its most challenging moments, leading to acute anxiety 'of being left behind, of overlooking "use by" dates, of being saddled with possessions that are no longer desirable' (2005, p.2). Moreover, with its rapid cycle of change, liquid life cannot retain 'its shape or stay on course for long' (2005, p.1) and the burden of responsibility that fluid modernism places on the individual comprises the need to replace traditional patterns with self-elected ones (2000, p.8).

The question then arises: how can the individual select, from the multiple patterns on offer, which best suits his current situation, while remaining ever ready to dismantle the various parts of the patchwork of options he has sewn together (Bauman, 2005, p.6)? In the face of 'erosive forces and disruptive pressures' (2005, p.6), the individual is in constant battle with the 'crumbling walls' of his identity (2005, p.13). Thus, he must 'master and practice the art of "liquid life"' with its attendant 'disorientation', and 'absence of itinerary and direction' (2005, p.4). This is a journey without end, 'a desert, a void, a wilderness, a yawning abyss into which only a few would muster the courage to leap of their own free will' (2005, p.5). But can we really accept this state, or do we simply founder in a state of disorientation? And is it possible to develop what Bauman terms 'immunity to vertigo', a tolerance for the absence of itinerary and direction, and for infinite travel without purpose? Therefore, how far can consciousness take us on these quests without including the unconscious?

To answer these questions, I will contextualize and critically examine Bauman's concept within Jungian, post-Jungian and relational psychoanalysis. According to *This Be The Verse* by British poet Philip Larkin (1971), parents negatively impact you. It may not be their intention, but it happens. Is Larkin correct in suggesting to leave your parents' home as soon as possible and refrain from having children of your own? This poem – written in the early 1970s and later turned into a song by British songwriter Anne Clark (1987) – pictured the mood of an epoch when rebellion against authority (including parental authority) was key. Thus, separation from the parents is the key to individuation because 'when the destructive instinct is projected outward, the problem of omnipotence is not solved, but merely relocated' (Benjamin, 1988, p.67). As suggested by Kast (1993, pp.5–6), to individuate means to:

1 Become independent from parents and from parental complexes
2 Become more competent in relationships
3 Become more of who[9] and what you are
4 Become more 'whole' (spiritual)

If an individual fails to accomplish this separation–individuation axis, life may be attended by the feeling of 'killing time', as depicted so vividly in Anne Clark's song of the same name (Album: Joined Up Writing; Song: *Killing Time* 1984): What are the symbolic meanings of ice, suicide, cross and flag in this song? Both the cross and flag could be collective symbols linked with religion and national identity, while ice and suicide relate to the paralysis of the need for renewal. Thus, this song shows both faith and trust in the new time – the wish to have *faith in the cross* and *trust in the flag* – as well as the fact that this cannot be, because – following Beck – we live in a time of individualism where such collective symbols are *dead*: thus, the only cross is your cross, the only flag your flag. This song demonstrates that without learning the art of *meditation*, we end up killing time or (even) ourselves as a consequence of anomie. This is important because, as Bauman (2005, p.6) noted, we live in a time of 'materially affluent yet spiritually impoverished and famished contemporaries, tired like the residents of Calvino's Eutropia of everything they have enjoyed thus far (like yoga, Buddhism, Zen, contemplation, Mao)'.

Jung also discussed the meditative life and the fact that superficial approaches thereto are merely a distraction. In his essay 'Self-knowledge' (*Mysterium Coniunctionis*, 1955, para.497 [hereafter CW14]), Jung claimed that 'what I call coming to terms with the unconscious the alchemists called "meditation"' and added, citing Ruland, that meditation is 'an Internal Talk of one person with another who is invisible, as in the invocation of the Deity, or communion with one's self, or with one's "good angel"'. In a post-biblical society, there is a fresh need for a renewed *internal talk*, and one way of engaging in such is through Jungian psychoanalysis. As Jung (CW14, para.498) noted, however, 'there are relatively few people who have experienced the effects of an analysis of the unconscious on themselves, and almost nobody hits on the idea of using the objective hints given by dreams as a theme for meditation'. It seems that more than 70 years after the publication of this essay, little has changed at least in the world of sociology.

Jung (CW14, para.498) claimed that modern meditation 'is practiced only in religious or philosophical circles, where a theme is subjectively chosen by the meditant or prescribed by an instructor'. He added that

> These methods are of value only for increasing concentration and consolidating consciousness, but have no significance as regards effecting a synthesis of the personality. On the contrary, their purpose is to shield consciousness from the unconscious and to suppress it.

That being the case, such methods are of no therapeutic value.

Although the reputation of meditation and contemplation has changed in the West since Jung wrote this paper, he believed them to have a bad reputation in the West. I propose that, today, the *à la mode* forms of meditation and contemplation – yoga at lunchtime, daily morning meditation, weekend or 'holiday' retreats – that have been adopted in the West do not facilitate *internal talk*. Instead, they merely facilitate a momentary calm before returning (recharged) to the jungle of an affluent society. Thus, these techniques resemble smartphone battery chargers: indispensable for recharging in our society, but never fully disconnecting. Therefore, I agree with Jung's (CW14, para.498) view that:

> No one has time for self-knowledge or believes that it could serve any sensible purpose. Also, one knows in advance that it is not worth the trouble to know oneself, for any fool can know what he is. We believe exclusively in doing and do not ask about the doer, who is judged only by achievements that

have collective value [...] Western man confronts himself as a stranger and that self-knowledge is one of the most difficult and exacting of the arts.

The Western approach to meditation and contemplation is paralleled in Anne Clark's song *Killing Time* (1984). I claim it is a commodity one can buy, consume (swallow) and defecate. As such, it has no lasting presence; instead, the circle of buying, swallowing and defecating must be continuously renewed.

To clarify, and particularly to reinforce Jung's claim that 'the doer [...] is judged only by achievements that have collective value', I again employ Anne Clark, using extracts from her song *Sleeper in Metropolis* (1983), which vividly describes the alienation of society described by Beck, Giddens and Bauman: "a sleeper in metropolis", "insignificance", "the system", "helpless safety"...'.

While 1960s', 1970s' and 1980s' society was one of rebellion against the parents and authority, it also looked 'east' to different kinds of spirituality to replace the Bible, which had become simply another symbol of authority. In this regard, Bauman (2005, p.7), citing Andrzej Stasiuk's idea of the 'spiritual Lumpenproleratiat', claims that those affected by this virus 'live in the present and by every present [...] They live to survive (as long as possible) and to get satisfaction (as much as possible)'. Bauman adds that they are 'filled to the brim with survival-and-gratification concerns' and are left with 'no room for worries about anything other than what can be, at least in principle, consumed and relished on the spot'.

In an interview I conducted with Orbach in June 2018, she noted that 'women today are exactly the same' as they were in the past, adding that:

> The whole issue of dependency and attachment and autonomy and work is still very much on the agenda. I come across young women that feel it is very bad to have any dependency needs. [...] They don't know that their work should occupy a huge amount of their life. [...] That's particularly women in their 20s and 30s when they have a judgement that what feminism is meant (or what it was or what the nuances are)... is that they should be ok with it. Whereas the world is not fine. They need to be brought up with the idea that the world is full of struggle. Psychological struggle as well. To manifest yourself. To dare to express your longings. To dare to connect with others in a way that is separate and connected. And this is where the struggle is both within feminism and psychoanalysis. You do need a separated attachment. You are not cut off but you are not merged.
>
> (Orbach, 2020, p.198)

Orbach thus confirms what Benjamin and Kast previously proclaimed: the need to separate from parents and parental complexes to become more competent in relationships, in order to individuate.

I therefore asked Orbach:

> How are women today, keeping in mind Carol and Maria from your own *The Impossibility of Sex* (1999). Therefore, how are those women that were able

to chose to have a full-time job, family commitments, kids, partners? Those women that – when following Beck, Bauman, and Giddens, can chose who to be, what to do and who to love?

Orbach answered:

> I had the experience with some young women that they have ticked all the boxes, but they don't exist. 'I have got the boyfriend, I have got the body, I have got the job', 'I have achieved'. But these things are not integrated, and this is partly because feminism, their mother (I am not blaming their mothers), and the historical moment when they were raised which was to project onto girls and foster their ambitions without actually underpinning them, so they feel a bit empty I think. A very good example is a recent book of mine in which a character Helen is in that situation. She is a lawyer, she has got everything going for her but she doesn't exist.
>
> (Orbach, 2020, p.199)

To investigate further the need for separation (from the parents) and integration (of different aspects of modern life) as a means to contrast the *emptiness* and *meaninglessness* of life with substance and purpose, I here employ Giegerich because he suggests making a person fully aware of her/his unconscious ideas. Giegerich (2010, p.232) agrees with Jung (1989, p.340) that 'meaninglessness inhibits the fullness of life and therefore is equivalent to illness'. He adds, however, that this sentence must be understood appropriately, 'against Jung's probable intention' that '[t]he feeling that there should be a higher meaning of life and that it is missing is the illness'. Thus, Giegerich (2010, p.234) queries whether lack of meaning is enough to make one neurotic. He claims that 'there has not been one case where the meaninglessness of life was the cause of illness' and that the quest for meaning 'is the expression of a neurotic pretentiousness, a claim to metaphysical grandiosity. It is the delusion that life is only life if there is, like in a dog race, that never-to-be reached one thing, the sausage, to race after'. Giegerich (2010, p.234) claims that Jung refused to see this, despite being aware of 'the danger of pointless seeking' (2010, p.233), which I compare to Beckett's 'waiting' for Godot: both actions are a sign of *légèresse*, indicating an impossible depth, substance or purpose in life. As de Beauvoir (1949) noted, 'une femme libre est exactement le contraire d'une femme légère'. Going beyond sex and gender, I believe that depth (substance) could be the antidote to *légèresse* and that an (absolutely) free individual is the opposite of a *légère* individual.

The concepts of *emptiness*, *meaning*, *searching* and *waiting* are interwoven: all show traits of ambivalence, wanting and rejecting. Thus, meaninglessness is linked to a never-ending *searching* and *waiting,* and ultimately to increased *légèresse,* until 'something' (perhaps the numinous) happens to the individual or a symbol appears. But what if this numinous event, this symbol, never arises? Or we are so conscious (and therefore distracted by the *daily noise* of our affluent lives) that we fail to recognize it when it does come?

In this regard, Giegerich (2010, p.233) recalls Jung's example of a woman who

> does not live the life that makes sense [...] because she is nothing (*empty* in Orbach's term). But if she could say, 'I am the daughter of the Moon. Every night I must help the Moon, my Mother, over the horizon' – ha, that is something else! Then she lives, then her life makes sense.
>
> (CW18, para.630)

Giegerich claims that this is, in fact, not a cure, as Jung claimed, but merely 'a repetition of that illness that he himself diagnosed' (2010, p.233).[10] According to Giegerich, the 'Pueblo-Indian model' cannot be applied to the modern woman because it would involve 'an endless, futile search' (2010, p.233); thus, 'Jung's suggestion feeds her neurotic craving, her "addiction"' (2010, p.234).

Instead, Giegerich (2010, p.234) proposes as a 'real cure' that she go in the *opposite direction*; that is, that she be made fully aware that her unconscious idea that 'she ought to be the daughter of the moon [...] is why she is desperately travelling'. Giegerich proposes confronting her 'with the exaltedness, inflatedness of the unconscious demands and expectations' and adds, 'why should she not be able, like everybody else, to find satisfaction, *contentedness*, in ordinary life?' (2010, p.234). This is the very opposite attitude to Anne Clark's *Killing Time* (1984). Giegerich's realism is helpful to frame and understand the limitations of Beck's, Bauman's and Giddens's work.

Hillman (1997b) also suggested learning to give something back to society, Magatti and Giaccardi (2014) suggested becoming generative and Orbach (2010, p.202) suggested learning 'to express your feelings in a non-hystericized form'. Therefore, Orbach emphasized, in Freudian fashion, the need to accept the ordinary unhappiness of life. In Giegerich's lexicon, this would imply a *sublation*, presenting the opportunity for development and the realization that one is not 'a secret Queen in search for her missing crown insigna and the recognition due but denied to her' (2010, p.234). This could permit one to accept one's ordinary unhappiness and even allow a fantasy of new and unexpected developments, even happiness, to arise. But how can this be achieved?

What if *substance* and *purpose* were to replace *emptiness* and *meaninglessness*? What if, following Jung, one needs to learn the art of meditation? Otherwise, as suggested by Bauman and Larkin, we will continually move from one life/identity to another in a perpetual cycle of dissatisfaction, of *killing time*. Is Bauman's liquidity, then, a 21st-century existentialism along the line of Kierkegaard, Nietzsche, Camus, Sartre and Laing? I propose that liquidity is the consequence of early existential theory (minus a purpose and substance): the more we turn to existentialism, the more we turn to anomie (anxiety, depression and suicide). This is because if, following Bauman, in the 21st century becoming never reaches completion, this is a symptom of our own lack of substance and purpose and the only certainty is impermanence. Meditation, however, would allow individuals to look inward, to find substance and purpose in life, and by this means to compensate for emptiness and meaninglessness with substance and purpose and with separation and integration. It is only possible to become creative where creativity is compensation for anomie. As Jung suggested, to become 'one's own task' is key (2009, p.188), therefore to 'live oneself', while Kast[11] noted that this means not allowing others to create us, thus avoiding our entrapment in our complexes. We must be our own creators, where 'the creative ego-will is responsible for its fate. We are the makers of fate, the makers of our life' (Jung, 1997, p.942). We must accept our fate (both positive and negative) and make the best of it: it is important not to be determined by the unconscious because 'our unconscious contents are potentialities that may be but are not yet, because they have no definiteness [...]. Definiteness only appears where matter appears' (Jung, 1997, p.194). By matter, Jung is here referring to speech (dreams), drawings, painting, etc.

To conclude, I propose that the anxiety and depression that are rife in our society should not be viewed as pathological, but merely as attitudes towards life. In sociological terms, we could describe them as a form of *anomie*, wherein individuals lose sight of the fact that they can actively shape their lives, that they are the makers of their own bed. Thus, when creativity, and the contents of the unconscious, are repressed, they result in anxiety and depression results and this enables anomie. As if wandering in a wasteland, instead of looking inward, individuals engage in brooding – 'a sterile activity [...] not *work* but a weakness, even a vice' (Jung, CW18, para.1810) – before becoming depressed and suicidal as per anomie.

Why, then, is psychoanalysis so fundamental in the context of a sociological view of society and as a means to contrast 21st-century anomie? Because the goal of psychotherapy, according to Jung (CW16, para.99), is 'to bring about a psychic state in which my patient begins to experiment with his own nature – a state of fluidity, change and growth where nothing is eternally fixed and hopelessly petrified'. This, Jung claims, is always related to the opportunity to express oneself creatively, be it through dreams, painting, active imagination, or the body. Jung notes that the creative fantasy is an

> intrusion from the unconscious, a sort of lucky hunch, different in kind from the slow reasoning of the conscious mind. Thus, the unconscious is seen as a creative factor, ever as a bold innovator, and yet it is at the same time the stronghold of ancestral conservatism.
>
> (CW16, para.62)

Thus, liquidity equals to the conscious mind, and fluidity to the unconscious mind. Moreover, authentic creativity (creative fantasy) is what is lacking in a liquid society, because, following George Berkeley (cited by Giegerich, 2010, p.2), 'few men think, yet all will have opinions'. Therefore, creativity and creative fantasy help fluidity (and pluralism), not liquidity. If fluidity is fostered, there will be a chance to contrast anxiety, depression, suicidality and, therefore, anomie. Anomie occurs when emotions are stuck, while, when one is able to 'translate the emotions into images – that is to say, to find the images which were concealed in the emotions' (Jung, 1989, p.171), one becomes inwardly calmed and reassured. This is the compensation for anomie, the antidote to liquidity and Calvino's Eutropia.

Notes

1 I contacted Beck-Gernsheim, requesting an interview on the theme of the unconscious, but she gently declined due to poor health.
2 Thus, I claim that the copyright of individualization theory (renamed by Giddens 'The reflexivity of the self' a few years after) is Beck's to own, not Giddens'. Is it not the case that Giddens defined Beck (in his obituary) as 'the greatest sociologist of his generation'.
3 I contacted Beck-Gernsheim, requesting an interview on the theme of the unconscious, but she gently declined due to poor health.
4 Initially I intended to look at contemporary authors such as sociologists Eva Illouz and Bzung-Chul Han, but I later decided not do so, to limit the scope of my research.
5 The reference to Marcuse is not indirect here, because I see the one-dimensionality in the absence of the bi-dimensionality of the conscious and unconscious.
6 Key here are the feminist movement, the liberation movement and activism in the 1960s and 1970s and the Black movement in the United States.
7 Although I claim that as we approach the turn of the second decade of the 21st century, this can be considered to have spread beyond the Western world.
8 See: Süddeutsche Zeitung, 5–6 January 2015, p.9.
9 For copyright reasons, I cannot include here the full poem. It can be found on the internet.
10 Giegerich refers to Jung here.
11 Seminar titled 'In creation you are created' (C. G. Jung Institute Zürich, Summer Semester 2018).

Chapter 3

Integrating sociology and depth psychology

From the Frankfurt School to psychosocial studies

Having briefly reconstructed the views on Beck, Giddens and Bauman, respectively, I leave open the question as to whether their frameworks of investigation are the best ones with which to examine the development of narratives of self-identity in the 21st century or if a fresh perspective is required.

Suffice it to say that Beck, Giddens and Bauman failed to recognize the unconscious as a fundamental source for agencies in the reflexive process. The same mistake, I propose, was perpetrated – although from a different point of view – by the early members of the Frankfurt School.

Beck, as underlined in Chapter 2, noted that individuation is a term close to depth psychology but he failed to investigate further. One could ask, therefore, whether Beck was influenced by Freud (or any other psychoanalytical school)? My research has proven that he was not. I have found no direct reference to psychology or psychoanalysis in his work[1] and this, I propose, makes Beck a *sociological sociologist* with his work rooted primarily in sociology and (obviously) philosophy.

In contrast and as underlined previously, Giddens and Bauman are interested in and draw from psychology and psychoanalysis. But have they understood Freud's teachings and 20th-century psychoanalytical approaches? I propose that they have from a theoretical point of view but not from a clinical one. In this regard, Hillman reminds us 'that the person that really knows Jung is the person who has been through Jungian analysis' (2013, p.143). I use this claim to question sociology's approach to psychoanalysis, which is merely theoretical, and to question those sociologists who employ psychology and psychoanalysis using a sociological approach and with a sociological goal in mind. This leads me to underline that Bauman's and Giddens' use of psychology and psychoanalysis is inadequate. This, I propose, is inherited from Durkheim's view on psychology (see Chapter 2) and Adorno's view on Freud (see below), therefore psychoanalysis.

I propose that sociology either avoids *tout court* employing psychoanalysis (see Beck) or draws from it (see Bauman and Giddens) without an in-depth understanding of clinical material and how to deal with it or what to do with the contents of the unconscious and emotions.[2] This is because traditional sociologists have no tools with which to examine the unconscious and emotions since they constantly view these theoretically instead of clinically. This is clear when one examines

DOI: 10.4324/9781003390770-4

the Frankfurters (minus Fromm and Reich). Therefore, I recognize a *fil rouge* – connecting Durkheim, Adorno, Horkheimer, Marcuse, Beck, Giddens and Bauman (and contemporaries Illouz and Han).[3] A totally different approach is the one of Parsons (see below).

In this chapter (the last of the critical review), I will examine Adorno, Horkheimer and Marcuse, to assess their perspectives on psychoanalysis. In contrast, I propose adopting Jung's psychosocial viewpoint in line with the work of Erich Fromm, Jessica Benjamin, Steven Frosh, Lynne Layton, Susie Orbach, Andrew Samuels, Mary Watkins, Chiara Giaccardi and Mauro Magatti (proposing that what is needed is a psychosocial not a sociological approach).

In so doing, I will challenge what I call sociology's *one-dimensional view* (where being is constituted by the ways in which an institution affects the individual). Instead, I propose that the mix of institutional and emotional contents which I call – following Samuels (1989) – the plural-dimensional view, is key to understanding the development of narratives of self-identity in the 21st century.

The Frankfurt School: an overview

Before looking at Adorno, it is fundamental to give a brief introduction to the so-called Frankfurt School,[4] which developed at the Goethe University Frankfurt in 1929.

As David Held noted (1980, p.14), the 'Frankfurt School comprised intellectuals, academics, and political dissidents dissatisfied with the contemporary socio-economic systems (capitalist, fascist, communist) of the 1930s'. As James Gordon Finlayson (2005) underlined, the Frankfurt theorists:

> proposed that social theory was inadequate for explaining the turbulent political factionalism and reactionary politics occurring in 20th century liberal capitalist societies. Critical of both capitalism and of Marxism–Leninism as philosophically inflexible systems of social organization, the School's critical theory research indicated alternative paths to realizing the social development of a society and a nation.

Finlayson (2005) also underlines that 'The Frankfurt School perspective of critical investigation (open-ended and self-critical) is based upon Freudian, Marxist and Hegelian premises of idealist philosophy', and 'to fill the omissions of 19th-century classical Marxism, which did not address 20th-century social problems, they applied the methods of antipositivist sociology, of psychoanalysis, and of existentialism' (*Encyclopædia Britannica*).

When looking at the Frankfurters, it is impossible to overlook the concept of revolution and *ideology*, which are key to their critical theory. In this regard, both the work of Marx and Freud (as well as Hegel) could be considered pillars for critical theory in terms of revolution and ideology, and to revolutionize modern societies.

The Frankfurters studied in depth late 19th- and early 20th-century ideologies (i.e. communism, socialism, fascism and Nazism), pairing them with Marx' and

Freud's work. They did so – among other reasons – to try to answer the following question: why does ideology have such a grip on our minds? To answer such a question, they looked at Freud and, although initially amused and satisfied with the father of psychoanalysis, they later became dissatisfied, and accused him to have failed to solve the sociological problem they enlisted Freud to help them solve. I propose that the reason why they failed, lies in their choice of Freud and Marx, and because they failed to put forward a theory that would enable individuals and society to cope with the challenges of the second part of the 20th century. Let's start from the latter.

It could be said that their work is very much in line with the world coming out of the 19th century and with the historical events of the first half of the 20th century: the October's Revolution in Russia, First and Second World Wars in a developing industrial society. A society – as Stefan Zweig underlined in his masterpiece *The World of Yesterday* – that went to war hoping for (shaping) a better future. Therefore, it could be said that they failed to develop a theory for a world that went through two world wars, the atomic bomb, the Jewish holocaust, and the split 'between the Western bloc hegemonized by the political, military, economic and cultural power of the United States, on the one hand, and the bloc of countries led by the Soviet Union and dominated by Marxist ideology' Crespi, Jedlowski, and Rauty (2000, p.294). Hence, I believe they failed to understand – although Parsons (their contemporary) did, as I will underline in greater detail below – that in the time following the world wars 'the great utopian-type ideologies', 'the idea of progress and of a purpose operating in history', the 'ideals of radical reformism of society' faded with the 'loss of the revolutionary role attributed by the Marxist tradition' and the evident 'difficulty of replacing the latter as a revolutionary subject with other classes, or other social categories or movements' as Crespi, Jedlowski, and Rauty (2000, p.294).

Now, let's look at Freud and the Frankfurters' dissatisfaction with the father of psychoanalysis. As I will underline in greater detail below, Marx' and Freud's work is helpful for Adorno to build his theory of emancipation, in the working class's pursuit of happiness. Adorno initially applauded Freud and his *revolutionary quid*, but – in my opinion – mistakes his intentions. This is because Adorno mistakenly believes that Freud attempts to support the emancipation of the individual against an authority (the oppressor in flesh and bones, as opposed to a meta-psychological one). Therefore, later, Adorno blames Freud for having stopped halfway and accuses the Austrian physician of not helping individuals to emancipate fully and reach happiness (see below and aphorism 37).

Additionally, for Horkheimer, psychoanalysis should help the transition to a post-ideological society (1979 [1972], p.134); that is: more collective, orderly, planned and just (1979 [1972], pp.134–135). Therefore, they accuse Freud of not having fully helped shaping a theory in which lies hope for a better future. Therefore, the Frankfurters – who were interested in emancipation, liberation in the pursuit of happiness, pleasure and a high standard of living, became disaffected with Freud because he did not give a concrete answer to their purpose (which in my opinion is top-down and forcefully imposed to each individual belonging to the working class), and because they accuse him of replicating the same imposition of bourgeois categories in the analytical room.

This is where – I propose – they fail, because it is a rigid model (in line with 19th and early 20th centuries ideologies). However, Parsons' model is not top-down and it recognizes the new times, which are open-ended (see later in this chapter).

Adorno and Freud: an overview

To provide a comprehensive and detailed view of Adorno's perspective on Freud is a task that would require a whole book. Here, therefore, I will simply examine Adorno's critique of Freud and psychoanalysis and its relationship with society. Consequently, I will point out that traditional sociology has not been able to examine anyone other than Freud. To redress this, I will employ Jung as a possible alternative when examining society.

I propose that Adorno took Freud and his dogma as the only source from which to draw in the context of psychoanalytic investigation. He omitted any other view (e.g. Jung and Adler as well as the post-Freudians) and made of Freud and his dogma a model (paralleled by Marx's view of society) that afforded no space to pluralism or to other emerging views in line with the developments of society and within psychoanalytic theory's own development. Adorno paired Marx's theory (also a dogma!) with Freud's to build a theory of emancipation in the pursuit of happiness, but failed to take into consideration that psychoanalysis does not simply equal Freud and does not lead to happiness. This view and approach have been the mainstream in sociology up to the present day. It is timely for mainstream sociology to broaden its views of psychoanalysis.

Adorno studied and respected Freud's work, although he did not agree with Freud's viewpoints and conclusions. Adorno criticized psychoanalysis and Freud in *Minima Moralia* (1978), which I have selected here as my main source of investigation[5] (and which I will parallel with Luigi Ceppa's introduction (1994) to Adorno's *Minima Moralia*) and Jessica Benjamin's *The End of Internalization: Adorno's Social Psychology* (1977).

Adorno concentrated much of his work on the concepts of emancipation (within modern capitalist societies), pleasure and the dichotomy between instinct and reason. It could be said that he was obsessed with the working-class struggle towards emancipation and pretensions of happiness. In fact, for Adorno, emancipation meant reaching a state of *happiness*, which he saw as a forbidden state due to the oppression of the working class by the bourgeoisie. Therefore, Adorno's vast body of work focused on power relations, the dichotomy between emancipation and liberation in the pursuit of happiness. Emancipation, for Adorno, can only occur when authority is internalized and accepted.

According to Adorno, 'Freud's limitation lies in not having fully developed the most radical and dialectical aspects of his investigation'[6] (Ceppa, 1994, p.XXXII), as if Freud had stopped halfway. In this regard, aphorism 37, titled 'the Side of the pleasure principle', is key. In this aphorism, Adorno initially discusses the concept of *transfer* and one's own annulment of oneself. He lashes out against this concept, in which he sees the perpetration of oppression and dominance by society to the detriment of the oppressed individual. Thus, Adorno emphasizes that the transference, leads 'to the annulment of the self which was once brought about involuntarily and beneficially by erotic self-abandonment, is already a pattern of the relax-dominated, follow-my-leader behavior which liquidates, together with all intellect, the analysts who have betrayed it'.

Adorno (again aphorism 37) attacks Freud in the context of the emancipation of the oppressed and the achievement – as the ultimate goal – of happiness and enjoyment. He (aphorism 37) emphasizes that

> as a late opponent of hypocrisy, [Freud] stands ambivalently between desire for the open emancipation of the oppressed, an apology for open oppression. Reason is for him a mere superstructure [...] because he rejects the end, remote to meaning, impervious to reason, which alone could prove the means, reason, to be reasonable: pleasure.

In this regard, Jessica Benjamin (1977, p.42) claims that at the core of 'critical theory's analysis of modern capitalism is a paradox about the nature of resistance to domination' and she underlines that there are aspects of 'consciousness where this resistance might be located – critical reason, individuation, integrity and ultimately resistance itself – [that] are tied to the process of internalising authority. As a result, the rejection of authority can only take place through its prior acceptance'. Hence, she continues, according to the Frankfurters, 'the only possible resistance to authority is located in the same process of internalization'. Therefore, emancipation can only occur if internalization and acceptance of the authority/dominator have previously taken place.

Rather than examining internalization and acceptance of authority, Benjamin (1977, p.43) proposes examining mutuality and, to this end, she poses the following question: 'Could not the potential of emancipation be grounded in an intersubjective theory of personality, rather than an individual psychology of internalization?' Her response is that 'this possibility would call into question one of the major themes of critical theory's acceptance of Freudian theory: that ultimately it is our natural impulses, our 'human nature' including love and desire, which betray us'.

I propose that today, emancipation from authority cannot occur due either to its internalization and acceptance as proposed by Adorno or due to its mutuality, as proposed by Benjamin. Instead, (the process of) *clarification/knowledge* is key. I will explore this idea in more depth below having first examined Adorno's views on instincts.

Adorno also confronted Freud on the concept of instinct, emphasizing that (aphorism 37):

> In the teeth of bourgeois ideology, he tracked down conscious actions materialistically to their unconscious instinctual basis, but at the same time concurred

with the bourgeois contempt of instinct which is itself a product of precisely the rationalization that he dismantled.

Adorno continues (again aphorism 37): 'He [Freud] explicitly aligns himself, in the words of the *Introductory Lectures,* with "the general evaluation ... which places social goals higher than the fundamentally selfish sexual ones"'. In this regard, aphorism 37 is again key. Ceppa (1994, p.XXXII) underlines that, according to Adorno:

> Freud has not been able to fully control the weight of the mutual mediation between Es and I, pleasure and spirit. Thus, he blocked the formative process under the constellation (specifically bourgeois) of the drive sacrifice and renunciation, instead of illuminating it in the eschatological perspective of the drive satisfaction.

Thus, as just underlined, Adorno criticized Freud because he (Freud) 'concurred with the bourgeois contempt of instinct'. This is an interesting point when one considers the current age. Based on my clinical experience, I propose that today too (more than 100 years after Freud's theorization and almost 70 years after Adorno's *Minima Moralia)*, we can still recognize people's 'contempt for instinct and physical pleasure'. As was the case 100 years ago, this has nothing to do with the bourgeoisie; it has to do with human nature and how societies are built.

Adorno claims that, for Freud, 'the instinctual sacrifice can develop for him in removal or sublimation' and from this 'the history of civilization coincides with the curse of Oedipus and with the threat of castration' (Ceppa, 1994, p.XXXII). Adorno, instead, proposes 'a mediation of pleasure and spirit (*Lust* and *Geist)* that moves from the extreme – ideal – points of their archaic identity and their future reconciliation' (Ceppa, 1994, p.XXXII). In aphorism 37, Adorno also underlines that:

> Truth is abandoned to relativity and people to power. He alone who could situate utopia in blind somatic pleasure, which, satisfying the ultimate intention, is intentionless, has a stable and valid idea of truth. In Freud's work, however, the dual hostility toward mind and pleasure, whose common root psychoanalysis has given us the means for discovering, is unintentionally repressed.

In *King, Warrior, Magician, Lover*, Robert Moore and Doug Gillette (1991, p.22) recognize that when Freud talked about the *Id*, 'he saw it as the "primitive" or "infantile" drives, amoral, forceful, and full of God-like pretentions'. They underline that it comprises 'the underlying push of impersonal Nature itself, concerned only with satisfying the unlimited needs of the child' (1991, p.22). Aligning with my proposal that the Frankfurters and sociology did not look beyond Freud's theory, they emphasize the need to examine Alfred Adler and his concept of 'the hidden "power drive" in each of us as the hidden superiority complex that covers our real sense of vulnerability, weakness, and inferiority' (1991, p.22). They also examine Heinz Kohut who discussed '"the grandiose self-organization", which is demanding of ourselves and others in ways that can never be fulfilled' (1991, p.22). Therefore, they both suggest investigating the most recent psychoanalytic theories and also Jung's concept of the Divine Child as 'a vital aspect of the Archetypal Self' (1991, p.22) in order to approach things from a plural perspective. In this spirit, I propose – as an alternative to Freud's and Adorno's views – examining Jung's approach in his essay 'Stages of life' (CW8, para.749–795) in which he proposes that instincts correspond to a primitive state which he calls *natura primitiva* (when humans are unconscious). Jung (CW8, para.749) argues that 'if psychic life consisted only of self-evident matters of fact which on a primitive level is still the case, we could content ourselves with a sturdy empiricism'. Jung also claims – and this I believe is crucial when examining Adorno, Freud, instinct and sublimation – that 'it is just man's turning away from instinct – his opposing himself to instinct – that creates consciousness'. To explain this *turning away from instinct that creates consciousness,* Jung uses the Adam and Eve allegory of the tree of knowledge and claims that (CW8, p.749) 'instinct is nature and seeks to perpetuate nature, whereas consciousness can only seek culture or its denial'. He then adds 'as long as we are still submerged in nature we are unconscious, and we live in the security of instinct which knows no problems'. In the allegory of Adam and Eve, they are kicked out of the garden of Eden because they cannot resist temptation (instinct). At the same time, this can be seen as a development from an unconscious state (parents' domination and control) to a conscious one where Adam and Eve need to become responsible for their actions (therefore, mature enough to live their lives, not under the protective control of parents or within their garden). Therefore, when leaving Paradise, they are confronted with the tasks of adulthood. In fact, ceding to temptation could also be seen as a type of emancipation.

In this regard, Jung (CW8, p.751) underlines that 'every problem, therefore, brings the possibility of a widening of consciousness, but also the necessity of saying goodbye to childlike unconsciousness and trust in nature'. Jung claims that when humans are in a state of *natura primitiva* [when humans are unconscious], they cannot do much else than to follow their instincts. Only when they develop and mature (which I refer to as the process of *clarification/knowledge*) can they become conscious. However, this becoming conscious – I propose – does not exclusively mean sublimation as described by Freud.

In aphorism 38, Adorno turns his gaze towards psychoanalysis, writing that it 'prides itself on restoring the capacity for pleasure, which is impaired by neurotic illness'. He then adds in aphorism 40:

> Psychoanalysis itself is castrated by its conventionalization: sexual motives, partly disavowed and partly approved, are made totally harmless but also totally insignificant. With the fear they instil vanishes the joy they might procure. Thus, psycho-analysis falls victim to the very replacement of the appropriate super-ego by a stubbornly adopted unrelated, external one, that it taught us itself to

understand. The last grandly-conceived theorem of bourgeois self-criticism has become a means of making bourgeois self-alienation, in its final phase, absolute, and of rendering ineffectual the lingering awareness of the ancient wound, in which lies hope of a better future.

I propose that Adorno's vision is limited and that he does not contemplate the different psychoanalytic approaches, particularly those antagonistic to the Freudian approach (e.g. Jung and Adler, both driven to the liberation of the individual from a non-materialistic whole). Therefore, Adorno's problem is that, despite talking about transcendence, he remains imprisoned in the class struggle for emancipation in the pursuit of happiness.

Adorno's vision seems to me idealistic, because psychoanalysis is quite different from how he pictures it. I propose psychoanalysis as a process of *transformation* in which *psychagogia* is key. In this regard, Watkins (2003) underlines that psychoanalysis is when the analyst *accompanies* the patient. For Giegerich,[7] psychoanalysis helps patients 'to get out of their own traps' and 'to understand who they are and what they want'.

In this regard, Stefan Zweig (2015, p.23) writes that the 'reason and mission' of Freud's psychoanalysis 'was merely to clarify the extremes, not to reconcile them'. He also adds that 'Freud's combative absolutism always requires a decisive pro or con, a yes or a no, never a "one side or the other", never a "maybe" and a "meanwhile"'. Zweig then goes on to underline that 'the half probable and approximate things have no value for him: only the full, one hundred percent truth attracts him'.[8] I wonder if this absolutistic vision is correct and up to speed with our current epoch or if it is, rather, a daughter of its time. I also wonder whether the Frankfurters are in line with Zweig's absolutistic proposal, namely of Freud and psychoanalysis as masters of the full truth. Marcuse's view, as we will see later in this chapter, is going this way. As an alternative, I propose employing Jung's *I do not know* attitude, an approach that bridges the full truth and its opposite, where what counts is not the fixation of opposites but how to bridge these in the interest of the patient seeking clarification and knowledge.

Zweig (2015, p.17) emphasizes that Freud's great achievement was to give to humanity the opportunity for clarification. Since Freud's focus was on clarifying and not on the pursuit of happiness, according to Zweig, Freud helped humanity to attain depth rather than happiness. For Zweig, Freud's work has given man the opportunity to clarify and deepen. Why, then, do the Frankfurters speak of emancipation and happiness? I propose that – basing my argument on insights derived from the clinical application of psychoanalysis – emancipation is not possible without clarification and knowledge. Otherwise, it is merely compensation and leads to sublimation of the unconscious elements. Internalization alone is not sufficient; it must also bring clarification of the unconscious contents. Only in this way can emancipation be achieved.

Building on Adorno's internalization and Jessica Benjamin's mutuality, I propose that, thanks to clarification and knowledge, one can know about the authority (consciously or unconsciously dominating), and on that basis build the premises for a dialectical relation which will eventually bring you to accept it (although not mandatorily internalizing it) and – even more eventually – to mutuality. However, for a mutual relation to occur, there is a need for both parties to accept that mutuality.

In my view, *emancipation* could be linked to what Watkins (2003) calls *liberation*. She suggests replacing the term 'development' with 'liberation', because 'with regard to economic and cultural progress, "development" of one group seems often to require an oppression of the other' (2003, p.3). She adds that 'a dominant culture's idea of development is too often imposed on a culture, depriving it of undertaking its own path of development' (2003, p.3). As underlined in the introduction of this work, liberation enables 'the polyphony of thought, comprised of multiple voices and perspectives, best mediated by dialogue' (2003, p.2) and is based 'on a paradigm of interdependence, where the liberation of one is intimately tied to the liberation of the other' (2003, p.4).

Additionally, I believe that an individual cannot *look for freedom*. Rather, one must *wait for freedom* while *seeking one's own liberation*. Nelson Mandela is a good example of this because he accepted his status as prisoner when there was no space for mutuality. Thus, he did not seek freedom; he simply waited for freedom while seeking his liberation. Freedom only arrived once mutuality became possible (not when he had internalized authority); that is, when the South African government was able to engage with him as per mutuality. Otto Gross is a good example of the opposite: of an individual who sought freedom from his father's authority – without clarifying his complexes – instead of seeking liberation.

Adorno (aphorism 39) emphasizes that psychoanalysis 'expropriates the individual by allocating him its happiness'. He (aphorism 40) also claims that 'instead of working to gain self-awareness, the initiates become adept at subsuming all instinctual conflicts as inferiority complex, mother-fixation, extroversion and introversion, to which they are in reality inaccessible'. This point is important for two reasons. First, because Adorno's view is opposite to that of Zweig. Second, because in his reference to the complex of inferiority, maternal bonds, extroverted and introverted, we may recognize his familiarity with some classical Jungian themes. But why did Adorno not look beyond Freud? I have proposed that this could be related to his loyalty to Durkheim's[9] view of psychology and the Frankfurt School's inability to go beyond Freud's dogma and examine the irrational side of the psyche. Finally, making Jung a *persona non grata* in 20th-century sociology, the Frankfurters saw Jung's psychology – following Walter Benjamin (cited in Samuels, 1993, pp.295–296) – as 'the devil's work' and an 'auxiliary service to National Socialism'.

If Adorno had looked seriously beyond Freud (and possibly at Jung), he might have realized that psychoanalysis undoubtedly provides the work of reflection on oneself (particularly Jung's school). This would have allowed Adorno to grasp that the patient – contrary to his assertion – does not '[end] up being satisfied with an illusory recovery obtained through the integration of the patient into his perverse environment' (Ceppa, 1994, p.XXXIV).

When examining psychoanalysis and society, Adorno (aphorism 39) writes, with psychology in mind, that 'in the bottomless frauds of mere inwardness [...] is reflected what bourgeois society has practiced for all time with outward property'. He then concludes by saying that 'psychology repeats in the case of properties what was done to property. It expropriates the individual by allocating him its happiness'.

I claim that this is an incorrect view (albeit in line with critical theory's approach), and I propose instead substituting this view with that of Jung as well as relational psychoanalysis (as underlined in Chapter 2); they claim that patient and analyst are equal coparticipants in the transformation of both, who mutually affect each other. Therefore, there is no top-down relation, as in Adorno's view. Instead, there is mutuality. Additionally, if Adorno had examined Jung, he might have realized that psychoanalysis does not merely help the patient to fit in with his/her own class and culture or society, but enables him/her to clarify who he/she is and what he/she wants, as suggested by Giegerich (2010, p.233). Hence, I propose, psychoanalysis investigates freedom and enables the individual to 'choose', although freedom is only for the courageous.

Ceppa (1994, p.XXXIV) also stresses that for Adorno, the 'psychology of the ego, runs the risk of betraying, in the name of social adaptation, the original anarchic, subversive, hedonistic inspiration of psychoanalysis'. However, psychoanalysis is not merely about social adaptation. Instead, following Jung (CW8, para.794), I propose that 'a life directed to an aim is in general better, richer, and healthier than an aimless one, and that it is better to go forwards with the stream of time than backwards against it'. This purpose is key to understanding why the wish for emancipation alone, without clarification, knowledge or one own's purpose, does not help to overcome oppression.

Moreover, following Shamdasani (2013, p.96), I wish to disrupt Adorno's vision of psychoanalysis and society (taking individuation and psychoanalysis as synonyms): 'Individuation is an opening to the contemporary world, an opening to the dead and history'. Following Hillman (2013, p.96), 'It is an opening to the dead and the deeply personal. And the deeply personal is connecting back through history, it's connecting to all that's been left out and forgotten'. Therefore, Hillman (2013, p.96) claims that individuation is 'the process of connection or restoration or remembrance. The process of remembering. Recollecting the forms that animate us, the forms that are neglected, forgotten, mainly feared. Not ours'. Hillman (2013, p.92) also underlines that the purpose of individuation 'is to enable someone to envisage new possibilities, is to imagine new ways of consideration'. However, this view is antithetic to Adorno's view and truly speaks of the emancipation of the oppressed. It is about the individual and his/her being in the world in connection with his/her own individuality, ancestors and community, the collective and the environment (therefore, culture and society), and it is also finalistic! Thus, Adorno's vision of psychoanalysis (anarchic, subversive and hedonistic) is merely naive, and does not allow the individual to recognize and deal with his/her shadow; that is, one's dark (immature, undeveloped) side.

While I agree with Adorno that psychoanalysis must be emancipatory (Ceppa, p.XXXIV), for me, it must be emancipatory – following Jung, Kast (1993) and

Hillman (1997b) – from one's own complexes. This emancipation leads to the discovery of one's own place in society. Therefore, psychoanalysis is emancipation only when it follows a process of clarification and knowledge gained about oneself (Hillman's concept of remembering is fundamental). Without this, there is no emancipation.

I also agree with Adorno (aphorisms 34) that 'the almost insoluble task is to let neither the power of other, nor our own powerlessness, stupefy us'.; however, for me – again – this is merely separation from one's own complexes and it might help to move away from a one-sided view of the world based on domination, on the idea of victim vs. perpetrator. This is why I claim that Adorno's view is *passé* in the 21st century's late modern societies. His view that the human being is objectively positioned by birth in *certainties* such as class, gender, religion, ethnicity and nation, was appropriate – as Beck underlined – within the constraints of modernity. However, in a second-modern, 21st-century society, Adorno's view no longer works and it is for two reasons. First, because (as underlined in the previous chapter when examining Beck), society has gone beyond the certainties of modernity. Second, because, it is time to go beyond the one-dimensionality of the conscious world. Therefore, I propose a multidimensional and pluralistic view (Samuels), where conscious and unconscious are interwoven and mutually affect each other. This begs the question: is it correct to claim – following Adorno (see Ceppa, 1994, p.XXIX) – that 'man is the social world'? Jung's concept of the collective unconscious is fundamental here because he proposes an approach that is multidimensional, historic and spiritual (as well as symbolic). It is not limited to the here-and-now and modern – enlightened – certainties. Rather, Jung's collective unconscious is a-temporal.

Leonardo Ceppa (1994, p.XXIX) underlines that:

> Spiritualism [...] is for Adorno a sort of empiricism of interiority. It rightly poses the problem of the subject and of the meaning of life, but errs when it moves unreflectively from the immediate data of consciousness, assuming that it originates from the sentimental experiences that are already the fruit of a complex historical-social mediation (or construction).

I find this interesting and I see a *fil rouge* from Nietzsche, Marx, Freud and Adorno. However, I propose challenging this view by examining Jung's collective unconscious and spirituality, to move beyond Adorno's historical–social mediation (or construction). Therefore, I propose that historical–social mediation (or construction) does not encapsulate one's soul and now even the soul of a culture. I prefer employing Jung's (CW8, para.805) view on religion. He claims that since the Age of Enlightenment, a peculiar point of view has developed, according to which:

> all religions are something like philosophical systems, and like them are concocted out of the head. At some time someone is supposed to have invented a God and sundry dogmas and to have led humanity around by the nose with this 'wish-fulfilling' fantasy. But this opinion is contradicted by the psychological

fact that the head is a particularly inadequate organ when it comes to thinking up religious symbols. They do not come from the head at all, but from some other place, perhaps the heart; certainly from a deep psychic level very little resembling consciousness, which is always only the top layer.

Thus, Jung claims, 'this is why religious symbols have a distinctly "revelatory" character; they are usually spontaneous products of unconscious psychic activity' and adds that 'anyone who cherishes a rationalistic opinion on this score has isolated himself psychologically and stands opposed to his own basic human nature' (CW8, p.807). This is another reason why Adorno went with Freud rather than Jung.

Ceppa (1994, p.XXXIII) emphasizes that:

> in the present circumstances every form of adaptation, integration, theoretical synthesis is for Adorno a figure of false consciousness. Psychic qualities can not be subordinated to social laws – as did Heinz Hartman's ego psychology or Talcott Parsons' sociology, integrally functionalizing the unconscious to control reality. Role behaviour. We can not deduce social laws from psychic laws, explaining capitalism on the basis of the *auri sacra fames* and an *innate selfish instinct*.

This point is crucial in this research. In Chapters 1 and 2, I proposed that psychic qualities and social laws can be merged – not in the sole understanding of explaining capitalism – but to explain what being in the world is for human beings, bridging inner and outer realms that are mutually influential.

Post-Freudian psychoanalysis has demonstrated that much of what we are derives from the kind of attachment we have to the mother. However, the Jungians go beyond this, to examine the concept of *daimon*, fate and destiny. This view (antithetic to Calvinism and enlightenment) is where, I believe, sociology – which concentrated on the ways in which structure and agency are related – fails to accept the power of the unconscious and of *God* (whatever God is). Adorno mistakenly believes that psychoanalysis should bring emancipation and happiness, but I propose that neither psychoanalysis nor class struggle should lead to happiness; instead, both must lead to clarification and knowledge and the recognition of one own's daimon. To this, Adorno thinks that:

> if sociologism betrays, betrays the unconscious and its claims of happiness, in the name of existing society and instrumental rationality, therapeutic psychology eludes – by contrast – the objective dimension of autonomous social irrationality. Thus it ends up being satisfied with an illusory recovery obtained through integration.
>
> (Ceppa, 1994, p.XXXIV)

In conclusion, before moving on to examine Horkheimer, Jessica Benjamin (1977, p.42) is again helpful as a contrast to Adorno's view. She underlines – similarly to Orbach (2014) – that:

analytic psychology contains the realisation that human beings affect one another, particularly in the process of child rearing, and therefore that what appear to be innate or natural *properties* of a person are actually the result of social interaction and human agency.

She also (1977, p.47) underlines that 'Horkheimer and Adorno see reason as a universal historical, ontologised process developing out of the opposition of nature' and that 'the impasse of authority grounded in the antinomy of reason and nature is central to critical theory's analysis of modern culture'. However, she also claims that 'while critical or emancipatory reason must be developed to counter instrumental or dominating reason, they both emerge out of a conflict with inner and outer nature' (Benjamin, 1977, p.43). This is something the Frankfurters and mainstream sociology failed to acknowledge or to study in depth.

Horkheimer and psychoanalysis: an overview

In 'Die Psychoanalyse aus der Sicht der Soziologie [Psychoanalysis from the perspective of sociology]', in the collection of essays *Gesellschaft im Übergang*[10] (1979, p.134), Horkheimer notes that before the advent of psychoanalysis 'knowledge of the human soul was a matter that concerned philosophers and novelists',[11] and credits Freud for developing a theory that 'does not study the sensitive facts and physiological relationships by developing tests and experiments, but investigate[s] the human soul and its structure'. Horkheimer (1979, p.132) also underlines that Freud was perfectly conscious that his doctrine was inextricably linked to the exclusiveness of the profession of faith in science, to which Jung and a few others were the exception. He (1979, p.333) adds that Freud's hope was that science would 'obtain a dictatorial preeminence on Men's psychic life'.

Horkheimer claims that psychoanalysis must be seen as 'an active intellectual force in the transition to a society that is no longer in need of ideology' (1979, p.134); that is, to a society that is 'more collective', 'orderly', 'planned', and 'more just' (1979, pp.134–135). Simultaneously, for Horkheimer (in typical Frankfurter fashion), 'the thinking individual, the autonomous subject of bourgeois philosophy is actually socially powerless' and 'the opposition of individual reason to authority' is what has forced this individual to adapt (Benjamin, 1977, p.49). But are we sure that ideologies have become obsolete? I propose that it is incorrect to declare the advent of a post-ideological society (as the Frankfurters did) or, for that matter, a post-traditional society (as Beck and Giddens did). Jung is helpful here in drawing a parallel between ideologies and myths. In his forward to *Symbols of Transformation* (CW5, p.XXIV) he wrote:

[I]t struck me what it means to live with a myth, and what it means to live without one. Myth says a Church Father, is 'what is believed always, everywhere, by everybody'; hence the man who thinks he can live without myth, is outside of it, is an exception. He is like one uprooted, having no true link either with the past, or with the ancestral life which continues within him, or yet with contemporary human society. He does not live in a house like other men, does not eat and drink like other men, but lives a life of his own, sunk in a subjective mania of his own devising, which he believes to be the newly discovered truth. This plaything of his reason never grips his vitals. It may occasionally lie heavy on his stomach, for that organ is apt to reject the profit of reason as indigestible. [...] So I suspected that myth had a meaning which I was sure to miss if I lived outside it in the haze of my own speculation. I was driven to ask myself in all seriousness: 'what is the myth you are living?' [...] I took it upon myself to get to know 'my myth', and I regarded this as the task of tasks.

According to Horkheimer (1979, p.131), 'sociological reflections on psychoanalysis begin with the doctor's relationship with those who rely on him' and asks: 'Is it possible to think of a more serious way of dealing with the individual and his psychic structure [...]' than psychoanalysis? He adds that we are living 'in a world in which individuality is losing ground due to the manifest tendencies of society'. It might be questioned why he prioritizes sociological perspectives over psychoanalysis? I propose, instead, that we are dealing with highly relational and psychosocial facts (see Chapter 1). Hence, I reiterate here my critique of Adorno and sociology who view psychoanalysis through a sociological lens.

Horkheimer (1979, p.131) then notes that

analysis preserves some decisive moments of what is positive in the bourgeois world, in which the transformation of society is also announced in a way that is no less evident. [...] The specific structures of the patient's thoughts and feelings subsist under fixed categories.

To challenge Horkheimer's idea of fixed categories, I again employ Langwieler's (2018) vision (see Chapter 1) of the analyst's task and his conviction that the 'self-critical, non-dogmatic attitude of the therapist' is crucial, and means remaining open to 'observations during psychotherapy which contradict his theoretical expectations'.

Like Adorno, Horkheimer finds pleasure key and believes the supreme goal – 'connected with the phase of economic miracle' of the 1960s – is the *standard of living* (1979, p.137). For him, 'the phenomenon of idolatry' connected with the economic miracle of the 1960s, 'has rarely been configured in a meaningful way' (1979, p.137). Horkheimer's focus on the desire for a high standard of living brings us back to Beck and the post-biblical society mentioned earlier. It also brings us – almost 50 years since Horkheimer wrote these words – to recognize that the focus on the standard of living (the emancipation of the working class) has been confused with the concept of individualization. Instead, one should speak of a *broken individualization* that prevents individuation and that is equated to 'the betrayed promise of freedom and happiness for all'.[12] If the supreme aim of the individual[13] is (exclusively) a high standard of living, there is no room for individuation because the standard of living hinges on the material rather than the spiritual needs of the individual. Hillman (following Jung) suggested that life should be devoted to a purpose. I, therefore, propose that individualization breaks when its only purpose is a high 'standard of living'. In this condition, there is no absolute freedom.

While one could agree with Horkheimer that, in the 1960s, after years of war, reconstruction, and economic miracle, what mattered most to individuals was the standard of living, in today's affluent society, his vision no longer works; namely, the standard of living is a process 'strongly conditioned by political factors, […] not to mention material and prestige factors' (1979, p.137). In my view, the search for a high standard of living which could, from a superficial perspective, be conditioned by Horkheimer's 'factors' is linked to Adler's compensation theory – that is, with the compensation of one own's inferiority and the wish to overcome it, to leave a mark and to gain much more than Andy Warhol's 15 minutes of fame. If this does not happen, anomie prevails (see Chapter 2). Thus, the current late modern society is based not on the emancipation of the oppressed, but on the wish of the oppressed to compensate their status. A life lived under the spell of compensation – and its constant search for pleasure and high standard of living – is a life at the mercy of illusion, which is constantly renewed in a society based on 'never enough'. In 21st-century advanced societies, it is this, not religion, that is the prevailing illusion.

Let us now reflect on the concept of religion. For Freud, religion is an illusion,[14] while for Marx, it is the opium of the people. The Frankfurters agreed with both Freud and Marx while Jung preferred to look at the *religious dimension*, which he claims is fundamental for the creative process and the development of the individual. Following Marx, Freud and Adorno, Horkheimer underlines that 'what subsists, what is worthwhile, what is right determines science; the rest, first and foremost religion, is imagination' (1979, p.132). Freud underlines that 'if one tries to frame religion in the educational path of humanity, […] this (religion) finds a confirmation in the neurosis through which every civilized man must pass, in his path from childhood to maturity' (1969, p.562). To this vision, I wish to contrapose Jung's concept of the *religious dimension*, which also helps to further clarify Adorno and instincts. In *Mysterium Coniunctionis* (CW14, para.603), Jung underlines that '"religion" on the primitive level means the psychic regulatory system that is coordinated with the dynamism of instincts'. Jung continues: 'On a higher level, this primary interdependence is sometimes lost, and then religion can easily become an antidote to instincts, whereupon the originally compensatory relationship degenerates into conflict, religion petrifies into formalism, and instinct is vitiated'. He then adds that 'a split of this kind is not due to mere accident, nor is it a meaningless catastrophe. It lies rather in the nature of the evolutionary process itself, in the increasing extension and differentiation of consciousness'. Jung concluded that the unconscious (particularly the collective) is intrinsically related to the inborn spiritual attitude of the soul, and that – if this attitude is suppressed *tout court* – neuroses might arise.

It is important to underline that Jung's vision of the spiritual attitude of the soul has little to do with religion as described by Nietzsche, Marx and Freud. Thus,

Jung (CW11, para.522 and CW12, paras.7–8) makes the distinction between *imitatio Christi*, a superficial imitation of externals, and *becoming Christ*, a deeper imitation that involves living one's own life as truly as Christ lived his (taking into consideration that according to Jung, genuine individuation is to go through your personal crucifixion). Therefore we can talk about a true and false *imitatio Christi*. The first is a superficial imitation and the latter is and is individuation.

In his suggestion of 'becoming Christ' – instead of imitating him – lies Jung's central individuation concept: to urge people to know and live their own myth, rather than borrowing one. For Jung, the individual must become Christ, not imitate him, to discover who he/she really is. This transition is fundamental as it allows the individual to become emancipated. This emancipation is not possible for Freud and the Frankfurters because they are linked to the concept of domination and perpetrator vs. victim, to a causal rather than a finalistic approach to life.

Horkheimer (1979, p.137) described contemporary society (of the 1970s) as that wherein for the bourgeoisie 'religion has stiffened to a convention' while 'for the workers, the Marxian doctrines have been reduced to dull clichés'. Thus, he recognized the beginning of a transformation that would later be described in detail by authors including Beck, Bauman and Giddens. Horkheimer's vision is interesting and – to a certain extent – correct within 20th-century rationalistic and enlightened society where both the bourgeoisie and working class adhered to what Jung called *imitatio Christi* and where the working class's priority – beyond emancipation – was to live the materialistic pleasures of a bourgeois life. Today, however, advanced societies, religious and Marxian doctrines (both can be seen as ideologies!) could be considered passé. Both the grandsons of the bourgeoisie and of the working classes now seek fulfilment of their wishes (high standard of living), the pursuit of which is far from religious or Marxist values. Therefore, as I proposed elsewhere (2004), the purpose of millions of people in 21st-century late modern society is to fulfil their 'ludic' wishes. To live a *ludic life*.

The *ludic life* is related to Freud's view that a healthy life involves a balance of work and enjoyment and the active pursuit of wish fulfilment. Horkheimer (1979, p.132) considered the purpose of analytic therapy to comprise 'the ability to operate in the existent, in an emotional life' and moreover to be able to react to the world as it is, 'without delusions'. Thus, Horkheimer (1979, p.133) emphasizes that Freud's theory is marked by 'modern positivistic thinking' and that for Freud 'putting the patient in a position to work and enjoy means healing him' (1979, p.133). In the 21st century, the work–play balance is out of sync. Work is seen as an impediment to one's wish to enjoy. This enjoyment, the ludic life, is not healthy because, almost like an addiction, it seeks pleasure for pleasure's sake while avoiding responsibilities, and when pleasure is missing, boredom and anomie arise.

For Freud, to live a life that makes sense is to live a life where work and enjoyment are in balance. Today, however, this balance has been lost. In this regard, Jung's example – which I already referred to (on pp.105–106) – of the woman who feels to be the daughter of the Moon, helps. As underlined before, Giegerich claims that the 'pueblo-Indian model' cannot be prescribed to the modern woman because it would involve 'an endless, futile search' (Giegerich, 2010, p.233), and thus 'Jung's suggestion feeds her neurotic craving, her "addiction"' (Giegerich, 2010, p.234).

Furthermore, Horkheimer underlines that 'it is difficult to establish what enjoyment means', adding, 'we can say that it goes from the satisfaction of hunger and sexuality to the aesthetic; it includes all kinds of entertainment, as long as you live it consciously as such' (1979, p.133). While I agree that enjoyment must be lived consciously, I disagree that it merely involves satisfaction of hunger, sexuality and aesthetic enjoyment, which I consider materialistic needs. Instead, hunger for knowledge (of oneself and of the 'world') – Eros as opposed to Sexuality – will allow one to connect with self, others, and the 'world', thus bringing one to a state of appreciation rather than pleasure. Appreciation always links to 'the good enough' and the 'enough'; thus, to limits. A life in balance between conscious and unconscious elements, a life in which unconscious elements are integrated into conscious life, must be the goal. This might lead to calmness and reassurance in a world that sociologists and philosophers claim to be out of joint.

In conclusion, I agree with Horkheimer (1979, p.136) that Freud, like Kant, saw that the transformations that are occurring today in the family structure and inter-sex relations 'are pregnant with cultural and psychological consequences'. This is the central theme of my book. I also agree that 'from the genesis of society, religion, fire and many other archaic developments, up to the most recent wars, Freud has contributed to the knowledge of collective psychology' (Horkheimer, 1979, p.136). I wonder, however, why the Frankfurters were unable to go beyond Freud and his dogma, keeping in mind that – as Jessica Benjamin (1977, p.42, in footnotes) underlines – 'Fromm's rejection of Freud's patricentric theory' was not accepted by Adorno and that 'when Adorno and Horkheimer began to systematically synthesize Freud's theory of society they were already dissatisfied by the efforts of Fromm and Reich to achieve this integration'. In fact, both Fromm and Reich, as will be seen in the following section on Marcuse, distanced themselves from Freud's dogma, a sin that Adorno and Horkheimer could not tolerate. They preferred Marcuse but Marcuse was no psychoanalyst and like Adorno and Horkheimer, he made the mistake of taking psychoanalysis sociologically.

Therefore, I do not understand how Horkheimer claimed that 'psychotherapists and sociologists must work together' (1979, p.138), taking into consideration their relationship with Fromm and Reich. Why has the Frankfurt School failed to integrate sociology and psychoanalysis as equal and mutually influencing disciplines, while imposing a top-down relation of sociology over psychoanalysis (as the title of the essay employed for this paragraph implies) and by imposing a dogmatic Freudian–Marxian conception of society where sociology has supremacy over psychoanalysis and where the voices of the psychoanalysts have been silenced? In contrast to Horkheimer's view that 'we cannot establish a priori if we will get precise psychological and sociological knowledge, and of what species', I employ the work of Craib, Frosh, J. Benjamin, Orbach and many others to confirm that sociology and psychoanalysis can merge into one new discipline called psychosocial studies.

Marcuse and 'Neo-Freudian Revisionism': an overview

In his essay 'Critique of Neo-Freudian Revisionism' (1974), Herbert Marcuse confirms how close to Freud's dogma the Frankfurters were, although Marcuse – instead of following Adorno and Horkheimer in openly criticizing Freud – became *the keeper of the dogma* against those who revisited, amplified or proposed an alternative vision to Freud's. I have selected this essay as my source of reference because, in it, Marcuse is particularly critical of any non-dogmatic view of psychoanalysis and because his reiteration to stick to Freudian dogma is at its best.

Marcuse (1974, pp.253–254) reminds us that Freudian 'psychoanalysis elucidates the universal in the individual experience' and that it 'is consistently oriented on early infancy – the formation of the universal fate of the individual'. He (1974, p.238) claims that the function of psychoanalysis changed in response to the 'fundamental social changes that occurred during the first half of the century' as reflected in 'the collapse of the liberal era and of its promises, the spreading totalitarian trend and the effort to counteract this trend'. According to Marcuse, before World War I, psychoanalysis developed its concepts for 'critique of the most highly praised achievement of the modern era: the individual' and 'Freud demonstrated that constraint, repression, and renunciation are the stuff from which the "free personality" is made'. In this sense, Marcuse rightly claims that psychoanalysis was radically critical theory.

Marcuse (1974, p.239) underlines that the subsequent revision to psychoanalysis began when 'the psychoanalytic conception of man [...] appeared as "reactionary"' and when it 'seemed to imply that the humanitarian ideals of socialism were humanly unattainable'. Here, I would underline the Frankfurters' inability to look beyond Freud to those who developed his theory and as such became his antagonists. For Freud and the Frankfurters, all those who diverged from the original teachings (dogma) were to be called traitors and expelled, as happened to Fromm and Reich when they presented their post-Freudian ideas to Adorno and Horkheimer, and to Jung when he published *Symbols of Transformation*. Strangely, something similar also happened to Freud when – returning to Vienna from Paris, after a stint working with Charcot – his report was dismissed by the Austrian Medical Society (Zweig, 2015).

Marcuse (1974, p.239) criticized Reich's view for neglecting 'the historical dynamic of the sex instincts and of their fusion with the destructive impulses' and for rejecting 'Freud's hypothesis of the death instinct and the whole depth dimension reviled in Freud's late metapsychology' as well as for adopting 'sexual liberation' as 'a panacea for individual and social ills'. His main gripe was that Reich minimized the problem of sublimation and reduced freedom to 'a mere release of sexuality'; in essence, that he distanced himself from certain aspects of Freud's theory which Marcuse considers essential.

For Marcuse, psychoanalysis is more a political tool than a cure, the aim of which is to realize socialism. This clarifies why the Frankfurters were unable to dissociate from Marx and Freud and why these two figures represent the only possible ideology, at a time when the symbolism of the Bible was ceasing to affect people's lives.

When examining Jung – described as 'right wing' compared to the 'left wing' Reich – Marcuse (1974, p.239) claims that his psychology is 'obscurantist pseudo-mythology', but unfortunately says no more. This adds to Walter Benjamin's opinion of Jung (see p.123). Marcuse (1974, p.240) attacks what he calls *the Neo-Freudian schools* for wishing to attain what Freud attained, by claiming that 'the psyche can […] be redeemed by idealistic ethics and religion: and the psychoanalytic theory of the mental apparatus can be rewritten as a philosophy of the soul'. This is clearly an explicit attack on Jung, but not only on him. Marcuse adds that 'the revisionists have discarded those of Freud's psychological tools that are incompatible with the anachronistic revival of philosophical idealism – the very tools with which Freud uncovered the explosive instinctual and social roots of the personality'.

As underlined in Chapter 1, Progoff claimed that Jung sees man's social quality as inherent in human nature, and thus 'the individual must be understood in terms of the social situation in which he lives' (1955, p.167).[15] Progoff also claimed that – for Jung – since the individual comes before society, it cannot live without society, or indeed culture (1955, p.161) and furthermore, Progoff (1955, pp.163–164) claims that 'in understanding the individual as a derivate of society', Jung 'is following his more fundamental idea that "consciousness comes from the unconscious"' (1955, p.161). In other words, just as psychic contents are brought to consciousness by 'clarifying of the ambiguities of the unconscious', 'the individual emerges out of society by a process of differentiation and individualization' (Progoff, 1955, pp.163–164). Here, again, we may claim that the individual (more than the personality as described by Marcuse) is the outcome of social and psychological roots which are individual and collective. It should also be reiterated that, for Jung, *the social* is a mix of traits from a specific society and culture and comprises the cradle within which an individual is born.

Marcuse (1974, p.240) continues that 'the "center" of revisionism took shape in the cultural and interpersonal schools' where psychoanalysis became an ideology.[16] These schools resurrected the personality 'in the face of a reality which has all but eliminated the conditions for the personality and its fulfilment'. For Freud, Marcuse underlines (1974, p.240)

> the work of repression is the highest values of Western civilization – which presupposes and perpetuates unfreedom and suffering. The Neo-Freudian schools promote the very same values as cure against unfreedom and suffering – as the triumph over repression. This intellectual feat is accomplished by expurgating the instinctual dynamic and reducing its part in the mental life.

Marcuse (1974, p.240) – who rejects this approach as a 'philosophy of the soul' – claims that the new schools switched their orientation to 'secondary factors and relationships […] to emphasize the influence of the social reality on the formation of the personality'. However, he adds – and this is of fundamental importance here – 'we believe that the exact opposite happens – that the impact of society on the psyche is weakened'.

Jung demonstrated that his therapeutic approach encapsulates a view of society (the collective unconscious) and links it with one's own individual unconscious, with the immediate environment and the environment at large, as well as with one own's purpose and finality (or lack thereof). To contrast Marcuse's view, I provide the following example from Jung's work. Jung (CW7, para.167) writes about a man who contacted him to cure his homosexuality. This man was

> little over twenty, still entirely boyish in appearance. There is even a touch of girlishness in his looks and manner of expression. [...] he is intelligent with pronounced intellectual and aesthetic interests [...] his feelings are tender and soft, given to the enthusiasms typical of puberty, but somehow effeminate. There is no trace of adolescent callowness.

Jung proceeded to frame a diagnosis that 'undoubtedly he is too young for his age, a clear case of retarded development'. The patient, telling Jung that he wanted to be cured of his homosexuality (CW7, p.169), added, giving association to his initial dream, 'naturally I remembered yesterday that I was going to you for treatment and was in search for cure' (CW7, para.168). In this regard, Jung writes that 'the patient merely came to the doctor to be treated for that unpleasant matter, his homosexuality, which is anything but poetical'.[17] For Jung, what is unpoetical is to go to a doctor for treatment, not the young man's homosexuality.

This point is also vital in freeing Jung from accusations of homophobia perpetrated by some of his detractors. Here, Jung does not suggest curing the patient of his homosexuality; he wants the patient to develop and mature according to his own nature. In this case, becoming a mature masculine means becoming a human of male sex (and whatever gender), responsible and prepared to cope with society. Prepared does not mean, as Adorno (see above) and Marcuse emphasized, repressing instincts in light of sublimation; rather, it means that this man – having clarified his nature, having understood who he is and what he wants – could live his life and fulfil his own purpose in a society that does not accept homosexuality and claims it to be a sickness that needs to be cured. Thus, while the patient knocks at Jung's door to be cured, Jung instead supports the patient to face and clarify his nature and thus to transform into a mature human being. In contrast to Marcuse, Jung also helps the patient to examine the impact of his nature (homosexuality) on his psyche and his immediate social context, which has led him to search for a cure. Jung (CW7, p.170) adds: 'the patient had of course nothing like an adequate understanding of the treatment to which he was about to submit himself'. This is very often the case. Patients enter therapy because of an inner pain and perhaps they can adduce ideas or reasons, but the real reason is often not apparent to them when they enter the analyst's room for the first time.[18] It is only analysis that will help to clarify why they have come.

For Jung, the initial dream gives the analyst the opportunity to understand his real problem, and in this case, it is not the patient's homosexuality; rather, his lack of separation from his mother and his mother complex have caused his retarded development. In fact, the patient confirms his closeness to his mother, as is the case for many males. Jung adds (CW7, p.171)

> by this we are not to understand a particularly good or intense conscious relationship, but something in the nature of a secret, subterranean tie which expresses itself consciously, perhaps, only in the retarded development of character, i.e., in a relative infantilism.

It is important to underline here that Jung is not speaking of homosexuality in general; he is speaking about this individual only, who appeared immature to him because he was too close to his mother and/or his mother complex. Jung (CW7, p.171) adds 'the developing personality naturally veers away from such an unconscious infantile bond; for nothing is more obstructive to development than persistence in an unconscious […] state'.

I propose that the link between psyche and the impact of society, and vice versa, is immense. We first recognize that the patient is too close to his mother and therefore is immature and unseparated. This is the psychic aspect. The social impact on the patient is provided by the patient's homosexuality in 20th-century Swiss society where homosexuality was not accepted. Therefore, the patient, who is well enough adapted (perhaps too adapted and therefore one-sided) to the social reality of his time, seeks therapy to be cured of this, instead of being cured of his real problem: his immaturity and the fact that he has not yet been born. Hence, he lives in an embryonic state (unseparated from his mother and the mother complex) and must separate.

Reiterating my earlier comment about Adorno, it is not correct to claim that psychoanalysis leads to the annulment of oneself and one's own instincts, to let sublimation prevail, or, following Horkheimer, that a high standard of living means the satisfaction of hunger, sexuality and the aesthetic, or, following Freud, that to enable the patient to work and enjoy means curing him. In fact, following Jung and contextualizing this in 21st-century, late modern society, therapy is a creative transformation that enables people to become themselves – clarifying who they are and what they want – while living in a social context that might not be entirely friendly to them.

Furthermore, building on the section on Adorno and the fact that, according to Jung (CW8, para.807), 'religious symbols have a distinctly "revelatory" character', the symbolism of the church is important here. According to the Frankfurt School, the church could be regarded as an oppressive institution, as the authority in society where one confesses one's sins and is redeemed from homosexuality. In Jung's terms (CW7, para.172), 'the Church represents a higher spiritual substitute for the purely natural, or "carnal" tie to the parents'. This could lead one to view the church as a place of initiation and Baptism as initiation, perhaps into adulthood. Here, the Church is where one accomplishes the 'rite of initiation into manhood' (CW7, para.172). Jung underlines that in ancient Greece, homosexuality and education were synonymous. He also claims that the 'homosexuality of adolescence is only a misunderstanding of the otherwise very appropriate need for masculine guidance' (CW7, para.173), a man's effort to balance his unconscious closeness to his mother and to improve relationships with women from an immature relationship to a mature one (CW7, para.173). Therefore, Jung (CW7, para.174) underlines – and here again is the link between psyche and society – that 'according to the dream, [...] what the initiation of the treatment signifies for the patient is the fulfilment of the true meaning of his homosexuality, i.e., his entry into the world of the adult man'.

Returning to Marcuse (1974, p.241) – when he re-examines the revisionists and particularly Fromm – he claims that in 'aiming at the reified, readymade form rather than at the origin of the societal institution and relations, [they] fail to comprehend what these institutions and relations have done to the personality that they are supposed to fulfil'. Marcuse (1974, p.243) criticized Fromm for distancing himself from Freud and weakening 'the psychoanalytic conception', particularly Freud's theory of sexuality, which he believed would lead to 'a weakening of the sociological critique and to a reduction of the social substance of psychoanalysis'. Fromm was not the first to do so, however. Before Fromm, Jung and Adler had been ousted by Freud's inner circle. Marcuse (1974, p.244) accuses Fromm of having distanced himself from another dogma of therapy, namely the fact that 'the analyst rejects patricentric-authoritarian taboos and enters into a positive rather than neutral relation with the patient'. Marcuse adds that this 'new conception' involves an 'unconditional affirmation of the patient's claim for happiness' (Fromm, 1935, cited in Marcuse (1974, p.244)). Here, let us pause and comment in depth. First, as underlined in Chapter 1, therapy is not a static relationship, nor is it a top-down relationship and it is certainly not neutral. Instead, it is a fluid relationship where each party affects the other.

Therefore, I would ask provocatively: what does Marcuse know about the patient–therapist relationship given that he was not a therapist, did not undergo training analysis himself and never worked therapeutically with patients? I propose that his view of the therapeutic relationship (although he refers to it as a taboo) – which he calls neutral although it is called 'abstinent' – is biased by the spirit of his time and his one-sided Freudian approach. It is fundamental not to confuse neutrality with abstinence and the relational school does so, putting at the centre the analyst and patient as a whole. Otherwise – contrary to Marcuse's view underlined above (and what we saw previously with Adorno) – the dichotomy of dominator/dominated already present in society is replicated in the analytical relationship.

Following Samuels (1989), I propose the need for a pluralistic approach that is the opposite to a dogmatic one, as proposed by the Frankfurters (wrapped in Marxian and Freudian ideology and theory).

Secondly, some patients get into analysis seeking happiness. This is also what Adorno proposed, when discussing the emancipation of the working class, or what Horkheimer foresaw when discussing the high standard of life. Therefore, there is a contradictory view within the Frankfurters themselves. Returning to Fromm and the fact that patients seek happiness – building on the example of the man who sought therapy to cure his homosexuality – it is important to mention that emancipation (and 21st-century individualization) has turned into the false myth of happiness (see my critique of sociology in Chapter 2), where happiness is seen as the compensation for the current state of anomie, which hinders happiness. Moreover, in 21st-century late modern societies, emancipation equates to the idealization of happiness. Therefore, I propose that some patients enter analysis in a state of anomie and are seeking happiness (to compensate for their dissatisfaction at not yet having reached a high standard of living which equates to emancipation, success and therefore – as its ultimate goal – happiness). Thanks to therapy, they might be cured of this idealization, namely, of happiness.

Marcuse (1974, pp.244–245) is wrong in saying that 'with these demands, psychoanalysis faces a fateful dilemma', the claim for happiness, that 'if truly affirmed, aggravates the conflict with a society which allows only controlled happiness, and the exposure of the moral taboos extends his conflict to an attack on the vital protective layers of society'. Happiness and controlled happiness are relative and very personal concepts and we should be on guard against seeking happiness as a compensation to the lack thereof. Under these circumstances, happiness is not attainable, and people become neurotic. Instead, as underlined in Chapter 2, this is like waiting for Godot.

Marcuse is also wrong that 'the affirmative attitude toward the claim for happiness then becomes practicable only if happiness and the "productive development of the personality" are redefined so that they become compatible with the prevailing values' and are 'internalized and idealized'. This vision is *passé* because, despite the need for a 'productive development of the personality', I question Marcuse's view that this development is linked to the prevailing values, a criticism I also levelled against Adorno. If analysts follow this path, and claim to 'know' what is right or wrong for the patient – hence to make him/her compatible with the prevailing values – the analysis will fail, since the analyst might impose knowledge that goes against the nature of the analysand and, borrowing from the previous example, would acknowledge the right to treat homosexuality so that the patient lives a life 'compatible with the prevailing values'. This, to me, is controlled happiness, as well as controlled freedom. Absolute happiness, therefore absolute freedom, means enabling the patient to come in contact with (and live) her/his own nature and to accept it unconditionally and critically. In this way, a sense of calmness and reassurance will arise as a consequence of the therapy. Therefore, as underlined previously when examining Adorno, it is not a matter of internalization; it is a matter of clarification/knowledge and acceptance of one own's nature.

Marcuse underlines that 'this redefinition must in turn entail a weakening of the explosive content of psychoanalytic theory as well as of its explosive social criticism' (1974, p.245). I propose that it is rather the opposite because when a person clarifies who she/he is and knows what he/she wants and his/her purpose, this person can live life freely and face the life tasks that arise in a more balanced way.

To Marcuse (1974, p.254) 'the revisionists fail to recognize (or fail to draw the consequences from) the actual state of alienation which makes the person into an exchangeable function and the personality into an ideology'. However, he fails to recognize that when the Frankfurters investigated the concepts of emancipation, high standard of living or happiness, they did not realize that they were theorizing people's alienation from their own nature in light of forced emancipation. Therefore, somehow, people must search for their own freedom and happiness. I question this as well as Marcuse's (1974, p.260) claim that 'the revisionists claim that their psychoanalysis is in itself a critique of society'. I agree with Clara Thompson's view that psychoanalysis

> goes beyond merely enabling man to submit to the restrictions of his society; in so far as it is possible it seeks to free him from its irrational demands and make him more able to develop his potentials and to assume leadership in building a more constructive society.
>
> (1950, p.153)

I also agree with Fromm – cited and criticized by Marcuse (1974, p.266) – that man's 'ability to take himself, his life and happiness seriously [...] rests upon his courage to be himself and to be for himself' (Fromm, 1941, p.250). This, one could say, is a very Jungian statement which links to another critique levelled at Fromm by Marcuse that '"the psychoanalytic cure of the soul" becomes education in the attainment of a "religious" attitude'. In my opinion, the religious attitude – or religious dimension – as seen previously, is a fundamental step in the maturational process, without which individuals will have – as their only purpose in life – the attainment and accumulation of capital (of whatever sort) but not cultivating their soul (Zoja, 1999).

In conclusion, I believe that the approach of the Frankfurt School was valid at a time when the Western world was divided into authoritarian and inflexible top-down relationships and into the dichotomy of unpaired categories such as bourgeoise vs. working class; male vs female; race, gender, etc. However, in 21st-century second-late-modern societies, the Frankfurters' model of authority/perpetrator versus victim no longer works.

From the Frankfurt School to Ulrich Beck

At this point, it is helpful to comment on the sociology of the Frankfurt School and the ways it differs from Beck's. The differences, I propose, are – mainly – about the concept of ideology. Beck's theory could be called post-ideological while the Frankfurters' one is imbued by ideology, and rose in a time when ideology mattered from a normative point of view. Beck's theory is post-ideological because it was formulated at a time when 20th-century ideologies were being eroded. On this, Parsons' sociology might help to understand what I mean by post-ideological.

While the Frankfurters were, in my opinion, locked in the past (between the end of 19th and the first half of the 20th century) and bound to first modern industrial society and ideologies (they built up their sociology on the premises of two: Marxism and Freud's psychoanalysis), Parsons – their contemporary – was able to understand that the world and contemporary society were changing, and he saw this quite differently than the Frankfurters.

Crespi, Jedlowski, and Rauty (2000, p.295), underline that, with respect to the changing world of the 1950s), Parsons' theory assumes:

a position equidistant from both the deterministic theories of the Marxist tradition and the individualism of the theories of the liberal tradition, Parsons develops a systemic and functionalist theory, which appears to be underpinned by his belief in the validity of the American democratic model. In the evolutionary perspective he adopted, he nurtured, in fact, a substantial optimism in the possibility that the contradictions, struggles, situations of anomie and deviance that characterised the society of his time could eventually be overcome in new forms of sociality, opening up ever wider spaces of individual and collective freedom.

What is described here, is sufficient to notice a change of paradigm. This is supported by the fact that the Frankfurters aimed at the emancipation of the working class (and to reach a state of happiness), while Parsons recognized that this is not possible from a normative point of view.

Therefore, as Crespi, Jedlowski, and Rauty (2000, p.297) underline, in *Structure of Social Action* (1967 [1937]), Parsons challenges mainstream sociological discourses of his time such as behaviourism, Marxist determinism, the individualism of the liberal tradition and develops singlehandedly 'a theory of action that takes into account both the subjective components and the conditioning of social action'. This is called Parsons' voluntaristic theory of social action, that 'without underestimating the material and structural conditions present in every concrete social situation', gives space 'to the relative freedom of choice of the individual, as moved not only by self-interest considerations, but also by reference to moral and normative values'. Parsons' definition of social action (that takes into account the natural environment, economic and technical resources, and the particular structures of the social and cultural context), is built on the following:

a   the social subject or act, which can be represented by an individual, a group or even a collectively;
b   the purpose of the action, the future result towards which the action is directed;
c   the situation, i.e. the objective conditions and means within which the action takes place.

In conclusion, Parsons – and this is the important link with Beck – similarly to Durkheim, thinks 'of the individual as being originally motivated by desires that tend to be a-social' (Crespi, Jedlowski, and Rauty, 2000, p.297).

In describing what he meant with individualization, Beck (2002, p.11) underlines that this is the amplification of what 'Parsons has called institutionalized individualism' (1978, p.321). Hence, Beck adds,

this means that in modern life the individual is confronted on many levels with the following challenge: You may and you must lead your own independent life, outside the old bonds of family, tribe, religion, origin and class; and you must do this within the new guidelines and rules which the state, the job market, the bureaucracy etc., lay down.

This is exactly what the Frankfurters were not able to understand (because looking backward at Hegel, Marx and Freud instead of looking forward): that society was turning towards a system where people are unchained from the traditions of the first modern society and embracing risks (personals and collective) on a daily basis.

Therefore, it can be said that Beck's work benefitted from many of Parsons' intuitions and he developed them further, without however – following the usual fashion of agency theory – looking at psychoanalysis as a tool for his investigation.[19]

I therefore propose that my own I+I, or the Beck and Jung merger, is an alternative set to challenge and balance the downsizes of traditional (first modern) sociology, bridging the sociological aspects dear to those that put forward the choice-biography-based-sociology in a post-ideology second-late-modernity, and analytical psychology of Jungian derivation.

With this, I do not intend to claim that the Frankfurt School is bad sociology as well as bad psychology. I mean that their view is structurally linked to the first modernity instead of building a bridge with the second, as they were not able to understand the need for this bridge.

As already underlined at the end of Chapter 2, Beck's claim that 'an awareness that full mastery of either consciousness or the world is not possible and hence a new bundle of social relationships forming around this dissolution of certainty (Beck and Lau, 2005)' (Sørensen and Christiansen, 2013, p.35), is helpful to understand that in second-late-modern societies *ambiguity* is key, and that this is what differentiates Beck's work from the Frankfurters'. It is this ambiguity that – if taken as a driving force in second-late-modern societies and paired with Jung's concept of individuation and *vox-dei* (see Chapters 4 and 5) – might help to shed light on the fact that the Frankfurters' model (we could call it the Marx-Freud fusion) is inferior or deficient in contrast to the merge of Beck's and Jung's work. This is because the Frankfurters' approach is based on rigid ideologies and goals, while the I+I is open-ended, enhancing individualization and individuation. The I+I takes into consideration that second-late-modern societies, as Beck underlined, are no more about progress and optimism. Instead, as underlined above, they 'turned our notion of progress pessimistic and made pessimism a fundamental governing principle' (Sørensen and Christiansen, 2013, p.19).

Having briefly illustrated the views of Adorno, Horkheimer and Marcuse on psychoanalysis, I want to underline that a change of paradigm is needed when examining the formation of narratives of self-identity at the beginning of the 21st century in second-late-modern societies and a new vision is required to contrast with that offered by sociology (that the world is out of joint (Beck, 2016)). I propose that Jung and the post-Jungians as well as psychosocial studies offer such a new paradigm, in line with relational psychoanalysis and Samuels's *plural turn*.

My claim is that a relational approach to sociology and psychoanalysis (hence to *relational psychosocial studies*) is necessary for several different reasons. In the next few pages, I will focus on this.

Notes

1 In 2018, I contacted Elizabeth Beck-Gernsheim on this matter but I have received no answer from her.
2 While it could be interesting to examine Foucault on emotions, I omit him here, because it would require another area of investigation which I prefer not to include in this work.
3 I initially intended to examine both Illouz and Han, although later I decided to omit here, because it would require another area of investigation which I prefer not to include in this work.
4 Among their members: Max Horkheimer, Theodor W. Adorno, Herbert Marcuse, Erich Fromm and Walter Benjamin.
5 I have decided to take *Minima Moralia* as my source of reference – instead of, for example, *The Authoritarian Personality* or *Dialectic of Enlightenment* where Adorno and his co-authors heavy draw on psychoanalysis – because of the way this aphorisms are written, as a stream of consciousness.
6 This and all future quotes from Ceppa's introduction to Adorno's *Minima Moralia* are my translations from the Italian.
7 Private conversation (2016).
8 My translation from Italian.
9 As underlined before, following Lukes' (1982) introduction to Durkheim's *The Rules of Sociological Method*, we understand that Durkheim sought to demarcate sociology from psychology, claiming sociology to be a 'special psychology, having its own subject-matter and a distinctive method' (Durkheim, 1982, p.253), while psychology is 'the science of the individual mind' whose object or domain is as follows (Durkheim, 1982, p.40): (1) states of individual consciousness; (2) explanation in terms of 'organico-psychic' factors, pre-social features of the individual organism, given at birth and independent of social influences; (3) explanation in terms of particular or 'individual' as opposed to general or 'social' conditions (focusing, say, on individuals' intentions or their particular circumstances); (4) explanation in terms of individual mental states or dispositions. However, if we look carefully into a psychosocial parallel between Durkheim and Jung, we might recognize that these four points can be linked respectively to Jung's concepts of (1) the personal unconscious, (2) archetypes and the collective unconscious, (3) the persona and (4) Jung's theory of neurosis and psychodynamics.
10 This essay is not translated into English. I choose this text among other of his essays because it directly examines the relation between sociology and psychoanalysis. It was presented in 1968 at a conference on this theme and later published as *Sociologie un Psychoanalyse aus der Sicht der Soziologie* in 'Jahrbuch der Psychoanalyse', V, Bern-Stuttgart, 1968, pp.9–19. I employed here the Italian translation (1979), titled *La Società di Transizione*.
11 This and all future quotes from Horkheimer's *Gesellschaft im Übergang* (*La Società di Transizione*) are my translations from the Italian because there is no English translation.
12 As Giaccardi noted at a conference titled 'Social Generativity. What it is and what it is good for' (2018).
13 Living in a second-late-modern society.
14 Freud meant that religious phenomena have been valued because they have been wished for, not because they have been demonstrated to be real.
15 Progoff (1955, p.161) also states that Freud's view was that the individual came first and only then society.

16 One could ask whether Freudian psychoanalysis also became an ideology (replacing religion and to the same extent as Marxism) for the Frankfurters, but I will not investigate
   this here.
17 Jung underlined that certain dreams are poetical and the one brought by this patient is so.
18 And if they do, as Jung suggested, they must go through the work of the analysis (instead
   of the intellectual work of understanding) and have a genuine wish to change their lives.
19 Crespi, Jedlowski, and Rauty (2000, p.298), underline that 'In particular, in dealing
   with the problems of the personality system, Parsons repeatedly makes recourse to the
   psychoanalytic categories elaborated by Sigmund Freud, which he also knew from his
   direct experience of analytic therapy'.

Chapter 4

The 'I+I'

A critical comparison of Ulrich Beck and C.G. Jung and theoretical formulation of the 'I+I'

In this chapter, I will synthesize and apply my findings by conducting a critical comparison of Beck's and Jung's theories, to ascertain the commonalities and differences between them. Here, it will be shown that while Beck (2002, p.X) recognizes the depth-psychological use of the term individuation, he does not expand the topic,[1] and therefore fails to acknowledge the importance of the unconscious (collective or individual). Having conducted a comparative analysis of Jung's and Beck's individuation and individualization theories respectively, in the second half of this chapter, I will introduce the 'I+I' concept, meaning individuation in a second-late-modern society. This comparison introduces a new configuration of psychosocial studies, wherein Jung is used to consider the psychic and Beck (and Bauman) the social. In attempting to demonstrate the validity of this approach, I will answer the following research question: What is the best tool to understand the nature of development of narratives of self-identity at the beginning of the 21st century? To better understand the current world (and in response to Beck's latest work *The Metamorphosis of the World* (2016)), I will claim that there is a necessity to build a bridge from sociology towards psychoanalysis, or from Beck's individualization to Jung's individuation (and not vice versa), in order to open the door to the unconscious with a psychosocial approach. At the end of this chapter, I will pay attention to the problem of Jung's prioritization of individual development over collective life.

To illustrate my findings, in Chapter 5, I will use a clinical vignette, inspired by a patient who – during our first session – reported a 'sense of emptiness', of 'feeling stuck' and that 'sentimental relationships don't last'. While this patient is sociologically individualized and (apparently) well adapted to a liquid society, it remains to be seen if she is individuated. I leave this question open while I recapitulate what individuation is for Jung and what it is for Ulrich Beck.

C. G. Jung's individuation

As outlined in Chapter 1, according to Jung, individuation is one's own 'identification with the totality of the personality, with the self' (Jung, 1990, p.138)

DOI: 10.4324/9781003390770-5

and a process 'of differentiation, having for its goal the development of the individual personality' (CW6, para.757). Thus, individuation is a time when the individual is at 'a point of intersection or a dividing line, neither conscious nor unconscious, but a bit of both' (CW7, para.507). Individuation can also be described as 'the process in which the patient becomes what he really is' (CW16, para.11).

Verena Kast (1993, pp.5–6) furthers this definition, stating that to individuate means to become (the person you have never been). This means that one must:

1   Become independent from parents and from parental complexes.
2   Become more competent in relationships.
3   Become more of who and what you are.
4   Become more 'whole' (spiritual).

James Hillman (1997b, pp.87–88), meanwhile, describes individuation as comprising the following steps:

1   Descend.
2   Make peace with your biological family.
3   Find a place you can call home.
4   Give something back to society.

Sonu Shamdasani (see Hillman and Shamdasani, 2013, p.92) underlined that individuation 'enables someone to envisage new possibilities, to imagine new ways of consideration' and that individuation is a way out of solipsism. In this regard, Ann Casement (2001, p.147) claims that in addition to becoming 'wholly and indivisibly oneself', individuation also means 'gathering the world to oneself in order to fulfil collective qualities more completely and satisfactorily'. Thus, individuation is intended to be intrinsically antithetical to any individualism that a given person may harbour.

Both Kast's and Hillman's concepts help to better understand Jung's individuation[2] and what needs to be done to become an individualized and liquid society. Both concepts will become helpful in the next chapter, when investigating the clinical vignette.

Ulrich Beck's individualization

Gabe Mythen (2020), underlines that

in mobilizing the concept of risk to understand the widespread and radical social changes documented above, Beck was able to stitch together underlying patterns and processes across a range of spheres, from the environment and security, to the family, politics and science.

She adds that

> working in unison with Lash and Giddens, Beck explored the consequences of
> the processes of reflexive modernization, fleshing out the impacts of receding
> social structures of the risk society's self-confrontational dynamic on individu-
> als, culture, communities and institutions.
>
> (Beck et al., 1994)

Sørensen and Christiansen (2013, p.29) underline that

> according to Beck, we are currently witnessing modernity's detaching from –
> and development beyond – its roots in industrial society. To Beck, only the so-
> ciety of first modernity can be called industrial, as the transition towards second
> modernity is actively shifting us towards a new kind of society: the risk society.

Additionally, according to Beck (Sørensen and Christiansen, 2013, p.35), first modernity means:

1 Territorially bound, state-centred nation-states (nation and society are
  convergent)
2 Collective life patterns in macro groups/class societies (programmatic
  individualization)
3 Gainful employment societies of full employment (gainful employment as a
  medium for social status and recognition)
4 Instrumentalized, marginalized idea of nature (nature as a perpetually available/
  open resource which must be harnessed and used); dichotomy of nature and
  society
5 Scientifically defined concept of rationality (focus on instrumental control);
  faith in science and progress
6 Functionally differentiated societies (increasing specialization)

Second modernity means:

1 The post-national world risk society (the impossibility of a nation-state-based
  organization of society and economy)
2 The dissolution of the communities and basic institutions of industrial society
  (the nuclear family, class, neighbourhood, etc.); gender revolution and a 'normal chaos of love'
3 The post-work/post-full-employment society (decreasing amounts of gainful
  employment and new, flexible kinds of underemployment)
4 The societalization of nature (nature as an internal and transitory phenomenon)
5 Science's disenchantment and the critique of rationality
7 De-differentiation; the traditional boundaries are put under pressure or wholly
  torn down.

In this context, as Woodman (2009, p.17) reminds us, 'ambiguity is central to the both/and logic of late modernity' as theorized by Beck. Therefore, as Woodman underlines (2009, p.17), for Beck second modernity is about the 'weakening of the classic distinction between risk (calculable) and uncertainty (un-calculable)'.

Beck contra Jung

Feminist and relational psychoanalyst Susie Orbach (2014, p.17) underlined that 'being is constituted out of the enactment and living of both conscious behavior and behavior of which we are unaware' and that agents mutually influence each other while structure and agency are also mutually influential. Orbach (2014, p.16), as already underlined, claims that 'the individual is born into a set of social and psychological circumstances. The human infant is a set of possibilities – not id based, not instinctually driven – but in order to become recognized as a human, will need to attach' and later to separate. Following this, I propose that traditional sociology is not equipped to consider the unconscious, because it relies exclusively on classical drive theory, and has an ontological bias towards the rational and cognitive aspects of human behaviour. To this could also be added its loyalty to Durkheim's[3] view of psychology and the Frankfurt school's inability to go beyond Freud's dogma and examine the irrational side of the psyche. Finally, making of Jung a *persona non grata* in 20th-century sociology, the Frankfurters saw – following Walter Benjamin (cited in Samuels, 1993) – Jung's psychology as 'the devil's work' and an 'auxiliary service to National Socialism'. In contrast, I propose adopting Jung's psychosocial and relational viewpoint (see Chapter 2).

I also propose that Beck (see Chapter 3), and traditional sociology lack the tools to examine the unconscious and emotions, since they look at these factors theoretically (sociologically) instead of clinically (symbolically). We must query why, at a time where people have gained freedom that were unthinkable in earlier times, suicide rates have increased by 25% across the United States over nearly two decades (U.S. Center for Disease Control and Prevention, 2018)?[4] This fact alone is sufficient reason to look anew at the concepts of individualization and individuation and to realize that to truly become liberated[5] in an individualized society, people need to individuate. Thus, Jung's individuation process comprises a valid theory for understanding the world as it is (thus opposing the idea that the world is 'out of joint', 'unhinged' or 'gone mad' (Beck, 2016)). I propose that Jung's individuation comprises a theory of metamorphosis of the individual and therefore of the world. Moreover, metamorphosis is always linked to self-responsibility, in opposition to anomie.

What, then, is the link between precarious freedom, self-responsibility and leading a life made up of a succession of new beginnings, disorientation, and the absence of itinerary and direction? As discussed before (above and in Chapter 3), Beck and Beck-Gernsheim (2002) claim that when living an experimental life, everything is a matter of self-responsibility. Self-responsibility, I propose, is where individualization cracks, because people have difficulty taking responsibility and instead engage in brooding, 'a sterile activity [...] not work but a weakness, even a vice' (Jung, CW18, para.1810), before succumbing to depression and suicidal ideation, as per anomie.

In this regard, both sociologist Mauro Magatti (2018) in his column 'there is no freedom without responsibility' (Corriere della Sera), and Kulturkritiker Erich Fromm (1941) in *Escape from Freedom* underlined that 'modern man still is anxious and tempted to surrender his freedom to dictators of all kinds'. Fromm (1941) also noted that 'if humanity cannot live with the dangers and responsibilities inherent in freedom, it will probably turn into authoritarianism'.

However, in the words of Magatti and media sociologist and anthropologist Chiara Giaccardi (2014), if, in Western society, we have already liberated ourselves, 'what other liberation must we therefore seek?' Why are people not yet free if they have liberated themselves – again following Fromm (1941) – from the political, economic and spiritual shackles that have bound them? Why are people not yet happy, as Czech dramaturg Václav Havel wrote already in 1976 in the play titled *Horský Hotel*? Why are anxiety, depression and suicide rates increasing? This is, I propose, when the dichotomy between the wish for autonomy and anomie becomes apparent. Therefore, when there is a broken individualization that equals to 'the betrayed promise of freedom and happiness for all',[6] there can be no individuation.[7] Thus, I propose:

- Individuation and individualization are antithetic.
- Individualization is a diagnosis while individuation is a prognosis.
- Individualization means *homo optionis* while individuation means *become who you are*.
- Individualization equates to the conscious mind and solipsism and leads to anomie (precarious freedom) while individuation equates to pluralism and creativity and leads to generativity (absolute freedom).
- Individualization is linked to *Bewusstsein* while individuation is linked to *Gewissen* (see below).

Based on the above, Jung's individuation could provide an answer, perhaps even an antidote, to the current broken individualization and consequent anomie. This might be because, following Watkins (2003), it is the capacity for dialogue, not reason, that distinguishes humankind from other living creatures. Furthermore, such dialogue takes place with oneself, with one's neighbour and with God (Niebuhr, 1955, cited in Watkins, 2003) and this 'capacity for dialogue is a necessary precondition for human liberation' (2003, p.87), particularly 'from rigid, stereotypic, and unidimensional narrowness'. In this view, development (which she calls liberation) is based 'on a paradigm of interdependence, where the liberation of one is intimately tied to the liberation of the other' (2003, p.88). In this sense, 'the other' may comprise 'economic, political, sociocultural, spiritual, and psychological' entities. Additionally, Samuels (1989, p.1) – who introduced the concept of the plural psyche to 'hold unity and diversity in balance' and underlined that 'our inner worlds and our private lives reel from the impact of policy decisions and the existing political culture' – suggested that within both the microcosm of an individual and the macrocosm of the global village, 'we are flooded by psychological themes'.

An example – taken from the literature concerned with the *finis Austriae* – might help to clarify this point and to discuss more fully the reasons why people have difficulty taking responsibility. Italian Jungian analyst Paolo Ferliga (2005, p.1), analysing Joseph Roth's 1932 novel titled *Radetzkymarsch* (1999) from a psycho-analytic point of view, underlines

> The protagonist, Carl Joseph Trotta, motherless, is initiated into the military by his father. A pupil at the cadet school, he is subjected by his father to a cold test of his knowledge and progress at school every time he returns home for the holidays. Only after this examination, conducted by his father with the fussiness of an accountant, is it possible to go to the table to eat in an atmosphere that is always cold and compassionate [Should this be 'compassionless'?]. His father Franz is in fact an impeccable official of the Empire, himself initiated by his father into an administrative career. Franz's father, Carl Joseph's grandfather, became a hero at Solferino for saving the life of the then young Emperor Franz Joseph. Made a nobleman by the Emperor for this gesture, Joseph Trotta became Baron of Sipolje. Nobility and marriage to the daughter of an old family of civil servants accentuate his distance from his old, now invalid father, who reminds him of his Slavic and peasant origins.

Therefore, Ferliga underlines that:

> Between fathers and sons, relations have the cold and impersonal character of the Habsburg bureaucracy. The fathers impose their will on the sons, who are not content to do what the fathers want. There is no initiation, but imposition. The invalid great-grandfather spends his time tending the grounds of a cas-tle, while Baron Joseph, having abandoned his military career, takes personal charge of his wife's estate, becoming in fact a Slovenian peasant. When his wife died, he put his son in a boarding school. Never a gift, never praise or blame for the report cards, words reduced to the bare minimum. The son cares nothing about becoming a 'good official'. Instead, he would like to devote himself to looking after his mother's estate. But the father, on his death, will donate it to a charitable institution. For him, the son had to become a bureaucrat of the Em-pire. It was his way of remaining loyal to the emperor. Franz, who had become a district captain, did the same to his own son, forcing him into a military career that he could not bear. Carl Joseph also prefers to return to nature by going to live in the country of his ancestors, Slovenian peasants. There is no communica-tion between fathers and sons in this glimpse of *finis Austriae*: fathers who do not speak to their sons, functions of authority instead of initiatory figures, sons who cannot and do not know how to speak to their fathers. Everyone would like to return, more or less consciously, to the world of their ancestors, to a simple, hard life, in close contact with nature.

Ferliga (2005, p.1) recalls that 'one day District Captain Franz decides to take his son Carl Joseph on a short trip to Vienna' and that this could be 'an opportunity for closer contact between father and son'. But this does not happen, and their relationship continues to lack *eros*. Later 'Carl Joseph matures the idea of leaving the army, but does not know how to tell his father' (Ferliga, 2005, p.1). Here we see a first indication of his own individuation, although suppressed at birth – because of the supremacy of the loyalty to *the Emperor* (literal and metaphorical). In this respect, Roth (1999, p.271) underlines:

> with such thoughts, it would have been impossible for him to see and speak to his father, although he felt a great fondness for him. He had a kind of nostalgia for his father, as one has for a homeland, but at the same time he knew that his father was no longer his homeland. The army was no longer his job.

What Watkins (2003, p.87) points out is helpful in this respect: the 'capacity for dialogue is a necessary precondition for human liberation', particularly 'from rigid, stereotypic, and unidimensional narrowness'. In fact, what lacks here is such capacity for dialogue! Because of this, Carl Joseph fails to do what Kast and Hillman suggest (see above), and he becomes suicidal as per anomie.

Ferliga (2005, p.1) points out that what happens to Carl Josef 'is an experience of waste (of money, energy, meaning) and total loss' and that 'in an increasingly useless and unmotivated army, Carl Joseph shares the experience of dissolution of many officers: the game, a woman to support, debts that are growing by the day without him realising it'. This, I propose, is anomie because there is no self-responsibility here. It is individual (Carl Joseph) and also collective (*finis Austriae*) experience of waste. Carl Joseph's story helps us to look at the fact that when people have difficulty taking responsibility succumb to depression and suicidal ideation. Therefore, it is in this context that we can understand Magatti's claim that 'there is no freedom without responsibility' and Erich Fromm's claim that 'modern man still is anxious and tempted to surrender his freedom to dictators of all kinds'. In fact, Carl Joseph surrendered his freedom to his father (the highest authority) who, in turn, surrendered his freedom to the Emperor (even growing sideburns as Franz Joseph), and they both surrender their freedom to the hero of Solferino, Joseph Trotta (Baron of Sipolje), as a way of remaining loyal to the Emperor and the Empire.

This also explains what happened to Europe since the end of the First World War and its turn to authoritarianism, brought by the difficulty to 'live with the dangers and responsibilities inherent in freedom' (Fromm, 1941) and with the wish to remain loyal to the order of the past.

If this is the case, however, why does mainstream sociology fail to investigate these themes? Why does Beck argue that individualization might 'unleash the conflicts and devils that lie slumbering among the details' but does not say more? To all this – and as an antidote to broken individualization (and the difficulty sociologists demonstrated when looking at the unconscious) – I suggest examining Jung's concept of meditation.

The 'I+I': meditation as self-knowledge

In the section of *Mysterium Coniunctionis* titled 'Self-knowledge', Jung (CW14, para.497) claimed that 'what I call coming to terms with the unconscious the alchemists called "meditation"' and added, citing Ruland, that meditation is 'an Internal talk of one person with another who is invisible, as in the invocation of the Deity, or communion with one's self, or with one's good angel"'. In an individualized society, there is a fresh need for renewed internal talk, and one way of engaging in such is through psychoanalysis. Jung (CW14, para.498) claimed that modern meditation methods are 'only for increasing concentration and consolidating consciousness, but have no significance as regards effecting a synthesis of the personality. On the contrary, their purpose is to shield consciousness from the unconscious and to suppress it'. That being the case, such methods are of no therapeutic value. Instead, Jung (CW14, para.498) proposes analysis as meditation, although 'there are relatively few people who have experienced the effects of an analysis of the unconscious on themselves, and almost nobody hits on the idea of using the objective hints given by dreams as a theme for meditation'.

More than 70 years since the publication of this essay, little has changed. While in Jung's day, meditation had a bad reputation in the West, today, the à la mode forms of meditation and contemplation – yoga at lunchtime, daily morning meditation, weekend or holistic 'holiday' retreats, etc. – that have been adopted in the West do not facilitate internal talk. Instead, they facilitate a momentary calmness before returning (recharged) to the jungle of an affluent electronic society. Thus, these techniques are akin to smartphone battery chargers: indispensable for recharging in our society, but never fully disconnecting.

Therefore, I agree with Jung's view that:

> No one has time for self-knowledge or believes that it could serve any sensible purpose. Also, one knows in advance that it is not worth the trouble to know oneself, for any fool can know what he is. We believe exclusively in doing and do not ask about the doer, who is judged only by achievements that have collective value [...]. Western man confronts himself as a stranger and that self-knowledge is one of the most difficult and exacting of the arts.
>
> (CW14, para.498)

Meditation and self-knowledge – which lead to individuation when the individual can work and internalize the objective hints given by dreams – might help people to produce *something* (values) that the individual decides to share with mankind. In this regard, the study on Jung and Nietzsche by Giovanni Colacicchi is helpful.

Colacicchi (2021, p.52) underlines that 'individuation appears to be the ethical and healthy tertium between mass-mindedness and individualism: ethical and healthy because it allows both individuals and the society in which they live in to flourish'. Colacicchi adds that 'Not only is the individuated subject capable of a better social performance: for Jung, he or she must produce something in favour of society'. In fact, Jung writes that 'the individuated personality must produce something equivalent in favour of society', otherwise 'individuation remains a pose so long as no positive values are created' (Jung, 1916a, p.1098). Therefore, Colacicchi (2021, p.52) claims that

> here Jung speaks, in a Nietzschean manner, of the creation of values. These values, if we keep in mind Jung's ideas on conflicts of duties, could be seen as the ethical and creative tertium which the 'hero', having endured many conflicts of duties during his journey of individuation, is capable of 'producing', and decides to share with mankind.

I propose that there is no opportunity for the *tertium* in current second-late-modern meditation practices, because such techniques do not facilitate self-knowledge (which is the investigation of 'the objective hints given by dreams' (CW14, para.498).[8]

Meditation in the sense used by Jung, however, would allow individuals to look inward, to find substance and purpose in life, and by this means to compensate for emptiness and meaninglessness. As Jung suggested in The Red Book, to become 'one's own creator' is key (2009, p.188).

Finally, I propose that the anxiety and depression related to anomie, which are rife in our society, should not be viewed as pathological, but rather as attitudes towards life, as an opportunity for development and liberation, and as a key aspect of intermediate (pre-individuated) states.

In sociological terms (as underlined in Chapters 2 and 3), anxiety and depression are linked to anomie, the state wherein individuals lose sight of the fact that they can actively shape their lives. Thus, when creativity and the contents of the unconscious are repressed, anxiety and depression result and this enables anomie.

In this context, Jung's individuation is fundamental because the goal of psychotherapy, according to Jung (CW16, para.99), is 'to bring about a psychic state in which my patient begins to experiment with his own nature – a state of fluidity, change and growth where nothing is eternally fixed and hopelessly petrified'. This, Jung claims, is always related to the opportunity to express oneself creatively, through dreams, painting, active imagination, or through the body. Moreover, Jung notes that the creative fantasy is an 'intrusion from the unconscious, a sort of lucky hunch, different in kind from the slow reasoning of the conscious mind' (CW16, para.16).

In conclusion, the 'I+I', the concept of individuation in a second-late-modern society, takes Beck's individualization's theory as a valid picture of second modernity and merges it with Jung's individuation process. Therefore, the 'I+I' is claims that to become free in second-late modernity – to fulfil one's destiny (in Jungian terms) – people need to individuate once being individualized.

By introducing the concept of 'I+I', my objective is to forge a novel notion that emerges from the merge of Beck and Jung's individual concepts. I opt for the term 'merger' because it implies a relational aspect. As per the Oxford dictionary, to merge signifies to 'combine or induce combination to create a unified entity' or to 'blend or induce blending gradually into something else until it becomes indistinguishable'. This accurately mirrors my specific intention when scrutinizing the theories of Jung and Beck. Consequently, a merger can only transpire through mutual agreement; it is not coerced but rather transformed into something entirely new: a third entity.

From Bewusstsein to Gewissen

Jung (CW10, para.677) underlines that 'with deeper self-knowledge, one is often confronted with the most difficult problems of all, namely conflicts of duty' which – he added – 'simply cannot be decided by any moral precepts, neither those of the decalogue nor of other authorities'. Therefore, he states that

> this is where ethical decisions really begin, for the mere observance of a codi-fied "thou shalt not" is not in any sense an ethical decision, but merely an act of obedience and, in certain circumstances, a convenient loophole that has nothing to do with ethics.
>
> (CW10, para.677)

In his paper 'A Psychological View of Conscience' (CW10), Jung looked at the concepts of *Bewusstsein* (consciousness or what is conscious) and *Gewissen* (con-science). Here I wish to look at the distinction he makes, to further clarify what I underlined above and hopefully also the concept of the 'I+I'. Therefore – following Susie Orbach (see above) who underlined that 'being is constituted out of the en-actment and living of both conscious behaviour and behaviour of which we are un-aware' – I shall propose that one can equate individualization with consciousness (*Bewusstsein*) therefore conscious behaviour, while individuation can be equated with the conscience (*Gewissen*) and behaviour of which we are unaware.

Jung (CW10, para.825) clarifies[9] that conscience (*Gewissen*) – 'is a special form of "knowledge" or "consciousness"' whose peculiarity 'is that it is a knowledge of, or certainty about, the emotional value of the ideas we have concerning the motives of our actions' and he adds that

> conscience is a complex phenomenon consisting on the one hand in an elemen-tary act of the will, or in an impulse to act for which no conscious reason can be given, and on the other hand in a judgment grounded on rational feeling. This judgment is a value judgment, and it differs from an intellectual judgment in that, besides having an objective, general, and impartial character, it reveals the subjective point of reference. A value judgment always implicates the subject, presupposing that something is good or beautiful for me. If, on the other hand, I say that it is good or beautiful for certain other people, this is not necessar-ily a value judgment but may just as well be an intellectual statement of fact. Conscience, therefore, is made up of two layers, the lower one comprising a

particular psychic event, while the upper one is a kind of superstructure repre-
senting the positive or negative judgment of the subject.

Based on this view, I propose that conscience (*Gewissen*) is what sociology cannot
grasp. It can only grasp consciousness or what is conscious (*Bewusstsein*). In fact,
Jung (CW10, para.832) claims that 'although people still labour under the delusion
that consciousness represents the whole of the psychic man, it is nevertheless only
a part, of whose relation to the whole we know very little'.

Therefore, Jung (CW10, para.826) underlines that conscience (*Gewissen*) 'may
appear as an act of conscious reflection which anticipates, accompanies, or follows
certain psychic events, or as a mere emotional concomitant of them, in which case
its moral character is not immediately evident'. This is important when looking at
the clinical case of Chapter 5.

Jung (CW10, para.826) adds that 'an apparently groundless anxiety state may
follow a certain action, without the subject being conscious of the least connection
between them. Often the moral judgement is displaced into a dream which the subject does not understand'. Here Jung brings the example of a businessman who had
a revelatory dream that – if understood – would have prevented him from fraud.
The same applies to Carla, the patient in Chapter 5.

Jung (CW10, para.856) underlines that

> 'Conscience', in ordinary usage, means the consciousness of a factor which in
> the case of a 'good conscience' affirms that a decision or an act accords with
> morality and, if it does not, condemns it as 'immoral'. This view, deriving as it
> does from the mores, from what is customary, can properly be called 'moral'.
> Distinct from this is the ethical form of conscience, which appears when two
> decisions or ways of acting, both affirmed to be moral and therefore regarded as
> 'duties', collide with one another. In these cases, not foreseen by the moral code
> because they are mostly very individual, a judgment is required which cannot
> properly be called 'moral' or in accord with custom. Here the decision has no
> custom at its disposal on which it could rely. The deciding factor appears to be
> something else: it proceeds not from the traditional moral code but from the
> unconscious foundation of the personality. The decision is drawn from dark and
> deep waters. It is true that these conflicts of duty are solved very often and very
> conveniently by a decision in accordance with custom, that is, by suppressing
> one of the opposites.

Jung (CW10, para.855) emphasizes that 'Conscience is a psychic reaction which
one can call moral because it always appears when the conscious mind leaves the
path of custom, of the mores, or suddenly recollects it'. He adds:

> conscience signifies primarily the reaction to a real or supposed deviation from
> the moral code, and is for the most part identical with the primitive fear of
> anything unusual, not customary, and hence 'immoral'. As this behavior is

instinctive and, at best, only partly the result of reflection, it may be 'moral' but can raise no claim to being ethical. It deserves this qualification only when it is reflective, when it is subjected to conscious scrutiny. And this happens only when a fundamental doubt arises as between two possible modes of moral behavior, that is to say in a conflict of duty. A situation like this can be 'solved' only by suppressing one moral reaction, upon which one has not reflected till now, in favour of another. In this case the moral code will be invoked in vain [...]. Only the creative power of the ethos that expresses the whole man can pronounce the final judgment.

Therefore, Jung (CW10, para.829) stresses that:

If conscience is a kind of knowledge, then it is not the empirical subject who is the knower, but rather an unconscious personality who, to all appearances, behaves like a conscious subject. It knows the dubious nature of the offer, it recognizes the acquisitive greed of the ego, which does not shrink even from illegality, and it causes the appropriate judgment to be pronounced. This means that the ego has been replaced by an unconscious personality who performs the necessary act of conscience.

Hence, Jung (CW10, para.838) asks: 'where does the true and authentic conscience, which rises above the moral code and refuses to submit to its dictates, get its justification from?' He answers (CW10, para.839) quoting John,[10] that 'since olden times conscience has been understood by many people less as a psychic function than as a divine intervention; indeed, its dictates were regarded as vox Dei, the voice of God'. He (CW10, para.840) also claims that 'the view of conscience as the voice of God becomes an extremely delicate problem'[11] and adds that 'conscience – no matter on what it is based – commands the individual to obey his inner voice even at the risk of going astray' (CW10, para.841) and that conscience, when seen as the voice of God (which is opposite to the moral code or moral conflict), 'often cuts sharply across our subjective intentions and may sometimes force an extremely disagreeable decision' (CW10, para.842). Therefore, Jung (CW10, para.84) points out that 'if the vox Dei conception of conscience is correct, we are faced logically with a metaphysical dilemma', namely that 'we must admit with Faust: "Two souls, alas, are housed within my breast," which no human charioteer can master, as the fate of Faust clearly indicates'. This is also important while looking at Carla's case in Chapter 5.

Therefore, Jung underlines that 'we can refuse to obey this command by an appeal to the moral code and the moral views on which it is founded, though with an uncomfortable feeling of having been disloyal' (CW10, para.841). But disloyal to whom? To one's own Self, is the answer.

Giovanni Colacicchi (2021, p.92) underlines that, in Jung, conscience is about 'the "interior space" in which we are in dialogue with God (in Jung, the *ethical*[12] dimension of conscience) and the "awareness of particular moral values" (in Jung, the *moral*[13] dimension of conscience)' and that 'Jung sees the ethical dimension of conscience as the decisive factor for individuation (see CW7, para.218)'.

Then Colacicchi (2021, p.29) reminds us that Jung 'distinguishes between two types of moral conflicts, those of neurotics and those of "normal people", where "the conflicting opposites are both conscious" (Jung, 1978, p.436)'. Colacicchi proposes that 'with reference to neurotic conflicts, the question that arises is: how does it occur that one side of a conflict is or becomes unconscious?' and adds

> one side of a conflict may have become unconscious due to the mechanism of repression, which Jung defines as 'a rather immoral *penchant*[14] for getting rid of disagreeable decisions' (CW11, para.129). Or it may have been unconscious in the first place.

Therefore Colacicchi (2021, p.29) reminds us that, according to Jung, 'since one side of the dilemma is relegated to the unconscious, there is no way that a solution can be found' and that 'these types of moral conflict are *irresolvable*[15] and neurosis, in Jungian terms, could thus be defined as the "non-solution" to an irresolvable conflict of duties which should instead become a conscious and so resolvable condition'.

Colacicchi (2021, p.29) also helps us to confirm that, according to Jung 'when both sides of the dilemma are conscious' they can be solved. He claims (2021, p.30) that

> conscious dilemmas can be solved in two ways. In the first, a horn is simply suppressed. Jung calls this the 'moral' solution (CW10, para.855–857). In the second case, the conscious conflict is endured, and eventually a third point of view is found, thanks to the cooperation of the irrational side of our psyche. Jung calls this the 'ethical' solution.
>
> (CW10, para.855–857)

Therefore, as Colacicchi (2021, p.29) proposes, 'the solution, according to Jung, can only "emerge" from the unconscious' and that 'this second type of solution to a moral conflict is "a special instance of [...] the transcendent function" (CW10, para.855), the function that allows a cooperation of consciousness and the unconscious'.

Colacicchi (2021, p.30) claims that 'the unconscious can intervene presumably because it is not part of the conflict. In other words, when both sides of the dilemma are conscious, the unconscious can provide a more impartial and creative contribution to the psychic system'.

This impartial and creative contribution, is, following Jung, the *vox Dei*. The only way (unless we – refusing to obey – prefer to be disloyal to our Self and to content ourselves to live with uncomfortable feelings leading to anomie)! In fact, Jung underlines that 'any other type of ethical decision would be conventional, meaning that it would depend on a traditional and collective code of moral values (Jung, 1990, p.300)'.

In this regard, it is also important to remember that Jung (CW10, para.845), following the vox Dei hypothesis, looks at the importance of 'the numinous character of the moral reaction' and at the fact that 'conscience is a manifestation of mana, of the "extraordinarily powerful," a quality which is the especial peculiarity of archetypal ideas'. When Jung (CW10, para.846) reduces 'the notion of the vox Dei to the hypothesis of the archetype' he underlines that 'the archetype is a pattern of behaviour that has always existed, that is morally indifferent as a biological phenomenon, but possesses a powerful dynamism by means of which it can profoundly influence human behaviour'. Therefore, he claims that in the archetype is the answer to a moral problem. In fact, when Jung (CW10, para.848) claims that 'the vox Dei hypothesis is then no more than an amplificatory tendency peculiar to the archetype – a mythological statement inseparably bound up with numinous experiences which expresses these occurrences and also seeks to explain them', he also shows the way out of feeling stuck (as per Carla's experience) and anomie.

In the next chapter I will show that, when learning to follow the insight brought by the unconscious, conflicts of duty can be solved, and when this happens one's own integrity[16] is restored.

Employing the dreams brought by my patient Carla, I will show that (1) repression made her neurotic, therefore unable to make decisions (stuck); (2) analysis helped her to make her dilemma conscious, to try to solve it; (3) at least initially, what Jung calls the *moral* solution was her preferred way to solve such conflict – although – (4) by working together and with the help of the transcendent function, a third point of view was found. This, as Colacicchi (2021, p.30) reminds us, happens 'thanks to the cooperation of the irrational side of our psyche' and is what Jung calls the *ethical* solution. Therefore, the *ethical* solution, is only possible when one is able to listen to the voice of God.

Hence, I shall propose that, once the ethical solution has been formulated, integrity (a consequence of meditation and self-knowledge) enables the shift between *Bewusstsein* and *Gewissen* and the shift from living in an individualized society (without individuating) to what I call the 'I+I'.

Jung's prioritization of individual development over collective life

At this stage, it is important to devote enough attention to the *alleged* problem of Jung's prioritization of individual development over collective life. This problem constitutes a massive hurdle to accepting Jung's thinking as making a valid contribution to the psychosocial. Therefore, the way Jung's individuation impacts on the outer collective has to be taken in serious consideration.

British author and Jungian analyst Mark Saban (2019, p.201) underlines that for Jung 'inner' and 'outer' were dichotomies at the time he engaged in his descent into the unconscious, from which stemmed the Red Book. Saban adds that Jung could appreciate their interdependence only later in his work (2019, p.188). According to Saban (2019, p.188) the early Jung solves 'the problems of outer conflict by prioritising an *inner* dialogue, while the later one emphasizes 'that the patient's projection onto the analyst gives the helpful *illusion* of outer engagement'. Hence, Saban (2019, p.189) notes that 'Jung's emphasis upon the importance of the other's "validity" is a recognition that inner and outer possess equal status, even recognizing a possible mutuality'.

Saban (2019, p.196) addresses that, according to Jung, individuation – understood as psychological growth – is not about an 'encounter with the outer other' (outer person or collective) and with this 'Jung explicitly rules out the notion of individuation-through-extraversion'. However, Saban (2019, p.196) continues, 'there are hints throughout the works of this period that such limitations are in fact misplaced and perhaps even incoherent given the overall thrust of his psychology'. In fact, I wish the case of Carla (Chapter 5), can be a proof 'that the possibility that the relationship between outer and inner collective is one of complex mutuality' (Saban, 2019, p.196) and that:

> although Jung expressly differentiates the outer function ('The collective function in relation to society') from the inner function ("The collective function in relation to the unconscious"), he acknowledges that 'from the 'mystical' or metapsychological point of view', (Jung, 1916a, para. 1101[17]) these two apparently different functions are in fact identical.

Saban points out that in a book of the same period, Jung (see 1916c, para.486) stresses that 'psyche is both individual and collective', and that its health is about their joint action.

In fact, I agree with Saban (2019, p.197) when he claims that:

> the relationship between individual (inner) and collective (outer) opens up the possibility that the process of individuation might necessarily consist in a process of confrontation and dialogue not only with the *inner* unknown other (collective unconscious as interiority) but with the *outer* unknown other (collective in the form of outer person or group). Under these circumstances, individuation might be expected to require either outer or inner confrontations depending upon which attitude type was, at the time, dominant. However, there is a clear contradiction between such an idea and the Jung's notion that introversion is uniquely the road to psychological transformation.

Having looked at the relationship between the concepts of individual (inner) and collective (outer) throughout Jung's trajectory, I now wish to focus on the concept of individuation from a psychosocial point of view.

Jung (CW7, para.266) underlines that 'there is a destination, a possible goal', beyond the alternative stages of life. This is, he claims, the way of individuation. According to Jung, 'individuation means becoming an "in-dividual," and, in so far as "individuality" embraces our innermost, last, and incomparable uniqueness, it also implies becoming one's own self. We could therefore translate individuation as "coming to selfhood" or "self-realization"'.

Therefore, the question is: what impact on collective affairs can [Jung's notion of] individuation have? This question helps investigate what might be the implications of Jung's highly individualistic notion of individuation within the collective realm. It is essential if wishing to achieve the goal of merging Jung and Beck into the I+I, because such an investigation is concerned with analysing implicit tensions within Jung's concept. The below discussion will attempt to answer this question, by looking at the tensions between Jung's ideas about society and his emphasis upon the individual.

Jung (CW/7, para.267) underlines that the individual goes through a process of 'alienations of the self' which means 'divesting the self of its reality in favour of an external role' (social recognition) 'or in favour of an imagined meaning' (a primordial image). For Jung the collective is dominant here – serving a social ideal – with its positive (social duty and virtue) and negative (egotistical) sides. Jung therefore claims that 'self-realization seems to stand in opposition to self-alienation' and adds that this is a misunderstanding due to the fact that 'we do not sufficiently distinguish between individualism and individuation'. Therefore, Jung clarifies that individualism equates to 'deliberately stressing and giving prominence to some supposed peculiarity rather than to collective considerations and obligations', while

individuation means the better and more complete fulfilment of the collective qualities of the human being, since adequate consideration of the peculiarity of the individual is more conducive to a better social performance than when the peculiarity is neglected or suppressed.

Therefore, individuation (Jung, CW/7, para.267) is psychic development 'that fulfils the individual qualities given'. It is a process 'by which a man becomes the definite, unique being he in fact is', 'fulfilling the peculiarity of his nature', and this differs 'from egotism or individualism'. While this happens, the person 'does not become "selfish" in the ordinary sense of the word'.

Therefore Jung (CW7, para.268) underlines that 'the human individual, as a living unit, is composed of purely universal factors, he is wholly collective and therefore in no sense opposed to collectivity'. Hence:

the individualistic emphasis on one's own peculiarity is a contradiction of this basic fact of the living being. Individuation, on the other hand, aims at a living co-operation of all factors. But since the universal factors always appear only in individual form, a full consideration of them will also produce an individual effect, and one which cannot be surpassed by anything else, least of all by individualism.

This answers the question posed above: the individual is (composed of) universal factors. It is collective. It is the collectivity. What makes it oppose the collectivity is its *ego wish* to stick to social values and norms that have nothing to do with the universal factors. But this seems to clash with Samuels' take on Jung's view of society and the individual.

In line with the early Jung described by Saban, Samuels (2014, p.104) underlines that 'the way in which Jung positioned the individual in relation to society, and the way in which society is reduced to "the mass" or "the masses", simply assumes that societies and individuals are inevitably antipathetic'. Therefore, he adds that 'at times, Jung seemed to suggest that a society or a nation is simply made up of the individuals in it, and there is nothing more to be said'.

Samuels (2014, p.104) argues that 'the impossibility of the individual in relation to society represents a premature concession by Jung' and asks: 'Can we recuperate the Jungian idea of the individual?' Doing this, he claims, 'would involve critiquing the relationship between individual and society as Jung set it out'.

Samuels (2014, p.106), reminds us – employing Camus – that people seek both social and spiritual ambitions. Could this be the connection between Beck (a sociological sociologist) and Jung (the psychoanalyst that more than anyone else looked at spirituality)? Samuels proposes that – what Camus termed 'religion' or 'philosophy' (1953, p.237), should be termed 'social spirituality'. Samuels therefore proposes that 'in social spirituality, individuals come together to take action in the social sphere, doing this in concert with other people'. I wonder whether this could be seen as an extension of what Beck called methodological utopianism. Therefore, the I+I (individualization + individuation) is the adoption of *methodological spiritualism* (which corresponds to methodological utopianism + spirituality). The methodological part is related to Beck's individualization, and the spiritual part is related to what Jung calls *vox-Dei* (see Chapter 5).

I concur with what Samuels underlined in 2014 (p.109), as an additional explanation for adopting the I+I as *methodological spirituality*. He claims that 'Governments constantly try to improve things in the political world, usually by redistributing wealth or changing legislative and constitutional structures or defusing warlike situations', but they fail to provide societies with 'the spiritual goods and a sense of meaning and purpose'. Instead, governments would use economic tools to tackle challenges within the state, but 'will not refresh those parts of the individual citizen that a psychological perspective can reach'. Samuels criticizes that these political measures 'only ruffle the surface' and would not bring about a change 'for which the individual political soul yearns'. Therefore Samuels (2014, p.101), underlines that the 'contemporary discourse stresses that individuals are embedded and constructed by and in social relationships, communal networks, task-oriented groups, and ecosystems', and asks 'has the potential of an individual to contribute actively to what happens in the collective been underestimated by this set of assumptions?' I propose this brings about Jung's social aspect to individuation.

Samuels (2014, p.101) states that 'if Jungian psychology could refashion its approach to the individual, then it could become a source of support and inspiration to embattled citizens whose experience of their battles is often that they are in it on their own'. This is exactly what I wish to accomplish with my own I+I.

Here I wish to pause for a moment and constitute that, in my opinion, Beck and Jung are working on the same problematic: to link the social/collective with the individual realms whether called individuation or individualization – or even called individualism.

Additionally, what is interesting here is the different methods they employ to establish this link. My view is that both are trying to incorporate individual phenomena (such as emotions for Jung and individual choices for Beck) with a form of early sociology-informed depth psychology (Jung) and with a form of depth psychology-informed sociology (Beck), although the latter never mentions it.

The main issue concerns whether, for Jung, there is a social aspect to individuation. Can one individuate outside of a concern for social and political issues? Can one individualize outside of the reflexive structure of the West?

Let's start from a first point: 'individuals in the West are today in agony', claims Samuels (2014, p.103). This is something that sociology has confirmed, as I underlined in Chapter 3. I propose that if Samuels and Beck would have had the chance to talk about this, they would agree. What they would disagree on is how to change things. Beck would propose an agenda that excludes the souls (emotions and affects) while Samuels (or Jung) would propose an agenda stemming from the material of the soul. Therefore, with my I+I – a psychosocial agenda informed by sociology and depth psychology – the issue could be tackled in a different way (at least theoretically).

In conclusion, the vignette portrayed in Chapter 5 might help to shed light on what Saban calls the enantiodromic and compensatory relation between *inner* and *outer*. In fact, Carla, who lives an extraverted life, had to undergo an introverted journey, to become herself. Without this, she would have continued to be extrovertedly neurotic.

My hope is that her case will help to show that, at the time she came into analysis, she was 'one-sided in the direction of the spirit of this time' (Saban, 2019, p.163). Therefore, this case helps to clarify that 'the relationship between outer and inner collective is one of complex mutuality' (Saban, 2019, p.196) and that 'the solution to the problem is not to become one-sided in the other direction' (Saban, 2019, p.163).

Additionally, I believe that the below case is a demonstration that – as Saban underlined (Saban, 2019, p.163):

according to the logic of the storm lantern dream, Jung should at this point seek to harness the hermeneutic strengths of *both* spirits, (both personalities, if Shamdasani is right) by bringing each into contact with the other. For example, historical (spirit of this time) factors might be brought into play with what Jung will go on to describe as archetypal (spirit of the depths) factors, in a potentially creative meeting between the social/political and the soul-oriented.

Notes

1 'There is a lot of misunderstanding about this concept of individualization. It does not mean individualism. It does not mean individuation – a term used by depth psychologists to describe the process of becoming an autonomous individual […]. Nor, lastly, does it mean emancipation as Jurgen Habermas describes it' (Beck, 2002, p.X).

2 I am aware that Murray Stein provides a concise and well-set-out account of individuation, with a therapeutic emphasis, in his chapter 'Individuation' in R. Papadopoulous (Ed.), *The Handbook of Jungian Psychology* (2006). I have decided to not employ Stein here.

3 Following Lukes' (1982) introduction to Durkheim's *The Rules of Sociological Method*, we understand that Durkheim sought to demarcate sociology from psychology, claiming sociology to be a 'special psychology, having its own subject-matter and a distinctive method' (Durkheim, 1982, p.253), while psychology is 'the science of the individual mind' whose object or domain is as follows (Durkheim, ibid., p.40): (1) states of individual consciousness; (2) explanation in terms of 'organico-psychic' factors, pre-social features of the individual organism, given at birth and independent of social influences; (3) explanation in terms of particular or 'individual' as opposed to general or 'social' conditions (focusing, say, on individuals' intentions or their particular circumstances); (4) explanation in terms of individual mental states or dispositions. However, if we look carefully into a psychosocial parallel between Durkheim and Jung, we might recognize that these four points can be linked respectively to Jung's concepts of (1) the personal unconscious; (2) archetypes and the collective unconscious; (3) the persona; (4) Jung's theory of neurosis and psychodynamics.

4 See: https://www.cdc.gov/media/releases/2018/p0607-suicide-prevention.html (retrieved from the internet on 10.1.2022).

5 *Liberation* is a term/concept I borrow from Mary Watkins (2003).

6 As Giaccardi underlined at a conference titled 'Social Generativity. What it is and what it is good for' (2018).

7 With this I do not imply that individualization is a prerequisite for individuation. In fact, below I propose that individuation can be an antidote for broken individualization, which implies that individuation can take place independently of individualization.

8 Or employing other techniques that help to get in contact with the materials (and symbols) brought up by the unconscious.

9 I will let Jung's own words speak here (without paraphrasing them) because I believe they speak for themselves and contribute to clarification.

10 'Try the spirits whether they are of God' (1 John 4:1).

11 I will not look at this problematic in detail and I remit the reader to CW10, para.840).

12 My italics.

13 Ibidem.

14 Ibid.

15 Ibid.

16 I will look into the concept of integrity in the concluding chapter (Chapter 6).

17 See: Jung, C. G. (1976 [1916]). *Collected Works, Volume 18: The Symbolic Life*, 2nd Edition.

Chapter 5

The 'I+I' as a metanarrative of 21st-century narratives of self-development

A clinical case

In this chapter, I will examine the biography of a former patient of mine from three different perspectives – individualization (Beck), individuation (Jung) and 'I+I'– to ascertain whether this patient could be considered individuated, individualized or 'I+I'. Employing this method will demonstrate the need to merge the first two theories into a third and to suggest that the merging of psychoanalysis and sociology into the Jungian–relational–psychosocial model is a useful tool to understand the nature of the development of narratives of self-identity at the beginning of the 21st century. It will also demonstrate that the 'I+I' is an alternative and competent way to examine the current development of narratives of self-development at the edge of psychoanalysis and sociology and thereby, to frame and contextualize my analytic generalization within the advanced electronic and individualized society context of the 21st century.

Carla appeared as sociologically individualized and well adapted to individualized and liquid society (according to Beck and Bauman, respectively), but not individuated (according to Jung). On the one hand, she had challenged the certainties of modern life, namely, the social order of the nation-state, class, gender, ethnicity and traditional family structure and had strived for self-fulfilment and achievement. Simultaneously, however, albeit unconsciously, she felt trapped in the impasse described by Bauman. During our first session, Carla described a sense of emptiness, feeling stuck and that her sentimental relationships did not last.

I propose that this case illustrates my thesis (i.e. precisely how this represents I+I) rather than a traditional Jungian treatment because – as already underlined in Chapter 2 – Beck-Gernsheim and Beck (1995, p.8) claim that individualization 'occurs in the wealthy western industrialized countries as a side effect of the modernization process designed to be long term' and that everyone born after 1950 has to be considered individualized. Therefore, the difference between this case (the I+I) and a traditional Jungian case, lies in the fact that Carla (as well as all people born after 1950 in the West) living in second-late-modern societies, are *de facto* individualized.

Carla: personal history

Carla was 40 when we met in April 2017 and started therapy. We ended therapy in the autumn of 2020. Born in Colombia, she recalls a 'nice' time there, although she

DOI: 10.4324/9781003390770-6

seldom gave details about it during our conversations. She moved to Spain with her family when she was 16 years old (after riots broke out in her hometown in 1989, because her parents were afraid to raise four children there.) She hated Spain, stating, 'Spain hated me' because

> kids made fun of my accent and they looked at me from top down, because south Americans were considered inferior. They used to tell me: 'go back to your country!' There was no middle class from South America in Spain. Only super rich and super poor south Americans. We lived in Madrid for two years, later we moved to Javea (a small town near the coast), because my father is originally from there.

At age 17, Carla went to Italy to study Italian for a month. She loved it and ended up staying there for two and a half months. She underlined that the host family welcomed her and loved her as an additional member of the family. She loved it there because she didn't feel the pressure of being under the power of the 'Spanish Colony' as in Madrid and Javea. Once back in Spain, she was 'forced' by her parents to study economics (she never graduated). Although she wanted to study fine arts, her parents would not allow it.

At 21, she moved to London where she lived for 16 years (before moving to Berlin), to study drama (theatre is her passion) and, she added, 'to live my life'. She also mentioned that her parents did not support her either financially or emotionally. Furthermore, the money her parents had saved for university fees for their children was used exclusively for Juan, 'the first male brother'. She noted that when Linda, 'the preferred daughter', decided to study engineering, their mother provided her with financial support.

As soon as she arrived in London she met and moved in with Jay (who was ten years older and an alcoholic). She commented that she soon realized she was not in love with him, although it was convenient for her to live with him despite the fact that he was an alcoholic and could be violent at times. She lived with Jay for two years, until one night when he tried to beat her while drunk. He was so drunk that he lost equilibrium and fell, bumping his head and losing consciousness. Carla, afraid he was dead, ran to call the neighbour. The neighbour helped her to call an ambulance and told her (as if he knew what was going on): 'take your stuff and leave this house now. This is the only way you can leave him'. She followed his advice and left. After this, Jay started following her and stalking her. She contacted the police, but the police didn't really help, because she recalls, 'they say it is difficult to sue a former partner'.

While in the UK, she married Mourice (her non-European gay-best-friend who needed a visa to stay in the UK). They divorced soon after the civil wedding, once Mourice had received a lifelong visa.

In London, she also had a relationship with Omar (for five years). Together they decided to move to Berlin, intending to move in together. Finally, however, he stayed back in London and they broke up. Only then he admitted to being unfaithful to her (having had affairs while they were a couple). She described Omar as a musician, always on tour, and a promiscuous man. In the course of therapy, she realized almost all her partners were unfaithful; 'like my father' she added.

In Berlin, she had a relationship with Timo, a neighbour in her building. It lasted ten months (she loved him and fantasized about building a future together). However, when Timo's ex-girlfriend came back to Berlin (from south America) he broke up with Carla. She commented: 'I was in love with him for what he represented: a different man than other men. He was good ("*bueno*") while in the past I was attracted by the bad ones ("*malotes*"). Timo is good. Omar is bad'.

An important note, in the course of the analysis, is that both Omar and Timo left her for another woman or cheated on her, and I wonder whether there could be here a trans-generational passing of a complex, where she is not able to find a man that will not cheat on her or leave her for another woman (like in the relationship of her mother and father) until she works on her complex?

When she visited me, she told me she just started going out with Neal (since April 2017) and that they were not in a relationship. She was longing for a relationship, but he was not. She commented she felt sad when he told her he doesn't want a 'serious relationship'. But she accepted this because she liked him. She said:

I am sad because I don't know if he wants something serious in the future. A part of me want[s] to run away from him (to not get hurt). Another wants to stay because I like him. I like to talk about culture, theatre and politics and all this stuff.

Then she added:

He wanted to have the typical German talk, whether to understand if we are a couple or not. He wanted to underline that we are not a couple. He was sincere. I felt like a kid who has the sweets taken away, and Mum says: 'No! I will give it to you later'. And the sweet is love. I don't trust men. I always get disappointed. I am tired of all relationships ending the same way. I am tired that a relationship never works and that all relationships are complicated and ugly (*feo*).

This is an important comment and links with what was underlined about Jay, Timo and Omar, together with the fact that she recognizes she cannot have a stable and long-lasting relationship with a man. Therefore, she added that she has a very difficult relationship with her father. They do not speak to each other. She is afraid that he will die soon and that they will not have the chance to become close again. She also has a difficult relationship with her mother. Her parents divorced when she was 27, although she recalls them fighting for a long time.

When we met, she told me she had different jobs to pay her bills (dramaturge, editor, web content manager, and later as a waiter in a bar and secretary in an office). Her passion is theatre, and she is an actress as well as the co-owner of an independent theatre company with her friend and colleague Rebekka. When we met, they were working to put together a new show (see initial dream).

Family history

Mother: When we started therapy, Carla's mother was still living in Colombia and had many difficulties. During the course of therapy, she first moved to Spain and later to Vienna, where she lived during winter 2017–2018 with Linda. She then moved back to Spain, where she lives in a residence for elderly people due to having been diagnosed with Alzheimer. Carla's mother is Colombian (of Spanish origin). Carla said that her mother was an academic before she got married and was forced by her husband to stop working to take care of the family. Carla recalls they didn't have a good relationship because Carla was always the rule-breaker.

Father: Carla's father was born in Spain and moved to Colombia as a kid. Carla underlines that she doesn't speak with her father (nor does her sister Linda) for the past two years, 'when he decided to stop talking to us because we took mum's side after their divorce. He told us "you are with me or with the devil (referring to our mother)"'. She then added:

> Father was able to put my brothers against mum. Later our younger brother (Nando) joined us. Juan is the only one close to father who still speaks to him. When my parents divorced my father was only able to say bad things about my mum. He never realised he was not able to manipulate my sister, my brother Nando and I. Therefore, he stopped talking to us. He now lives in the south of Spain. My father is toxic. He is now doing everything possible to get the inheritance my grandmother gave to my aunt (father's brother, who was born male and had a gender operation at the age of 40).

Carla also added that her father is good at humiliating family members and manipulating them. She also added:

> I used to adore my father when I was a girl. I never had a good relationship with my mother when young, until later when I discovered my father was a monster. When I was a kid, I thought the monster was my mum, but when my parents separated, I realized that the monster was my father and not my mother because he was making her life impossible. Since they separated, I have a better relationship with mum, although she is not a saint. After the separation my father did everything possible to make us kids take his side and used to call mum *Mussolini*. He said he stayed with mum because of us and that meanwhile he was having affairs and sex with prostitutes. I recall that this was the time when Nando almost died in the hospital and father was away with a prostitute (with whom he had a long relationship). My mother was home alone with four kids. Mum, after the separation, never told us to stop talking with Dad.

Brother Juan: Carla doesn't talk much about Juan. He lives in Colombia and is the only brother close to their father. She mentioned that Juan, being the eldest brother, takes on the macho role in the family.

Sister Linda:

We are very close to one another. I adore her. She is nine years younger than me and without her I would go crazy in such a macho family. She is like my daughter and we mutually help each other. We have different relationships with our mother: Mum and I never had a good relationship because I have always been a rebel breaking the rules; but Linda is the youngest of four siblings and always had a good relationship with Mum. Linda is the only one who supported me with my wish to be a theatre actress and producer. Linda and I lived together eight years while in London. I could live with her all my life. She has been married seven years.

Brother Nando:

My brother was always sick as a kid. He was frequently hospitalized and my grandma and aunt used to stay with us and help. I wonder whether he is gay, although father taught him he had to be a real man. Nando and Linda are twins and very connected.

Reason for seeking therapy

Carla came to me to address the following: (1) a sense of emptiness; (2) feeling stuck; (3) sentimental relationships that do not last. From the first meeting, it was clear that she was aware of having a problem (inner pain) and that she was seeking a solution. I propose that the psychological problem could be linked with her negative father complex (but not limited to it. In fact, the inferiority, exile/foreigner/colony, betrayal/cheating, feminist, mother complexes are also present, although all linked to her father complex), and the fact that she expects (hopes and expectations) a man to take care of her and make her happy and change her life. She claimed: 'I don't trust men. I always get disillusioned and disappointed. I like a man and after six month[s] I do not'. At the same time, it is clear that she hates men and she believes that men are like her father. Her neurosis is related to this. It is related to her need to understand that there are different types of men around and that not everyone is like her father. Therefore, she needs to separate from her father (by looking at her father complex) and strengthen her ego while also looking into her shadow. She needs to learn to trust people and stop using people. At the same time, she needs to realize that the world is not an idyllic place where she is always a victim of abuse. She needs to integrate all these different aspects to be able to transform and heal.

First impression, appearance, problem, transference and countertransference

Carla's comment that she doesn't trust men had a strong impression on me, because I am a man. Why choose a (white heterosexual) male analyst if you don't trust men? Therefore, I noted this and started to believe that her negative father complex and the fact that she was raised in a *macho society* was not the only problem. I slowly started to believe that 'becoming herself' was the reason why she came to me and the fact that she has been running away from this. She has been running away from looking at her difficulties and therefore she has no honest relationship with people. She uses people. And when she doesn't need them anymore she gets disillusioned, always feeling like the victim.

I propose that her hate for her father is a compensation for her love for him. For a longing to return to a time when she adored him and when everything was perfect. This father complex was also visible in theatre (as an institution run and ruled by men) where she was always the victim of men's power.

Course of therapy

I will now look at the analysis of unconscious material (21 dreams out of 70+) – employing the perspective of analytical psychology– including a consideration for self-regulation of the psyche and prospective aspects of the process and potential for development. I have chosen to employ dreams (as my primary source) because – as Jung stated – they are the *via regia* to the complex. Dreams help to understand the problem (diagnosis) and the way forward (prognosis). In doing so, I will also take into account the transference/countertransference aspects of the case to a lesser degree compared to dream material. Transference and countertransference – as underlined before – is fundamental in analysis, as

> the patient, by bringing an activated unconscious content to bear upon the doctor, constellates the corresponding unconscious material in him, owing to the inductive effect which always emanates from projections in a greater or lesser sense. Doctor and patient thus find themselves in a relationship founded on mutual unconsciousness.
>
> (CW16, para.364)

Clinical work with an individual – especially when employing dreams (paralleled by a look and acknowledgement of the social situation of the patient) and transference and countertransference – offers the opportunity to look at the psychosocial dimension of individuation and the self-healing attitude of the soul. Dreams provide an example of what Colacicchi (2021, p.52) calls the *tertium*. This (tertium) 'can only "emerge" from the unconscious' and brings a solution 'to a moral conflict' (CW10, para.855) with which the patient has been wrestling with.

Initial dream

We are at a rave party in Hatown in a huge space adjacent to Rebekka's parents (where we're staying). It's a weird rave party, in a huge cylindrical black container (like a water storing container), and somehow it seems like it's a Halloween party.

But I'm not in fancy dress. Not everyone is. Rebekka, Clara, Penny and Cloe are there (we're about to start rehearsing tomorrow) *and there are other friends from Berlin and London. Suddenly Mourice says 'careful', pointing at someone who's standing on some kind of a pulpit and I see the 'Joker' (from Batman) pointing at me with a water gun. I duck and cover my head, but I feel a gooey substance covering me and it's vomit. I stand up and I'm covered in vomit. I'm wearing a cream-white jumper and it's covered and I can even smell it. And I'm walking trying to figure out how to get out or clean myself, but I don't know where the exit or the toilets are.*

In analysing the dream, the keywords that arose for Carla were humiliation and shame. I propose that these keywords are what the dream wants to bring: they are concrete feelings, not subjective. For example, the smell of vomit is an object-related feeling.

Carla commented that Hatown was where her theatre company had recently spent a week rehearsing, and that they had stayed at Rebekka's parents' country house. What, then, is the symbolic meaning of the weird rave party? It is somewhere you lose yourself. It is a powerful experience. Thus, it symbolizes Carla's becoming unconscious (planning to get lost, taking drugs/drinking). Here, the contrast between work (rehearsal) and the rave is evident. The patient is supposed to be at Hatown for work but she goes to a rave.

Mourice is Carla's ex-husband, a non-European gay man (her best friend at the time) whom she married so that he could renew his visa and avoid deportation. At first glance, Mourice seems to be a helper: he warns her of the impending danger. But is he really a helper? Given their history, he could symbolize how Carla has given up on relationships, since her 'sham' marriage occupied her libido space, thus preventing her from fully committing to a relationship based on mutuality.

The pulpit is linked to the theme of church, preacher, sin and to a religious mother context that begs the question: is the sin that she has committed her participation in the rave, rather than working or living her own life? Thereby, losing herself and unconsciously acting against her own dignity?

The joker could express Carla's disgust with herself. He is the trickster that helps to break the rigid order. But why vomit? She feels and smells it and is disgusted by it. To return to the religious context, could we consider the vomit a type of baptism; perhaps reflecting the fact that the patient needs to become conscious of her own naïveté? Thus, the soul showers the dream ego in vomit to present it as disgusting, while the cream-white jumper symbolizes her ego's wish to be clean. However, Carla does not know where to clean herself or where the toilets are; hence she has no knowledge or consciousness and must bear the vomit sticking to her for a while.

This initial dream is a statement and a clear request for transformation, particularly if we examine the feelings of humiliation and shame, paralleled with the patient´s sense of emptiness, feeling stuck and that sentimental relationships do not last. But why the need for transformation (individuation), if she is already individualized (see Beck's concept of *homo optionis*, 2002)?

In light of the theoretical discussion above (see Chapter 4), we may say that it is because she is not conscious of her emotions – and following Beck's view that in an individualized society, individuals are driven by the wish of self-achievement – there is an emptiness to her achievement. This viewpoint is echoed in a recent conversation with Susie Orbach (2020, p.198), which links to Beck's and Bauman's concepts:

> I've had the experience with some young women, that they have ticked all the boxes, but they don't exist. I've got the boyfriend, I've got the body, I've got the job, but I don't – it's not even that I'm not happy. It's: I have achieved, but those things are not integrated, they are not part of me […].

Orbach then added:

> I come across young women who feel it's very bad to have any dependency needs. […] They needed to have been brought up to know that the world is full of struggle, and there are psychological struggles as well; to manifest themselves, to dare to express their longings, to dare to connect with others in a way that is both separate and connected.

Building on Orbach's comment, I will now examine Hillman and Shamdasani (2013, p.92) who claimed – respectively – that individuation is to take 'someone out of solipsism' where solipsism is 'modern suffering. Being only an individual'. Is then Carla only an individual? It may be that the initial projection of freedom (her wish to leave her parents and live her own life as far as possible from them) stemmed from the desire for individualization, which became solipsism and then led to anomie. What then if, following Giegerich (see Chapter 4), substance (vomit, therefore matter) and purpose were to replace emptiness and meaninglessness (the rave)? What if, in the sense used by Jung (see above Chapter 4), Carla needs to learn the art of meditation? I propose, following Kast (see above Chapter 4), that Carla needs to separate from her parents and parental complexes, to become more competent in relationships, and particularly to become more 'whole' (spiritual). This will allow her, following Hillman (see above Chapter 4), to find a place she can call home and to give something back to society.

This dream also helps us to contextualize what I underlined in the previous chapter: namely that 'with deeper self-knowledge, one is often confronted with the most difficult problems of all, namely conflicts of duty' (Jung CW10, para.677). This initial dream also helps to state the beginning of Carla's development of conscience (*Gewissen*), that is, as Jung proposes, 'an act of conscious reflection which anticipates, accompanies, or follows certain psychic events, or as a mere emotional concomitant of them, in which case its moral character is not immediately evident'.

Following Colacicchi (2021, p.29), in the previous chapter, I reminded that according to Jung, 'since one side of the dilemma is relegated to the unconscious, there is no way that a solution can be found' and that 'these types of moral conflict are *irresolvable*[1] and neurosis' which is 'the "non-solution"', is the only solution at hand in this very moment. Therefore this is a case of non-solution, which is a neurotic solution and the reason why the patient started the analysis.

Dream 2

The need to 'become independent from parents and the parental complex'[2] was confirmed in the next dream, where the psychological content is *coming home to her Self*, to really be alone (to be adult means to be alone), to really separate – as Erich Fromm, underlined in *Man for Himself* (2020).

My mum tells me I have to look for my own flat because I am too old to keep living with her. I think, well... also my sister is too old. Then I realize that the flat we live in is under my name. The contract is in my name and I tell my mum to look for a flat because I will not leave. It is my mum's idea that I have to leave. It is not my idea to separate from her.

In this dream, the good inner mother (as opposed to Carla's real mother with whom she has a difficult relationship) sends Carla on her own path. Looking for her own flat symbolizes psychological independence from the parents and parental complexes. The good mother says: go! (separate). The patient also dreams, however, 'also my sister is old enough', and here we see a portrait of her inner defences. Therefore, as underlined in the previous chapter, she is not yet conscious of her problem (or of having a problem). Here is when, following Colacicchi (2021, p.29) it becomes apparent that 'since one side of the dilemma is relegated to the unconscious, there is no way that a solution can be found' and when she opts for a non-solution of the moral conflict (that is *irresolvable*).

Dream 3

I was suspended in the air. My feet fall off. I see them falling.

Here the soul makes her lose her feet. Here she is floating. To be suspended in the air means not being able to support herself. And it means to be up in the air (although safe because sitting). She is not sitting with her feet on the ground. And her feet fall and are lost irretrievably. Therefore, she cannot stand. I also wonder whether feet, as a sexual symbol, have something to do with her current relationship with Neal? Or with her father, since, after she told me this dream I looked at her feet and noticed they were covered by psoriasis. Therefore, she told me that psoriasis is her inheritance from her father.

Dream 4

The need to improve relationships is evident from the following dream:

I'm there with someone. In my room. There's a woman who comes in. She's blonde. Short hair. Big. She looks like a serial killer. I know she didn't ring the bell. I know she used to live here before. She walks in as if it's her place and I tell her she can't just come in. I ask how she came in. She doesn't answer and pushes on.

I stop her and I walk her out. I ask again how she got in. She says nothing. She has a ring full of keys in her hand. I take them off her and I close the door in her face. I find the key to my front door and I wake up.

Being there with someone, means socialization and relationships. And *to be in my room,* means to be in herself. Then a woman comes in. Who is she? An intruder Carla said. Another intruder? Perhaps a bringer of a message? The dream-I-attitude is defensive. Carla believes she is a serial killer. It is a projection related to fear. The dream I doesn't want her, although Carla knows, this woman was living there before. This woman is 60, dressed up like a housewife (from the 1950s). She is strong and wants to go to the kitchen. Carla asks her how she got in, but she doesn't answer and pushes on. Here we see another defence from Carla, asking her how she got in. The woman ignores Carla´s question. It is the impossibility of communication. Therefore, Carla walks her out. Rejection. Therefore, Carla finds the key of her own door in a chain of keys that this woman had. The projection shows her fear. Shows what is in her. It is not objective. And this brings to the fact that the intruder avoids the question. She has a mission. There is estrangement between the dream I and the other.

Carla is not allowing the woman in, therefore she is not following what Watkins suggests. Namely having the 'capacity for dialogue' as 'a necessary precondition for human liberation' (Watkins, 2003, p.87). I suggested to Carla that it might be worthwhile to allow the other to enter and to not reject her, because she is not threatening. This dream – what Jung calls the 'moral' solution (CW10, para.855–857), is an example of when a problem is simply suppressed.

Dream 5

The need to 'become spiritual' is evident in the next dreams.

I was sleeping on my sofa when my neighbours invaded my house from the door and window.

Carla is sleeping, therefore not conscious, active or ready to respond. When asked who the neighbours are, she said they were the kids from the building and the very elderly woman living next door. Thus, both the kids (energy) and an elderly woman (the experienced feminine) enter the flat. There is a tension between her young life (that is not integrated) and the old woman. However, these forces are seen as invading and she perceives them as ghosts, therefore as immaterial.

Following Shamdasani (2013, p.92) this is when, the individuation process (although only in embryo), 'enables someone to envisage new possibilities, to imagine new ways of consideration' and that 'individuation is a way out of solipsism'. However individuation is not possible further because, as per the previous dream, she still has to gain the ability for dialogue.

Dream 6

I was asleep and then I woke up (in my dream) to see that the front door of my apartment had been broken in. The door was ajar, and the lock was still visible from the side of the door (as if it had been broken into but not broken). I get up and go out the door and I see my neighbour (the elderly women who lives across the hall) and I tell her that I've been broken into and she just looks at me as if that's normal and carries on walking down the stairs.

Again, Carla is *asleep*, therefore unconscious, but the fact that she wakes up (in the dream) signifies a movement from an unconscious state to awareness. This is a development from the previous dream. *To see* means to become really aware of the intrusion (*broken in*), another development since the previous dream. The fact that the door was *ajar* means change. The door has been broken in but it is not broken, meaning that the patient can close the door again (a request for inner space). To go out of the door is a reasonable reaction and there she finds her neighbour (again the elderly woman), the experienced feminine. This woman looks at Carla as if what has happened is normal, as if she knows how it works and that the patient's shell has been broken into, but not the Self.

Both dreams beautifully portray the self-healing attitude of the soul, which knows it all. The patient needs to change her attitude and to gain substance and a sense of purpose to fight her sense of emptiness and fear of being stuck. This will allow her to find her own meaning for her life and possibly to develop, separated from her parents and parental complexes and more connected to her Self. Additionally, both dreams provide an example of what Colacicchi (2021, p.52) terms the *tertium*. Although, as I underlined in the previous chapter, at this point of her analysis, there is yet no opportunity for the *tertium* to be internalized as an opportunity of development, because she is still unaware of her problem.

Dream 7

I'm in my flat, it's exactly the flat where I live now, but a little different, maybe slightly bigger. I realize that in the middle of the ceiling there's the branch of a tree that comes through the upper floor (as if the ceiling had been cut around to make space for the tree branch to grow through it). When I look at it, I'm not sure if it's always been there, but I'm sure I think it's weird that there's been a hole in my ceiling all along. Suddenly I look up at the ceiling and I realize it's not solid, but made of gauze and above I can see a man who's dressed in white, sitting on a white hammock reading a book and observing me.

The meaning of this dream is about an opening up. A new insight. *I realize*, means an emerging awareness. It means that change is coming into consciousness. *A tree* means nature and life. The great mother. But why is this tree/branch in the ceiling and not in the floor? It sounds like an upside-down idea, although this could be connected to the alchemical tree that has its roots in heaven and the top in earth.

The upper floor is the awareness of a new floor (a new space) and the fact that she doesn't know if it has always been there, means a new development, change and sudden insight (as a possible expansion of consciousness). Therefore, the fact that she realizes that the ceiling is not solid gives the opportunity to open up to a new dimension.

Important is also the man –60 years old-ish– dressed in white who is reading a book and observing her. She recalled he was a kind of angel looking at her gently but also seemed distant, and that looks like Samuel Beckett. And Beckett,[3] she recalls, is the author who broke all rules in theatre. Therefore, I propose this man implies a critical and sober critique. It is a higher consciousness (as the elderly woman in the previous two dreams). This man and woman are important symbols of future development and knowledge, they are opposite to her biological parents, both know. Both are superior beings and serene. Possibly this is the first hint of *the vox Dei* and the shift from *Bewusstsein* to *Gewissen*.

Dream 8

The father and feminist complex is beautifully portrayed in the next dream.

I dreamt of Thomas Ostermeier. I'm in the Schaubühne but it looks a bit like a city/theatre. At one point I meet him with Bush and I know I'm angry with him. I don't remember what I say. There's an installation piece that's inside a space that seems more like a living room but open on one end. I almost fall out of the edge. I'm not sure how I think I slide. At some point I bump into Thomas and we go to see a show together in this space. I don't know what happens after but there's some kind of romantic development and we end up kissing and then I wake up.

This dream touches what could be called Carla's feminist complex and her abuse complex. It is partially related to the father complex, but it is important to look at this as an autonomous complex. This dream brings the issue of women working in theatre as well as her anger and anxiety for not being seen and understood.

Anger and anxiety are very important and helpful emotions here, often correlated, and to not be underestimated. As described in the previous chapter, Jung (CW10, para.826) states that 'an apparently groundless anxiety state may follow a certain action, without the subject being conscious of the least connection between them' and that 'often the moral judgment is displaced into a dream which the subject does not understand'. Both moral judgement and anxiety (as well as anger) are displaced in the dream. This is so that the dreamer might be able to come up with a creative answer – led by the unconscious – to solve the conflict/problem at task.

Thomas Ostermeier, she recalls,

is the most important theater director in Germany. I liked him. Now I don't. I met him years ago at a workshop he organized and there he was nice and helpful. After that workshop I had a good memory of him. Later I realized that he only produced male artists and directors at his theatre; that he hadn't produced any play written or directed by a woman. I wrote him an angry letter, but I never sent it to him.

Here we see the impossibility of communication as a consequence of fear and anxiety. Here the dream shows that, when Carla is trapped in her emotion, she gets angry and paralyzed. Therefore, she flees. This dream shows that her anger is dangerous because she almost falls out of the edge.

Here, again becomes imminent what Watkins (2003, p.87) proposes. Additionally, when dialogue is not fostered, liberation is impossible and the patient is left with a 'rigid, stereotypic, and unidimensional narrowness'. Hence, instead of confronting – or at least starting a conversation with – Ostermeier, she engages with him sexually. They kiss and the issue is lost. I wonder whether there is an Elektra complex here, but I don't want to look into this deeper. For sure there is a projection of the father complex both in Ostermeier and in theatre as an institution. I therefore prefer to propose that being angry or anxious means not being free in relation to the topic at stake. If she was free she might have found a way to express her concern without getting angry. Getting angry is pathological. It is a symbol of her suffering, experience, emotion and inner pain. Emotions are on the way to pathology[4] and in this case to her feminist complex. Which relates to her upbringing in Colombia and a patriarchal family forbidding her to study fine arts and drama.

Also, anger could be seen as a substitute for love (kiss). I wonder whether a relationship based on love and not on anger might help to stop her anger. She needs a real romantic involvement which she is not capable of. Her anger is caused because she feels she is not seen and understood. Therefore, anger is caused because she cannot give up the loving father who she idealizes (although she hates him). Because of this, she doesn't see the other person. She is blind. She is selfish, therefore unable to love. Love is only possible for a real person.

After Carla had this dream, while she was walking in a street in Berlin a man touched her bottom and ran away. She reported feeling abused and paralyzed. When discussing this with my supervisor, he proposed that her abuse complex was touched; that the feeling of being abused is part of her complex, and this complex feeds her anger towards men.

My supervisor added:

> She sees abuse everywhere but she cannot do anything about it. She gets paralyzed. Therefore, she felt abused by Ostermeier, and now by this man in the street. Who is the next abuser and when is she going to confront the abuser?

Both associations (the man touching her bottom and Ostermaier) are about violation and express the patient's difficulty in tolerating frustration. Therefore, it is important to pay attention to the psychosocial (outer) factors (i.e. misogyny, patriarchy) alongside – and in play with – her own (inner) neurotic factors. This psychodynamic explanation operates psychosocially as follows: the psychic and the social are intertwined in a never-ending (because neurotic) stuck-ness.

Following this (hoping to support her liberating herself from her psychosocial stuck-ness), I proposed her to write the letter to Ostermeier and that she should bring it to therapy (so that we could look at it together). The purpose of this is related to the fact that her anger towards Ostermeier (and the man on the street) is a complex reaction and I hoped engaging in writing such a letter would help her to understand this and to look at her anger from a different perspective.

Dream 9

The betrayal and cheating complex –'I don't trust men'– is portrayed in this dream. Although this dream proposed the first symbols of transformation:

I'm in a house I don't know. It's huge. I'm in the kitchen, sitting on a sofa with two small children. They're blonde and I'm obviously some kind of nanny to them – because the mother comes in to check on us. They are a rich family. The kids are around 2–3 and they're playing at feeding me and each other gummies of different colours and flavours. By the kitchen sofa, there's a kind of small bar on the wall and a window – balcony and there's someone I know there. I hear a familiar voice laughing out loud but I'm busy with the kids so I can't look. At one point the children are not there anymore and I see that the person laughing is Tom – but this time he has very long hair – but it's him/ his face – and he's sitting on a stool with the feet on the bar and he's sunbathing on the balcony. At one point there's a woman wearing a bikini sitting next to him but then she also disappears, and he starts talking to me and telling me he's angry with me – but also laughing – and that it's so stupid that he's angry with me. He says 'It's so stupid to be angry with your lover for such a stupid thing' but I don't know what the thing is. He says he's going to get us some Asian food and leaves but the mother of the kids comes to tell me I have to join them at the table so I go and sit at their lunch table. It's a huge room upstairs from the kitchen and it has massive windows from ceiling to floor onto the garden. The nature outside looks very much like a painting. The grass is very green and bushy and the tree bark is very dark. It makes me think of England or Ireland because this grass is the grass that grows in places where it rains – but it's very sunny. I look out of the window and walk out into the garden. I follow a path and it leads to a gate. I stop at the gate and look out, smoking a cigarette and looking. In front of me, there's a beautiful tree. The bark is very dark, almost black and the rest is very green. There's a stranger outside the gate but I'm not scared. I continue to smoke and look at the tree.

Again in this dream, there is a remarkable sexual context, as well as cheating and betrayal. But in this case, I am interested in the end of the dream, when she notices a tree. This time the tree is bottom up and next to it there is a gate. She reached the gate after following a path.

The tree, according to Jung, is one of the possible symbols of the process of individuation. I propose that with this dream she reached a threshold. From here starts her own metamorphosis. This metamorphosis – in opposition to the one proposed by Beck (2016) – is supported by the hints provided by the unconscious and because – by working together and with the help of the transcendent function – a third point of view was found. This is when the *tertium* (by her looking and being interested in the tree) or the *vox Dei*, starts to grab her attention and it is not disregarded *tout court*.

The metamorphosis of the individual that could precede and set in motion what Beck termed *The Metamorphosis of the World* (2016), can only happen – as Colacicchi (2021, p.30) suggested – 'thanks to the cooperation of the irrational side of our psyche', and it is what Jung called the *ethical* solution.

I propose that Carla's act of getting closer to this tree (of knowledge), although standing from a distance, is also getting closer to her *ethical* solution, which is only possible when one is able to listen to the voice of God. At the same time, metamorphosis is always linked to self-responsibility (therefore in opposition to anomie) but Carla, here, is not yet able to become self-responsible. This is why she looks at the tree from a distance.

This dream is also important, because I recently realized she was starting to accept and receive my proposals as insight, without confronting me (angrily). Without letting her animus deal – in acrimony – with me. She recently started to trust me enough and to see that she was learning to better cope with frustrations (with Rebekka, her mother and also with men). She also learned to not run away from men but to have a conversation with them about the status of their relationship.

I wonder whether the end of this dream meant that she is starting to be in contact with herself without getting distracted by others. She is also learning to not fear the unknown; therefore, to manage her anxiety towards the unknown.

After our session, Carla received an email from her boss Jo (owner of a café called *Le Blond*). In the email, Jo fired her and accused her of stealing money. Carla felt abused and lost. She said she never took the money. Jo also defamed Carla in front of all colleagues saying that she stole money.

This is important, because Carla realized that also women can harm her. And this brought memories of the difficulties with her mother. From this moment there is the transition from the negative father complex only to the negative mother complex. Hence, to the parental complex and the recognition of the need to separate from them.

We therefore worked on the fact that she cannot shut the door on people who (apparently) harm her and the fact that she needs to take care of herself. I feared she was going to not take care of herself on this matter and therefore to turn the page and to not look into the accusations from Jo. But she found the strength to start a legal action to defend herself. She was able to contact her workers' union and to look into the case. She found a lawyer (a man) who helped her with this matter and to win the lawsuit. I saw this as a development, although this gave her a lot of anxiety. Therefore, we talked about the fact that, when anxious, she feels paralyzed and then she runs away without facing the problem. I believe this is an important step in our work, but this was also paralleled by a dream (see below).

Dream 10

Several sessions after this incident were devoted to the issue of theft.

I'm at Le Blond which is not Le Blond but looks different but somehow, I'm there. I'm talking to a colleague, but it's already happened (getting fired) and I'm waiting to speak to Jo and finally I do and I tell her everything. I'm loud but I'm not shouting. I tell her that her accusing me is just because of where I come from and that it's so stupid that she blames me for it and so stupid that she did what she did. I find a 90€ note somewhere outside and also a 900€ note that's sewn into the fold of the middle of my skirt.

After telling me this dream she reiterated she didn't take anything from *Le Blond*. But the dream says something different. It says two things. First, she is there to talk to Jo and to tell her that being fired has to do with the fact that she is a foreigner (the exile/foreigner/colony complex – as when she arrived in Madrid from Colombia). I sense this is interesting, because in real life she would not dare to do so and this links her back to an open wound. Second, this dream says that she took money and that this money is sewed into her skirt.

But my question is: what is it that she stole? Did she perhaps take advantage of a situation? Has she not been honest about it? I wonder whether this is related to her ability to take shortcuts or advantage of her relationships with people (like with Rebekka and Jo). After discussing this dream, we had the chance to talk about the possibility that she might wish to go her way. To find her way instead of partnering with people who can take advantage of her. She said out loud that she joined Rebekka's production company 'only because this way would be easier to receive grants from institutions'. Something similar happened in relation to Jo, when Carla decided to work at her café illegally, without a contract. Perhaps the same applies to her relationships with men, with whom she is attached to get some advantage, not because she loves them.

After this, analysis follows – for almost two years – a thread of dreams related (similarly to dream 10) to looking for or starting a new relationship (Mat, Neal and Marko) with a man who is idealized but whom her soul cannot trust. She – like in the case of Neal – wants a relationship but he doesn't. I propose that the unconscious helps her with insight in this regard, although she cannot grasp these yet. But the insights are there (see below).

Dream 11

I'm in a museum bar with Marko and we get a beer. We sit down and I see my friend Maria but he sees her first and gets up and sits at her table. I get up to go to the bathroom and when I come back he's talking to her and I just catch the word orgy. I go to her, say hello and apologize and tell her he's not a bad person and continue to talk to her for a while. At one point I turn around and he's at the table with several people showing their admiration for his work. I feel a little sad for him.

This dream is about the absence of a relationship between Carla and Marko. They are there together but there is no meeting of minds and feelings. They sit down together (at a table) but do not have contact. There is no eros. Therefore, Marko leaves her to reach another woman: Maria. It is like a divorce and Carla lets him go. This could be sufficient – as an insight – to understand what her soul is telling her: let him go. But this does not happen.

Immediately, her attention goes to Maria. She gets distracted and angry about Maria, who she describes as the 'typical married woman – in a long-lasting relationship with the same man since I met her at university who still loves him and he loves her'. This is interesting when considering that she came to see me because her 'relationships don't last'. Why do relationships not last? This dream gives the answer thanks to the *vox Dei* (which gives a very clear hint from the unconscious): Let him go! This is what Jung calls the ethical solution (CW10, para.855–857), and, following Colacicchi, an example of the *tertium*.

When Marko approaches Maria, at the literal level, he is not interested in Carla and their relationship. From the intrapsychic level, could this mean that she is not able to give enough to him to make him stay and be interested in her? There is no exchange and no feeling between them. No eros. Jung (1984) talks about eros as relatedness.

It seems that the real relation – for Marko – is with Maria. In fact, Marko and Maria talk while Marko and Carla do not. Therefore, Maria is attractive to Marko (and vice versa). This is because she is the *image* of a woman that can have a stable relationship with a man. This dream depicts Maria as potential and separate from what Carla is *now* – in the absolute present – and in this relationship. Maria is the answer to her coming to analysis. She is the union of opposites. Her shadow.

In the second part of the dream, Carla hears the word 'orgy.' and she apologizes for Marko's behaviour. Following Jung (CW10, para.826), this is when 'the moral judgment is displaced into a dream which the subject does not understand'. Why is it so? Orgy links to sexuality, lust and transgressing the bond of a monogamic relationship. An orgy is something different than such a relationship: it is to let desire take over; it is wild and not civilized and it means propinquity. She apologizes for this, for the uncivilized masculine, although 'he is a good person'.

This dream could also help her gain the following insight: listen to him without judging and the need to apologize. Be *interested in him as he is*, with his good and not civilized sides. *Him as a whole.* Listen to him when he comes to you without being annoyed and he might get interested in you. It is clear that Maria can listen and not get annoyed by the non-civilized sides.

Therefore, this dream is also about the task of the *we* – as a couple – and sheds light (and insight) on what should be done to break the pattern of relationships that do not last. It clearly shows the absence of a relationship (eros) between Marko and Carla.

Dream 12

I get a WhatsApp message from Marko inviting me to meet him somewhere, I don't remember exactly what or where but I know that I go and there's a black man (reminds me of Le Gateau Chocolat[*]) who is sort of cross-dressing as Marko (wig/ clothes) but also has make-up on. He pretends to be Marko but I know he's not. I'm confused but then I see it's a ruse to distract me from Marko who's there with someone else, but when I look, it's not a real person but rather a rag doll, made out of very simple brown material with a very simple shape, just giant. Then Marko turns into a rag doll. And I wake up and I feel a profound sadness upon waking up, a little bit of anxiety too and I'm not able to go back to sleep.

This is all I remember from the dream but I know there are parts in the middle that I've missed.

[*] Cabaret Star. Le Gateau Chocolat is a one-man, larger-than-life musical phenomenon, wrapped in dazzling sequinned lycra. The six-and-half foot tall, six-inch heeled, wig-clad wonder swings wildly from one end of the musical spectrum to another, from disco, opera, musicals and pop. https://legateauchocolat.com

Carla commented she woke up very, very sad. And she added that this sadness is about Marko. Then she added: 'I try not to think of him during the day but I dream of him'. Why does she dream of him, when her wish is to forget about him? Because, I propose, there is something unworked. There is something she has to do before she can move on and *reach closure* about him and what he represents.

It is interesting that Marko is dressed up like a drag queen, and it is interesting that Marko is not Marko. He – this man – pretends to be Marko. On top of that, who is a drag queen? It is a (biological) man who dresses up, wears makeup, and acts like a woman. A pantomime of a woman – as underlined by the *Cambridge Dictionary*: a theatrical entertainment, which involves music, topical jokes and slapstick comedy; or dramatic entertainment in which performers express meaning through gestures accompanied by music. Pantomime as a vehicle of (and for) emotions. The drag queen – a man, often a gay man, who dresses as a woman for entertainment, as underlined by the *Cambridge Dictionary* – is a caricature of a woman, not a woman. A drag queen is similar to a clown. And their similarity lies – amongst other things – in sadness as their core emotion.

What if the sadness Carla feels in this context is related to the fact that *we are all transitioning* in search of our (Self) identity, and it is only when *dropping our own hopes and expectations* (wanting to be a woman but being a man: the impossibility of wholeness and *conjunctio oppositorum*) that we might be able to let longings arise. In fact, this would imply a process of *humbling* and *the end of ego-supremacy*. I propose that Carla´s sadness is related to ego-supremacy and to living in *possibility* instead of in *reality*. Sadness is a necessary tool to *become oneself*: a separate individual who *obeys necessity*.

This dream is about her *transition,* and the drag queen might also symbolize that Carla is in love (or believes herself to be in love) not with a man, but with a projection. And *love does not exist when it is a projection*. This is also why she is sad: sad of continuously falling in love with her own projection of/on men and her own hopes and expectations on men. Marko as drag queen precludes her reaching his soul and to have a relation based on Eros. This happened already in her life, when she married Mourice.

Dream 13

I'm sleeping in Marko's studio (but it looks different than his studio) and in the middle of the night he walks in and I hear him talk out loud to someone saying 'Carla is here' (as if that's something that I do sometimes) so they quickly walk past me into another room and as I open my eyes I see the back of a woman's head, long blond hair, the door closing just behind her. Marko comes out and talks to me, I don't remember exactly what he's saying to me, but I know that he's not alone and would like me to go. I wake up.

The fact that she is sleeping at Marko's studio is a contrast: a split. She pretends to be at home there, but she is not. In fact, she should not be there and recalls she was and feels like an intruder! This dream depicts the *power aspect* (not love) in her relationship with Marko (as well as her previous ones): *power as possession of something*. She wants to possess him, not to love him. To do so she intrudes into his home when he is not there. The problem is that she does not love him: she wants to possess him. The other problem is that she is an emotionless observer. The opening of her eyes, another contrast/split depicts a lack of feelings and her flatness. Marko would like her to go. She is there and doesn't move. This theme is constant in her recent dreams. Carla invades Marko´s space: 'Here she is again' she tells me laughing referring to herself in third person, during the session. And she adds: 'I avoid him in real life. I meet him in dreams'.

Meeting Marko at night is a compensation to her conscious wish not to meet during the day. Therefore, I asked her why she was looking for him. She answered: 'to ask for forgiveness'. I remained silent and remembered dream 12, when she apologized to Marko´s behaviour. Then she added: 'And I don't know why I should ask for forgiveness. I do not even want him to forgive me. I simply need to ask him for forgiveness'. Could her need to ask for forgiveness (not for apologizing for Marko´s behaviour) be related to her soul's need to drop all her hopes and expectations of what a relationship must be? To drop the archetype of a relationship? Could asking for forgiveness (without expecting to be forgiven) be a fundamental step towards individuation? Therefore, to apologize to Marko (not Maria) for not being able to love him and accepting him as he is?

A couple of weeks after this dream, Marko broke up with her. When I asked her how she felt, she commented: 'I am confused. I got upset initially. Now I am sad but also peaceful. I need to accept'. Hearing this I felt a punch in my stomach and wanted to shout *fuck off*, but I didn't. Was this reaction a countertransference reaction?

She is confused. She has mixed emotions and tries to control her emotions wishing to be peaceful. My countertransference told me she was not peaceful at all. In fact, she would have wished to shout. She avoids realizing, telling me 'I am upset' – she is alone now that this relationship didn't work out. She, therefore, needs to become aware of her loneliness and stay with it (instead of covering it with a new man, as she did in the past. Doing so would mean being guided by her fantasies.)

Change (being alone) is difficult because clearly she doesn't see the reality: her relationships don't last because they are out of her fantasy of possessing a man. She feels confused but there is nothing to be confused about. She should be shocked and depressed.

From the last few dreams, it is clear that she is captivated by *the idea of a man*. Additionally, she doesn't want to wound herself (like children who cannot accept a wound). Therefore, she is not able to leave the relationship with Marko – or with any of the previous boyfriends – on her own (despite the many insights!). To leave him would mean that she is able to accept her own pain and to stay with it. Confusion is a way to not allow a cut in the relationship. She really has to accept loneliness and the consequences of such a situation; to say: this (these) relationship(s) didn't work, and therefore I am alone. She needs to become aware and to stay with it. Then, suddenly, she had the following dreams, which mark a *change of paradigm*.

Dream 14

I dreamed my professor of drama died.

Who (really) died? Which part of her died or needs to die? Without digging deeper into this aspect of the dream, I shall propose that this dream is about the need to *grow or die within*. To move 'from potentiality into reality' (Giegerich, 2020, p.94). To grow means to acquire a clear position on (about) oneself and to move from a life lived being shaped and possessed by emotions towards a life lived on the basis of experience and insight.

This dream also brings another important aspect, Carla's memory of a man with whom she had a positive relation: her teacher as a positive father figure. In this regard, Daniela Eulert-Fuchs (2020, p.160), during her keynote speech at IAAP's congress in Vienna (2019), shared the case history of a patient of hers that 'was unable to form the representation of caring for others due to an overlong absence'. This dream, I propose, is the first appearance of such a caring other/father figure. Additionally – linking to dream 13 – his man, Carla reported, is a clown and a mime (as well as teacher), and might help to look at dream 13 where Marko was a drag queen.

I take this dream as a reminder that, despite the death of a beloved one (a caring figure), we remain connected to this person because he/she is internalized. Hence the caring aspect of a positive father figure is introduced here in opposition to 'the cheaters' (Father and her partners).

Dream 15

I am in the pit of a dry, clay river, and in that pit, I (but as a girl/child me as a spiritual child, as if it were my soul) am 'pacing back and forth' in the river pit and talking to someone, who is not physical, but an entity that is there, and saying: 'no, I don't want to go back' to life I think. 'I don't want to be born again', I am thinking of re-incarnation and that life is too painful. And so, I go on, from one side to the other. I felt, in the dream, the pain that I had felt all day, like a huge hollow/hole in my chest, like an empty, aching cavity – and when I woke up, I thought about that cavity in my chest and the one in the river and thought that maybe that was what it represented. I woke up confused, still hurting and strange because it was a very strange dream.

The funny thing is that in this dream I am more like the image of the drawing under the tree I made. I have short hair like now (I never had it like that as a child) and although I am small/not really young – more like ageless, it gave me the impression that I dreamt with my soul, somehow.

This dream is of fundamental importance! It is directly related to her being stuck and alone. The girl/child aspect refers to being unborn; therefore, not able to move. The tree links to the symbolism of the great mother, which is also apparent in the next dream. The dry pit, being an empty river, relates to a river and the fact that a river needs to be crossed. At the same time, being in a dry pit means that the soul needs dryness. A dry pit is sterile, lifeless and life needs water.

Then she cries and it is authentic. When she cries she is genuine and one with herself. To cry and not want to go back to life means an urge to stay with the problem and to not overcome it. It is the same as to bare the vomit of the first dream. It also means: I do not want to enter life and the world. This is related to the need for a spontaneous birth into life which is the opposite of ego and will (ego-supremacy). The second part of life is about the birth of death. She will be able to leave the dry pit only when she has gained a clear idea of who she is and what she wants. This dream is a clear resistance to enter life. She is not ready to cross the river, therefore not ready to enter the second half of her life (the cultural aim). She has *resistance* about joining life.

Dream 16

I'm walking to the U-Bahn station, in Berlin, the way is through a park and in the park there's a large tree. It's autumn and the floor is covered with leaves: orange, brown and yellow, and it's very cold but beautiful. I go to the base of the tree and start to dig a whole right under it – a burrow – carefully as to avoid to damage the roots – and once the burrow is ready, I crawl under it and curl up to sleep.

When I wake up, I'm under a mangrove (manglar) in Colombia. The roots are much higher and I'm on white wet sand and I know I'm home. I come out of it and I'm in a place I've been many times before: Puerto Betin, in Santa Marta (Colombia). Then I'm in Santa Marta near where you take the Ferry back to Cartagena, where there's lots of street vendors. I'm also in Maracaibo at some point. La Cora – is the place where we – as a family – went to the beach all the time. There's always lots of people, it's very warm, light, sunny, loud, very loud, traffic jams and I go back at some point to the mangrove, curl up under it and fall asleep. I wake up in Berlin, in the burrow under the park tree in Berlin.

This dream – which is highly symbolic when looking at the tree and the colours of its leaves – was dreamt in March 2020 (at the start of Covid lockdown) and helps to look at the need to come home, to get at the roots and to connect with her soul. The tree, again the great mother, hugs her with her roots and contains her. In this dream, which follows the dream of the dry pit, I propose that she went back home (where she comes from) to reconnect with her roots/family and also to bring her soul with her back to Berlin. This is an example of *Back to the Future*. The need to go back to the past to change the future, and get out of solipsism.

Dream 17

I'm in an art space. Like a warehouse converted into an art space. I'm with Marko and we're looking at art, then I go to find the toilet. The toilets are kind of run-down but clean. I go to a cubicle and the lock on the door is right at the bottom of the door. I slide the lock and proceed to use the toilet. There's a gap between the bottom of the door and the floor. I hear a voice and I know it's Rebekka's voice and she's asking if the toilet is busy, shakes the door and unlocks the lock in my cubicle. I say it's busy and lock it again but she unlocks it again. I think by this time I'm finished

in the toilet and I open the door, look at her and tell her 'what are you doing here?'
and walk past her back to the art space.

The first question is: what is an art space? A space dedicated to the intellect, therefore, ego-supremacy. The second question is: what is a toilet? A place dedicated to body functions (urination and defecation). Therefore, the opposite of ego-supremacy. This dream is about the fact that the soul is interested that the door can be opened from the outside and that Carla is not in control of this.

Rebekka represents a soul content that wants to get closer; a body content, not intellectual, therefore allowing something to get to Carla that Rebekka represents. Here something new and unseen emerges from the relationship with Rebekka. The question is: what could Rebekka represent?

The *physical and body level* is important here, as well as the wanting to get into a private and the integration of something, somehow, known to her (although not yet conscious); the content Rebekka insists on in overcoming the barrier. The will of the soul is to overcome the barrier but the dream I (Carla) doesn't get it and leaves before Rebekka can answer such a fundamental question: 'What are you doing here?' Doing so, she misses an opportunity for a change of paradigm, a change she cannot (yet) cope with.

Dream 18

We are at our job's Xmas party. I go with Kam to the reception where he works. We start to kiss. Stefan comes in. He doesn't see us kissing. We stop and act as if nothing happened, as if we are looking for something there. Stefan, who is a very good friend of Kam, offers him to smoke a cigarette. I wake up.

In the previous chapter, I stressed that, according to Jung (CW10, para.829) 'conscience is a kind of knowledge', and that 'it is not the empirical subject who is the knower, but rather an unconscious personality who, to all appearances, behaves like a conscious subject'. I propose this is the essence of this dream, because, it is when conscience can be seen 'as the voice of God' – which is opposite to the moral code or moral conflict – commanding 'the individual to obey his inner voice' (CW10, para.841).

On top of this, it is also important to remind that Jung (CW10, para.845), following the *vox Dei* hypothesis, looks at the importance of 'the numinous character of the moral reaction' and at the fact that 'conscience is a manifestation of mana, of the "extraordinarily powerful," a quality which is the especial peculiarity of archetypal ideas'.

This dream, following Colacicchi (2021, p.29) helps to clarify Jung's view that the solution to a conflict, or *tertium*, 'can only "emerge" from the unconscious' and that such solution 'to a moral conflict is "a special instance of [...] the transcendent function" (CW10, para.855), the function that allows a cooperation of consciousness and the unconscious'.

A kiss means intimacy and attraction. It could indicate the most intimate sign and symbol at the beginning of a relationship; a higher level. This contradicts her need – portrayed in an earlier[5] dream – to 'feel safe on a date'. This feeling safe could mean that she has a plan when going on a date. Therefore, she has hopes and expectations, which are conscious (a conscious wish) and are linked to the *will to power* (and opposite to *will to mutuality*). Also, it means that a date is a danger. In this dream, Kam is not a date; he is a colleague. And they kiss unexpectedly, without hopes and expectations. This kiss is unexpected and – on the contrary to the above-mentioned orgy (dream 12), it is appropriate (although embarrassing). It comes from a longing; therefore, from the soul.

Upon hearing this dream, I intuitively felt it would mark a change: a change of paradigm; but I didn't say much about it. I kept the feeling of butterflies in my stomach for myself and I simply asked her: 'Who is Kam?'

The fluttering sensation, unmistakably my countertransference, could also be construed as intuition. I posit that this perspective adds to Lopes Pedraza's emphasis on 'sticking to the image' as the 'golden rule of archetypal psychology' (Hillman, 1997a, p.18) and underscores the significance of following intuition as 'the golden rule of the neo-Jungian approach'.

Also interesting is Stefan (my homonym), who disturbs and interrupts them but also is a witness. Additionally, when Stefan steps in disturbing them, they act in a silly way (although this is also understandable). They act as if nothing happened. Actually, something big happened! I propose they kiss each other out of mutual attraction and that such attraction should be seen as longing coming from the soul (instead of a kiss programmed out of hopes and expectations and premeditated, as usual for Carla). Therefore, what was I there to witness? I propose I was witnessing a change of paradigm. I was there to witness her new *desire*! The etymology of the word 'desire' comes from Latin and is composed of the preposition *de-* (which in Latin has a negative meaning), and from *sidus* (which means star). Desire, therefore, literally means *lack of stars*, in the sense of *feeling the lack of stars*.

This dream, I propose, equates to Dante Alighieri's last verse of his Divine Comedy's *Inferno*: 'E quindi uscimmo a riveder le stelle' (*Inferno*, XXXIV, 139). This is when Dante and Vergil exit Hell and contemplate the stars. Contemplating the stars, Bianca Garavelli underlines (1993, p.501) is intended 'as pure bliss of the eye'. This dream gives the following insight: *love is not about searching. It is about finding* (although this might be embarrassing when being discovered or when discovering it). Kiss as bliss. Kiss as the contemplation of stars. Also, in this dream, there is a sense of ease and a new way to deal with the destructive forces. Could this mean that analysis is reaching a turning point or – even – the end?

Dream 19

We're in our work but I don't work there anymore, I'm coming with Kam. At one point some guy (who's supposed to have been my boss's boss) tells me he was upset I left because there was something important he needed me to do. Then I go to my old desk and there are several leaving presents and boxes of chocolates and cards. I start to eat some from a box and realize I need to go to the toilet. For some reason,

I strip naked and walk downstairs to the toilet and enter the male toilet by error. When I realize and walk out, Kam is coming out of a cubicle and sees me. I cover myself and go to the female toilet. Then I return to my old desk and dress again. I go to Kam's desk and we're holding hands and hugging as if we were together. At some point, we're in a forest and I'm showing him my house, which is completely open air. A bed and a sofa and some other stuff but no walls or ceiling. I tell him how nice it is to wake up in the forest. I don't remember the end of the dream.

We means a sense of community and bonding. She returns to a place where she doesn't work anymore and this mean a sense of separation because it is a place from which she has separated. The dream is interested in the actual separation that is overcome by going back. It is a negation (separation) from a Hegelian point of view. And a negation of the negation (separation of and from the separation).

The boss of the boss is sorry. It is a great compliment. It shows she is needed and wanted (opposite to what happens at *Le Blonde*, see dream 10). This high evaluation means she is important. And this is a compensation from how she perceived herself at the beginning of the analysis.

On her old desk, there are presents from colleagues, as a sign of appreciation and friendliness. This can be seen as a reached compensation from dream 10.

Eating (something sweet) means that she takes in the feeling of being welcome: pleasure and recognition. It is a compensation to the original difficulties with Rebekka, Jo and the negative feminine. Chocolate is a sign of appreciation, and the most important fact is that she accepts the gift.

Then she needs to visit the toilet. Needing to go to the toilet is related again to her body sense. She becomes physically aware of her body (in the previous toilet dreams she was not).

There she strips naked (which is absurd from a literal level, although not from an intrapsychic one). She strips naked in a place where it is totally inappropriate. In fact, when she realizes it, she covers up. At this point is important to recall Carla's initial dream. When covered in vomit, she looked for a toilet,[6] but she couldn't find one. And I proposed that she needed to stay covered in vomit long enough to allow transformation. I proposed vomit ought to be seen as baptism. Now she can strip naked, and she does so in a place where she doesn't work anymore (her former workplace).

Here nature puts pressure on her and by stripping naked she shows herself the truth. She uncovers which is the opposite of what she did in the initial dream – *I duck and cover my head, but I feel a gooey substance covering me and it's vomit* as a sign of protection from the Joker. In the current dream, she uncovers. She leaves her clothes, not minding the social convention. She strips naked from social and institutional conventions. Therefore, she moves from what Jung called the natural aim towards the cultural aim. From the first part of her life to her second: when humans become aware of their mortality (see dream 15). To be naked means to be honest about herself and to have come home to herself. She enters the male toilet by error. By doing so, she crosses a border that is prohibited for women. There she meets the masculine. Trespassing/crossing a border (not by plan) happens by error and not thinking. When she becomes aware of it, she tries to correct the mistake. Entering the toilet she comes very close together to the level of body needs. Kam can see she is naked. He can see her in her own truth (uncovered).

I'm coming with Kam means a beginning. Coming together and being there together. Holding hands means coming together after showing herself in her truth. There is no flirting or fantasies. There is a meeting via nakedness and body level. There is no intellectual desire/fantasy. She doesn't like Kam because of their conversation about culture (as with Marko or the previous ones). The encounter with Kam happens showing herself in her nakedness, therefore honesty. Honesty as a basis of a relation. It is clear that Kam plays a deeper role in her life because their coming together is calm and spontaneous. They meet at the level of need and nature.

Dream 20

I am in my house in the forest. It is late spring. This house has no windows nor ceiling.

Carla is alone in nature. This dream means being at home with herself. Finally alone! The forest is pleasant, and she is settled there and feeling free (of enactments with people) and recalls feeling safe. 'There is no *bullshit* in the forest', she underlines. She is in total contact with nature as there are no windows nor ceilings. This dream means that she is open. As open as the house. In the open air with no walls and no ceiling. This last dream fits her nakedness of the previous dream and compensates for the dreams she had during the first years of analysis,[7] when *spirits* and neighbours were invading and breaking into her flat in Berlin. She is in the forest where she wakes up every day with no planning and without nonsense. On top, what is new here, is the freedom from *fantasies of love* (delusional hopes and expectations).

Living in a house with no walls and ceilings has drawbacks and it brings a dangerous aspect. A house should be able to protect people: it is naïve to live in a house with no walls and no ceiling. Of course, it is a wonderful image of freedom, but you need walls and a ceiling! At this very point, it is ok to have no walls and ceiling. But when the weather or the situation changes, you need to be able to close the windows and protect yourself from possible danger. Right now, there is no need for preoccupation or hesitation; just be! Kam is there as the internalized positive masculine!

This and the previous dream give me a feeling that my job is done. She is *cured,* but I do not tell her. When the session is over, I look at her and say, as usual – see you next week. She looks at me and says: 'Kam is waiting downstairs, waiting for me'. Hearing this, I have the certainty this analysis is over and that she does not need me anymore. Kam will take care of (and accompany) her from now on. But I keep this for me.

Dream 21 (last dream)

I am at the Schaubühne, sitting in one of the armchairs in the cafeteria at the entrance. A woman appears and hands me a copy of a Shakespeare play, which I have to adapt. It is printed on loose white sheets, as if it were a rough draft. Then she gives me another sheet of paper, on which are printed the names of several actors in the theatre ensemble, all of whom are men. I don't say anything, I receive everything and as she leaves she says something that I half understand, but I don't remember, and I'm left with a bit of anxiety about the names. The next thing is that I'm writing the adaptation at home, at my desk. There are a lot of women in the adaptation I'm writing. I go back to the Schaubühne and hand the draft of the adaptation to the same woman. Thomas Ostermeier appears, dressed in beige (I think the same one I've seen him wear several times) and I give him the paper with the numbers and tell him that I couldn't include the actors on the sheet. I wake up.

This dream was the last one before I suggested that our work was over. This dream is a good example of what Giegerich – borrowing the term from Hegel – calls *sublation*.

In fact, this dream helps to confirm the good work and consequent compensation of the initial situation:

- The negative father complex (projected here on *Thomas Ostermeier* – and not only on him during five years' work together – and consequent overcompensation by grandiosity) is here solved by approaching the matter with experience and insight.
- Carla's grandiosity (projected here on the *Schaubühne* – the most important independent German theatre), helps to look at her inferiority complex. Here there is no compensation for inferiority with grandiosity (as the fulfilment of hopes and expectations – which are related to ego-supremacy). To be able to work for this theatre is the result of good and honest work.
- Being hired for such a prestigious institution, while not being German, is a compensation of her exile/foreigner/colony complex.
- This dream also helps to look at what I called the *feminist* complex, from a different point of view. She doesn't say anymore 'I don't trust men. I always get disillusioned and disappointed'. She realizes that on the list she is given, there are 'several actors (...) all of whom are men'. Therefore, she acknowledges it and works on her own list. And the fact that she can work and present her own list means that the masculine has been integrated. Positive and negative masculine are not polarizations but are bridged by her experience and the capacity to get insights.
- This dream is also about *abuse* and *betrayal/cheating* complex. This complex, present in all dreams involving Marko, has been compensated by the fact that an institution such as this (directed by a man who she called Patriarch), can hire her. This is only possible since a positive caring figure had become internalized (see dream 14). This is also possible because of the appearance – which is a consequence of our work together – in her life (and in her dreams) of Kam. Men

can be trusted now and are not only seen as abusers. This is also possible with the help of the development of conscience and what Colacicchi calls the *tertium*.
–   The woman in the dream could be a threat (as Rebekka and Jo), but she is not. Carla can concentrate and work, although this woman says something Carla does not understand.
–   Very important is that Carla can feel and say 'I'm left with a bit of anxiety about the names', but she can work and deliver what is according to her integrity. The news is that she doesn't freeze and keeps her integrity.

In conclusion, Carla is now connected to her feelings and emotions – she can feel anxious and can also verbalize it. Additionally, she has no hopes nor expectations here. She does her job, has learned to ask for forgiveness and has regained integrity.

Consideration for psychiatric and psychodynamic diagnosis

Kaplan and Sadock's *Pocket Handbook of Clinical Psychiatry* (Sadock, Ahmad, and Sadock, 2001, p.150) underline that 'anxiety is a response to a threat that is unknown, vague, or conflicting'. At the beginning of our work together, Carla reported feeling anxious when waking up in the morning or when meeting a love/work partner.

At the beginning of the therapy, Carla demonstrated an excessive anxiety and worry about her relationship with Neal and Rebekka. She was unable to control such worry. Symptoms, in case of generalized anxiety disorder (GAD) are: sleep disturbance (waking up feeling unrested and waking up in the middle of the night without being able to go back to sleep and nightmares), muscle tension (she disclosed she felt tense especially in the back and neck, and for this she needed yoga), being easily fatigued (need to have naps). Having considered all this, I believe this is a case of GAD because her anxiety and worry cause her distress in social and occupational areas.

I also wonder whether this GAD, could be related to a possible adjustment disorder, therefore a post traumatic stress disorder, following the move from Colombia to Spain. I wished to investigate a possible adjustment disorder relating to the time when her family moved to Spain, especially looking into the psychosocial factor of not being able 'to tolerate frustration in adult life correlates with gratification of basic needs in infant life' and 'poor mothering experiences' (Sadock, Ahmad, and Sadock, 2001, p.222). The differential diagnosis of an adjustment disorder also brings me to look into the move to Spain as the consequence of the riots in Colombia as a stressor outside the range of normal human behaviour (Sadock, Ahmad, and Sadock, 2001, p.222).

Linked to this, I also see a relational problem, when looking at her (mainly ambivalent, but also sometimes avoidant) relationship with her parents and those that remind her of them in her daily life.

Keeping in mind the self-regulation of the psyche, and in light of self-development, I proposed working with Carla to look into her anxieties and fears, hoping to support her in making peace with her family, finding her own home and giving something back to society (Hillman, 1997b). Alternatively put, following Kast (1993), to become aware of her parental complex and to separate from them as well as to their parents, to improve relationships and to become more whole (therefore spiritual). She needed to separate from her parents and from parental complexes, to become more competent in relationships and especially become more *whole* (spiritual). This way she would be able to develop a sense of self and be in contact with herself. In doing so I needed to keep in mind her above-mentioned complexes.

Conclusions and comments on the 'I+I' as metanarrative of Self-development

As underlined before, Carla presented herself in 2016 as a patient who was sociologically individualized and well adapted into individualized and liquid society: she had challenged the certainties of modern life; namely, the social order of the nation-state, class, gender, ethnicity and traditional family structure and had strived for Self-fulfilment and achievement. This helped us to consider her individualized (according to Beck), although not individuated (according to Jung).

Employing the Jungian–relational–psychosocial model, helped (as a tool) to attempt to understand this case, as well as to shed light on the nature of the development of narratives of self-identity at the beginning of the 21st century.[8]

With this vignette, I demonstrated that the 'I+I' is an alternative and competent way to examine the current development of narratives of self-development, in the attempt to bridge psychoanalysis and sociology, and thereby to frame and contextualize my analytic generalization within the 21st century advanced individualized society context.

More in detail, once the process of separation gets going for Carla, from an intrapsychic level, as well as underlined by Kast and Hillman, it is with dream 14 (death), when there was a change of paradigm. From this point, dream after dream, she enacted an intrapsychic-repairment-process and increased degree of separation and started to understand the insight her soul was sharing with her. Here is when she was able to feel she needed to ask for forgiveness. And this led her to re-gain her own integrity. Therefore, little by little, thanks to dreamwork, she was able to feel a sense of calmness and reassurance.

She also started to live her life taking into account providence (as opposed to linear thinking), renewed desire (appreciating the bliss of looking at stars), without having to come to an understanding, which is what Rilke suggested in the *Letters to a Young Poet*. She learned to obey (her) necessity: kiss Kam, and live accordingly. This case is helpful to underline that psychoanalysis is – as I will underline in the next and final chapter – *psychoagogia*: accompaniment of the soul.

Notes

1 Ibid.
2 See above (Chapter 4) Kast' and Hillman's definition of individuation, as comprising of four steps.

3 Of course, more could be made of the image of/association to Beckett? After all, he is a figure almost emblematic of late modernism. But I prefer to refrain from this, and only stating Carla´s comment about him.

4 I employ the word *pathology* not from a medical point of view. Therefore, I do not look at emotions as the study of disease, nor as the medical characteristics of a disease. I employ pathology looking at the etymology of this word. Therefore it´s Greek root in *pathos*: *suffering*, *experience*, or *emotion*.

5 Not included here.

6 'I'm walking trying to figure out how to get out or clean myself, but I don't know where the exit or the toilets are'.

7 See dreams 4, 5, 6, 7, 8.

8 The attentive reader might ask: What are the specific signs that this model is being applied, as distinct from alternative Jungian approaches? The answer lies in the recognition that the Jungian–relational–psychosocial model is able to recognize that a patient might be individualized but not yet individuated. Therefore, it proposes a (Jungian) psychosocial and relational approach when investigating the nature of development of narratives of self-identity at the beginning of the 21st century. Hence, it forces to look at the sociological context from a depth-psychological point of view, and, vice versa, it forces to look at *soul* from a sociological point of view.

Chapter 6

Conclusions

Absolute freedom is 'freedom after freedom'

In this work, I have proposed that in current 21st-century second-late-modern so-cieties, there is a renewed need for individuation. Therefore, this book provides an in-depth look at the concepts of individualization, individuation and freedom.

Additionally, I proposed that there is a gap when examining freedom from the psychoanalytical and sociological perspectives. This gap has to do with the bridg-ing (or lack thereof) of the two fields. I came to observe that therapists are not usually interested in freedom per se (as a sociological category) and sociologists are not interested in freedom from a psychological (or logical metaphysical) point of view.

In this work, I have proposed that in current 21st-century second-late-modern societies, there is a renewed need for individuation. Therefore, this book provides an in-depth look at the concepts of individualization, individuation and freedom.

In attempting to demonstrate the validity of this approach, I answered the follow-ing research question: What is the best tool to understand the nature of development of narratives of self-identity at the beginning of the 21st century? To do so, I claimed, there is a necessity to build a bridge from sociology towards psychoanalysis, or from Beck's individualization to Jung's individuation (and not vice versa), and in so doing, leave behind traditional sociology[1] in order to open the door to the unconscious with a psychosocial approach. To illustrate my findings, I used a clinical vignette, inspired by a patient who – during our first session – reported a 'sense of emptiness', of 'feel-ing stuck' and that 'sentimental relationships don't last'. In Chapter 5, I demonstrated that while this patient is sociologically individualized and (apparently) well adapted in a liquid society, she was not individuated when we first met.

Italian sociologists Chiara Giaccardi and Mauro Magatti, in their book, *Gen-erativi di tutto il mondo unitevi* (2014, p.68), asked themselves 'but if we have already freed ourselves, from what are we seeking freedom?' This work attempted to answer this question (proposing a 'Jungian–relational–psychosocial' model) and examined freedom not so much to answer the question what freedom is, but – if anything – to understand what freedom is after freedom – that is, the freedom ac-quired in the West since the Second World War, the events of 1968, the collapse of the communist/capitalist dualism and the fall of the Berlin Wall, when people have acquired physical but probably not absolute (psychological) freedom.

DOI: 10.4324/9781003390770-7

Wolfgang Giegerich (2020, p.58) claims that psychotherapy 'should fundamentally be comprehended as improvisation', which, for him, 'is the opposite of the application of a technique or of expert knowledge'. Therefore, when stressing that 'it is of course not enough if the *patient* starts to swim. The *therapist* has to do the same thing', he underlines that therapy is about co-participation and mutuality. Is freedom, too, about improvisation and co-participation? I intentionally leave this question unanswered, hoping that future research/researchers on this topic will continue this work and find their own answer.

Therefore, Giegerich suggests 'keep in mind the difference between the psychological (or logical metaphysical) level and a pragmatic level' (2020, p.92). Borrowing from Giegerich, I propose we must keep in mind the psychological (or logical metaphysical) level and a pragmatic level of freedom. Nelson Mandela (one of the giants associated with freedom in the 20th-century) helps us in this regard. In his autobiography *Long Walk to Freedom* (1995), he reminds us that 'to be free is not merely to cast off one's chains, but to live in a way that respects and enhances the freedom of others' – which to me sounds like *co-participation*. The chains of which Mandela speaks and from which we have freed ourselves are Giegerich's pragmatic level; the rest, I propose, is psychological freedom and that we must earn ourselves.

The theme of this work – retrospectively – is as follows: it is not sufficient to acquire pragmatic (physical) freedom, it is our duty to become absolutely free, which means becoming free at the psychological or logical metaphysical level. I will later describe what I propose absolute freedom to be.

Boris Groys, in his book *Antiphilosophy* (2012, pp.XXII–XXIII) reminds us of what Husserl coined *phenomenological reduction*. This consists,

in the subject's taking a mental distance from his own life interests – even the interests in his own survival – and in this way opening up a perspective in considering the world that is no longer confined by the needs of his empirical ego. By way of this broad phenomenological prospective one obtains the ability to do justice to all commands, by starting to experiment freely both in obeying them and refusing them. At the same time, the subject of the phenomenological reduction finds himself no longer required to transform the commands he receives into his conduct of life, or, conversely, to oppose them, since the phenomenological ego thinks as if it were not living. In this way one acquires for one's phenomenological ego a real 'as if' – an imaginary perspective of limitless life, in which all decisions of life lose their urgency, so that the opposition between carrying out and rejecting a command dissolves into the infinite play of life possibilities.

This, I propose, is psychoanalysis's supreme duty (and the 'Jungian-relational-psychosocial' model's task).

It can be said that once Husserl's *phenomenological reduction* has been reached, and only then, will it be possible to reach another step that corresponds to 'releasing oneself, namely one's releasing to or rather into oneself' (Giegerich, 2020, p.82). Giegerich underlines that this means 'releasing ourselves from our imprisonment in our subjectivity' and he adds that 'Jung wanted that we learn to face ourselves objectively, see ourselves from outside, as an objective vis-à-vis'. This means, according to the German therapist, becoming 'an other for myself, that is to say, I have to take myself as an objective fact' (Giegerich, 2020, p.82).

However, Giegerich also emphasizes that this is no easy task (as it is not easy to reach *phenomenological reduction*), because – he claims – 'we are enclosed within in our own subjectivity' and because 'we see ourselves only subjectively, in terms of our self-image, our ego-ideal and our demands upon ourselves' (Giegerich, 2020, p.82). Therefore, Giegerich adds, 'many people feel guilty or ashamed because they are not the way they ought to be' and this is when 'they think that *they* should be able to decide how they are', forgetting that 'their subjective thoughts and wishes' are 'molded after general moral principles or the values of one's social environment, which shows that our subjectivity is by no means isolated, solely subjective, but from the outset socially constructed' (Giegerich, 2020, p.82).

Only following this is it possible to understand a comment made by Giegerich in clinical supervision: he suggested that the patients *must drop all hopes and expectations*. This means, I propose, allowing *longings to arise* from one's own soul. When examining this, it is possible to understand that hopes and expectations are ego-driven while longings are related to the Self and arise from the soul. Thus, they come from God. As underlined in Chapter 4, longings are *vox Dei*, the voice of God, 'which often cuts sharply across our subjective intentions and may sometimes force an extremely disagreeable decision' (CW10, para.842).

Only then – as suggested in Chapter 4 – will people stop feeling in a constant void and suspended in a never-ending vacuum (similar to Italo Calvino's *Eutropia – see his book titled Invisible Cities* (1978)). Only then will the sublation happen and will people move from the *pragmatic level of freedom* to psychological (or logical metaphysical) freedom, which I term *absolute freedom* (which also equates to becoming individuated in an individualized second-late-modern society). Only then will people lose the neurotic need to move from city to city (as described by Calvino in *Invisible Cities* (1978)).

Italian Jungian psychotherapist Luigi Zoja wrote in his book *La morte del prossimo* (2009), that the French Revolution helped to subvert the vertical order of power and that the rigid, top-down patriarchal order that prevailed in 20th-century families and society was 'without uncertainty: and, in this sense, reassuring' (2009, p.84).[2] Zoja then reminds us that people have social duties but also 'the right to personal inspiration' and that 'the tension between freedom of desires and solidarity cannot find solutions, it can only reach balance' (2009, p.84). Zoja also reminds us that 'unlike solidarity, which can respond to some objective measurement and which supports personal limits shoulder to shoulder… Individual frenzies insinuate themselves into unconscious motivations and ultimately end up poisoning the very organisms that feed on them' (2009, p.85).

In line with Giegerich's suggestion to *drop all hopes and expectations*, Zoja proposes that we should replace desire, or animal appetites, with learning 'how to behave with others' and eschewing herd mentality (2009, pp.85–86). He also notes the 'tragic antinomy' between solidarity and equality on the one hand and 'the modern "right" to desire' on the other (2009, pp.85–86), with the 21st century favouring individual needs over the freedom that comes with fraternity and equality (2009, p.84). This, he says, is what positions us 'all on the side of evil: all responsible for the environmental and cultural degeneration of the planet' (2009, p.103) and he claims that 'self-criticism and personal assumption of responsibility are indispensable for a transformation to be lasting. This is not only a necessary condition in psychoanalytic therapy: it is even more so in attempts to transform society' (2009, pp.100–101). Thus, 'what is necessary is to de-individualise' (2009, p.100).

I concur with Zoja and propose that the concept of the 'I+I', which leads to freedom after freedom, therefore of *absolute freedom*, is related to self-criticism and personal assumption as well as the phenomenological reduction in a society such as the post-1989 one. Therefore, the 'I+I', freedom after freedom, *absolute freedom* is about *Laetitia*, which, as Spinoza puts it, is when 'the Mind moves on to greater perfection' (*Ethica*, III, prop.11). It could also be said it is when the soul moves on to greater perfection, ending ego-supremacy. It is the soul's move to an expansion of knowledge and gathering of insights.

In the concluding part of this concluding chapter, I wish to look at what I term as *absolute freedom* (by starting to focus on Marcuse's and Arendt's view on freedom).

Herbert Marcuse, in *Psychoanalysis and Politics*, underlines that 'freedom is always in relation to domination and authority' (1957, p.13) and Hannah Arendt, in *On Revolution*, affirms that: 'the existential conflict of modern times is not between different economical systems or classes, but between freedom and authorities' (2009, p.22). Are Marcuse's and Arendt's points of view still valid today?

Marcuse's statement can be certainly valid today but I challenge whether domination and authority have to be seen as an outer force – a *given* condition dependent on outer conditions (e.g. government, school, teacher, father/mother, partner, etc.) of authoritarian regimes – or whether we should consider such domination and authority as something a person has internalized and that is consciously or unconsciously activated, therefore inhibiting the subject form reaching freedom (in a non-authoritarian second-late-modern society).

When looking at Arendt's quote, I propose that such a statement could only be valid up to 1989 (in fact, it was written in 1963 from a post-war, East vs. West, good vs. bad, capitalism vs. communism and intellectual/elitist point of view), and I wish to stress that such a statement must be confined to the western world (Europe and the USA), and that careful attention must be paid to those countries (Russia or Turkey, just to name a couple) where the conflict – is again and anew – between freedom and authorities. See, for example, the oppressed and prosecuted freedom of speech or un-binary sexual orientation. Therefore, nowadays, certain countries that were democratic since 1989 are moving backwards to a condition of freedom in a state of pseudo-compulsion. Therefore, Arendt's quote is only applicable to modernity and second and late modernity (and not to a second-late modernity). In fact, if we exclude these three regions, we find that Arendt's claim remains relevant today (based on the evidence that the conflict between freedom and authorities still exists as a modern category today – not as a late or second-late-modern one). Hence, where authorities persist, there is no freedom for those affected by the coercion of the authority. And these individuals desperately seek to reach those places where this kind of freedom is granted. And sufficient to confirm this are the many examples of individuals escaping from current wars or authoritarian regimes, such as Syria, Afghanistan, Pakistan, Egypt and even Turkey now! These people (who become refugees and asylum seekers) are desperate to reach Europe, where freedom – physical, of speech and of movement – has been granted by law (although not fully by morality and culture) to all individuals, since 1945 or 1989.

Therefore, keeping in mind Beck's thesis: if, in late modernity, people have become liberated from traditional social ties and are now free to decide who to be and to become, why are people not yet *free*? Hence, quoting again Magatti and Giaccardi: 'if we already liberated ourselves, what other "liberation" must we therefore seek?' (2014, p.29).[3] Furthermore, this is – in my opinion – the main point for which it is necessary to build a bridge from sociology towards psychoanalysis (from Beck's individualization to Jung's individuation and not vice versa) because, to answer this question, one must leave behind sociology in order to open the door to the unconscious with a psychosocial approach.

When applying Arendt's quote to a late-modern society, does such a quote remain relevant even today? I propose that, in late modernity, where freedom (physical, of speech and of movement) is a given, individuals according to Beck, individualize – that is become *homo optionis*, in a society where 'biographies are removed from traditional precepts and certainties, from external control and general moral laws, becoming open and dependent on decision-making, and are assigned as a task for each individual' (Beck and Beck-Gernsheim, 2002, p.5) – therefore are the only owner of their future and of their freedom. But in so doing, Beck's research shows (as well as Barbara Hannah (1971)), that people might misinterpret Nietzsche´ claim that God is dead, and so they become their own God; hence, they have superpowers and feel immortal. Invulnerable. Rather, Nietzsche critiqued traditional religious and moral systems, encouraging individuals to create their own meanings and values in a world without inherent divine purpose. This emphasis on personal empowerment and existential freedom doesn't necessarily equate to individuals becoming their own gods, but rather taking responsibility for their own lives and actions in the absence of traditional religious frameworks. Here, Jung's compensation theory is once more important, particularly when examining the Lehman Brothers' crash, because in late modernity, people want more and more material gain as well as to *become someone* (thus avoiding becoming themselves, as alternatively suggested by Jung). Furthermore, while trying to become someone, they lose themselves in the never-ending race for supremacy (or 'the sausage', as underlined before (Giegerich, 2010, p.233)). The race to become the first and the best. In engaging in this race, they worship symbols (like the *golden calf* adored by Moses' people while he was climbing Mount Sinai). Hence, Magatti and Giaccardi (2014, p.29) suggest that in late modernity, 'freedom is reduced to consumption'.[4]

It is necessary then – keeping in mind Jung's question: 'but are we really free?' (CW18, para.1339) – to distinguish between two concepts: material freedom (when freedom is reduced to consumption) in contraposition to *absolute freedom*.

What I call absolute freedom is a possible merging of individualization and individuation: the 'I+I'. It is the process of becoming individuated in a second-late-modern society. It is our innate *striving for wholeness*, and the capacity to fulfil one's own destiny (Hillman, 1997b) in an electronically advanced, individualized second-late-modern 21st-century society. It is a sense of one's own inner realization (authentic not material). Therefore, not in a will-to-power effort but in an intimate process (that per Jung's individuation process might occur unnoticed or during analysis) to fulfil one's own destiny.

I propose that absolute freedom is a non-linear, uroboric process that starts much before one's birth. It is a trans-generational path, inherited from our parents, grandparents and ancestors, and that we leave in the hands of our children and grandchildren. When one is absolutely free, one becomes God. One becomes one-Self: whole. This correlates with Jung's idea that the Self is (the archetype of) the God-image.[5]

I employ the term *absolute freedom* not to mean that an individual should become like God, or God himself, but to reach a knowledge of oneself (and an acceptance of what one is) that will allow us to live our lives with an awareness of some of the most devouring complexes that limit our path to freedom.

However, just as absolute certainty is impossible, *absolute freedom* is also impossible. This is because people can reach a state of absolute freedom during their lifetimes, but they can also lose it (due to inner or outer circumstances) and gain it and lose it again (in an uroboric circle). Thomas Bernhard (1970) is eloquent in this regard when he claims that our whole life is nothing but a continuous effort to find ourselves again and again. We can also look at Ribi (2020), who claims that life must be a continuous transformation; otherwise, stagnation will bring death.

Therefore, absolute freedom, which is a generative process, means becoming individuated ('a process by which man lives out his innate human nature' (von Franz, in Jung, 1978, p.164)) in an individualized society. It is the opportunity to become oneself (*farsi sé*) in an individualized society; thus, a society where 'man and woman are released from the gender roles prescribed by industrial society for life in the nuclear family' while simultaneously

> forced, under pain of material disadvantage, to build up a life of their own by way of the labor market, training and mobility, and if need be to pursue this life at the cost of their commitments to family, relations and friends.
>
> (Beck-Gernsheim and Beck, 1995, p.6)

Absolute freedom occurs when people can live a life free from authorities. By this, I mean that it is a state of psychological freedom from the negative influence (or rather devouring influence) of authorities and of social (cultural) freedom beyond the class and gender roles prescribed by industrial (modern) society.

Absolute freedom is psychological and social (psychosocial) freedom from the effects that authorities have on us; it is psychological and social disenchainment (unleashing) from authorities. Therefore, it is a state of psychological and social freedom from the constellating complexes (or, at least, an opportunity to look at their devouring aspects) in relation to authorities. Authorities, in this regard, are not to be seen as *authoritarian regimes* only, as underlined above with Arendt.

Authorities, in this case, are anything – a person, an institution or their imago – that constellates our complexes (and that limits our psychosocial freedom): family, father, mother, partner, teacher, siblings, boss, school, institutions, communities, the government, etc. An authority is therefore anything that oppresses our individuation (particularly if we consider individuation to be a conscious/unconscious process, as Jung observed).

This does not mean – as one could imply – that what we need to do is to free ourselves from our complexes rather than from authorities (because is impossible! And those that tried to do so moving to the other side of the planet failed it – being devoured by nightmares). Rather, what I propose is that – when, as Colachicchi (2021) suggested, we let ourselves be supported by the hints suggested by the unconscious, we might be able solve a conflict related to a complex. Therefore, when we free ourselves from the authority complex, 'authorities' cease to have psychological authority over us. If we free ourselves from authorities in any other sense (than freeing ourselves from our complexes), our complexes and their authority over us will remain.

An example is the one of Nelson Mandela. He was under the 'social authority' of the South-African government that imprisoned him, but he was not under the psychological authority of such government. And this is what enabled him to endure captivity. He was imprisoned from a *social* point of view but free from a psychological one.

The concept of absolute freedom, then, is directly related to the Jungian concept of complexes (via regia to the unconscious) and Beck's individualization.

Absolute freedom, I propose, is also linked to the concepts of integrity, eros and *psychagogia*. Without indulging too much (hoping someone will do it after me), in this very last part of this book, I wish to look at these three concepts.

David H. Rosen (2002, p.XI) in the preface to Beebe's *Integrity in Depth* (2002) wrote that 'both integrity and the Self are spiritual concepts that unify and facilitate transcendence and transformation'. Beebe underlines that 'Integrity must be pursued as a desideratum in itself' (2002, p.15) and adds that 'the implication is that the real pleasure in exercising integrity in dealings with others is the discovery of integrity in itself' (2002, p.15).

Beebe underlines that integrity 'means, literally, the stage of being untouched' (2002, p.6) and he agrees with Robert Grudin (1999, pp.73–75), that 'integrity may be defined as psychological and ethical wholeness, sustained in time... integrity... is not a painfully upheld standard so much as a prolonged and focused delight' (2002, p.17).

From this, he (2002, p.19) looks at integrity versus violation and proposes that

when an individual's own integrity flourishes in relationship, both patient and therapist share the discovery of the integrity of interpersonal process as well. This shared field of integrity is the ground of any depth psychotherapy, and it is impossible to understand the burgeoning of psychotherapy in our century if one does not recognise the profound pleasure that the discovery of integrity brings.

Then Beebe adds that 'just as frequently (and some might argue, more frequently) integrity is located through the experience of violation. We may not even know we have a self until it becomes anxious, or angry – or until it has been raped' (2002, p.19). The violation of one's own integrity, therefore, compromises the possibility to attain any depth, therefore, to wish for absolute freedom. Depth psychotherapy (with the help of the Jungian-psychosocial-relational model), I proposed in the past few chapters, might help to attain – anew – such integrity. To attempt to repair rape! It is only in this context, that it is possible to understand what Beebe meant claiming that 'psychotherapy has been forced to realise [...] that its principle subject matter has always been, not, as Freud thought, pleasure and unpleasure but rather integrity and violation' (2002, p.19). Therefore, Beebe underlines: 'When psychotherapy is conducted with integrity, the miracle [of Tuccia's sieve] occurs. The unconscious libido is free to flow, yet stays contained' (Beebe, 2002, pp.52–53).

In *The Myth of Analysis*, James Hillman (1983, p.297) underlines that 'we can see the psyche going into therapy in search of eros' and that 'we have been looking for love of the soul'. He therefore claims that 'this is the myth of analysis'. In the previously mentioned vignette (Chapter 5), the patient – going into analysis – was exactly doing so (although unconsciously). She went in search for the eros and in search for love of the soul.

I propose that this, Hillman's 'myth of analysis' must turn into what I term *the new myth of analysis*. A return to the search for the eros and to go anew in search for love of the soul. But this will only be possible after recovery, which is 'if pleasure is the thesis, and violation the antithesis of the psychological experience of integrity, recovery is the synthesis' (Beebe, 2002, p.21).

I propose that in a 21st-century affluent and individualized society, there is a need for a *new myth of analysis*. When this will happen, *psychagogia*[6] will be possible.

Psychagogia translates as 'guidance of the soul' or 'soul-leading', as accompaniment of the patient's soul by the therapist, thanks to the art of rhetoric. Kalsched (2020, pp.147–148) gave an excellent example of this in his keynote paper at the International Association for Analytical Psychology (IAAP)'s congress in Vienna, 2019. When his patient dissociated because of her injury to her capacity to feel,

sensing that Beth was still struggling, I moved my chair closer to her and said, 'Beth please, just look at me!' Slowly her gaze met mine. 'Listen', I said, 'this is no longer just your problem... or just your lonely struggle... because my eyes have seen it too. I'm in this with you now, and I'm invested in what happens. It's our story now, and we're in it together. If we're going to get that child in you some help we'll have to do it together – so come back to me' I extended my hand and slowly, she reached over and took it.

This is not only an amazing example of rhetoric leading to *psychagogia* (accompaniment of the soul), but it is also an example of eros between two human beings, who happen to be a patient and a therapist.

What Kalsched underlines confirms Giegerich's (2020, p.58) proposal: that psychotherapy 'should fundamentally be comprehended as improvisation' and 'the opposite of the application of a technique or of expert knowledge'.

In essence, I propose that *psychagogia* might help (or be the opportunity) to move from Freud's 20th-century conception of 'ordinary unhappiness' to what I like call *ordinary spensieratezza*,[7] which brings about a state of calmness and reassurance (hence serenity). In this regard, Jung (1989, p.177) underlined,

to the extent that I managed to translate the emotions into images – that is to say, to find the images which were concealed in the emotions – I was inwardly calmed and reassured. Had I left those images hidden in the emotions, I might have been torn to pieces by them. There is a chance that I might have succeeded in splitting them off; but in that case I would inexorably have fallen into a neurosis and so been ultimately destroyed by them. As a result of my experiment I learned how helpful it can be, from the therapeutic point of view, to find the particular images which lie behind the emotions.

Therefore, this is when unconscious elements are integrated into conscious life. This, I propose, is comparable to Spinoza's *Laetitia* and could be linked to Husserl's *phenomenological reduction*, as well as Giegerich's suggestion to move from a subjective to an objective point of view.

I propose that Giegerich's claim to moving away from a subjective to an objective point of view is comparable with Husserl's phenomenological reduction, which consists

in the subject's taking a mental distance from his own life interests – even the interests in his own survival – and in this way opening up a perspective in considering the world that is no longer confined by the needs of his empirical ego.

(Groys, 2012, pp.XXII–XXIII)

When this happens, this is when 'the Mind moves on to greater perfection' (Spinoza, Ethica, III, prop.11)'. Therefore, it could also be said, it is when the soul moves on to greater perfection, ending ego-supremacy.

Therefore, *psychagogia* (which is the accompaniment of the soul) is an attempt – when looking at it from Shakespeare's point of view – to put right a time that is out of joint. The 'I+I' (that is about absolute freedom as freedom after freedom) also aims to put right time out of joint, although, as Hungarian philosopher Agnes Heller underlines, 'time is not set right in the sense of being returned to its former place, "new men" usher in new times' (2002, p.1).

In this regard, Heller adds that Hamlet 'was *born* to set right time out of joint' (2002, p.45) and that 'time is out of joint when reason and unreason are heterogeneous, when actors do not understand what they are doing and understand even less what others are doing or have done'. This, in essence, is why Carla came to analysis: to set time right, with the help of *psychagogia*. To restore eros, to regain her own integrity and ask for forgiveness (without the hope and expectation to be forgiven).

Heller – linking with Jung, Spinoza, Husserl and Giegerich – underlines that 'time is set right when Hamlet is able to know himself better' (2002, p.45). Therefore, I propose that, when 'Hamlet describes the chaos of the soul – a chaos that everyone who ever cast a sincere glance at himself recognizes in himself' (2002, p.45), he becomes absolutely free. Heller underlines that

> one of Hamlet's selves is alienated from the other, and all his lonely attempts to put them together, to mend the self thus torn, are in vain. They are in vain because he himself breaks the thread to sew the selves together. Hamlet cannot gather together his personality by his own effort.
>
> (2002, p.45)

Isn't this what happens when a patient comes into analysis? Isn't this a fair description of neurosis? When we take Carla's five years of analysis and compare it with Hamlet's journey (to freedom), we understand that becoming *absolutely free* is not possible alone. It requires the struggle of the soul and its trinity (ego, shadow, self) in a *psychagogic* relation. When taking Carla's five years of analysis, we understand that she came – beyond her dayworld claims – to ask herself a self-reflective question: *who am I?*

Notes

1 Sociology, I proposed, is unable to look at the unconscious.
2 My translation from Italian for this and all following quotes from Zoja.
3 Original quote in Italian: 'ma se ci siamo già liberati, di quale altra "liberazione" dobbiamo, dunque parlare?'
4 Original quote in Italian: 'la libertà è ridotta a consumo'.
5 See, for example, although not limited: Aion, para.109.
6 Socrates (in Plato's Phaedrus, 261a): claims that 'Is not rhetoric in its entire nature an art which leads the soul by means of words, not only in law courts and the various other public assemblages'.
7 In Italian, it means being carefree in a positive sense, i.e. free from serious thoughts or worries. To not be confused with carelessness. Synonyms: cheerfulness, gaiety, Letitia and serenity. Antonyms: pensiveness, worry, affliction and melancholy.

References

Abercrombie, N., Hill, S. and Turner, B. S. (2000). *The Penguin Dictionary of Sociology*. London: Penguin.

Adorno, T. W. (1978 [1944]). *Mínima Moralia*. London and New York: Verso.

Adorno, T. W., Frenkel-Brunswik, E., Levinson, D. J. and Nevitt Sanford, R. (2019 [1950]). *The Authoritarian Personality*. New York: Verso.

Adorno, T. W. and Horkheimer, M. (1976 [1944]). *Dialectic of Enlightenment*. London and New York: Continuum International Publishing Group Ltd.

Aldridge, J. (2014). 'The Intellectual Property of Women as It Relates to the Role of Sabina Spielrein in the Lives and Works of 20th Century Males Psychologists', *International Journal of Psychology and Counselling*, 6(5), pp.59–65.

Alighieri, D. (1993). *Divina Commedia: Inferno*. Bompiani: Milano.

Arendt, H. (2009 [1963]). *On Revolution*. London: Penguin Classics.

Aron, L. and Mitchell, S. A. (1999). *Relational Psychoanalysis, Volume 14: The Emergence of a Tradition*. New York and London: Routledge.

Asper, K. (1993). *The Abandoned Child Within*. New York: Fromm International Publishing Corporation.

Baudelaire, C. (1995 [1863]). *The Painter of Modern Life*. New York: Phaidon Press.

Bauman, Z. (2000). *Liquid Modernity*. Cambridge: Polity.

Bauman, Z. (2002). *Society under Siege*. Cambridge: Polity.

Bauman, Z. (2003). *Liquid Love*. Cambridge: Polity Press.

Bauman, Z. (2005). *Liquid Life*. Cambridge: Polity Press.

Bauman, Z. (2006). *Liquid Fears*. Cambridge: Polity Press.

Bauman, Z. (2007). *Liquid Times*. Cambridge: Polity Press.

Beck, U. (1992). *Risk Society: Towards a New Modernity*. London: Sage.

Beck, U. (1994). 'The reinvention of politics', in Beck, U., Giddens, A. and Lash, S. (Eds.), *Reflexive Modernization: Politics, Tradition and Aesthetics in the Modern Social Order*. Cambridge: Polity Press.

Beck, U. (2006). *Cosmopolitan Vision*. Cambridge: Polity Press.

Beck, U. (2007). 'The cosmopolitan condition: Why methodological nationalism fails', *Theory, Culture & Society*, 24(7–8), pp.286–290.

Beck, U. (2009). *World at Risk*. Cambridge: Polity Press.

Beck, U. (2016). *The Metamorphosis of the World*. Cambridge: Polity Press.

Beck, U. and Beck-Gernsheim, E. (2002). *Individualization: Institutionalized Individualism and Its Social and Political Consequences*. London: Sage.

Beck, U., Bonß, W., and Lau, C. (2003). 'The theory of reflexive modernization: Problematic, hypotheses and research programme', *Theory, Culture & Society*, 20(2), pp. 1–33.

Beck, U., and Lau, C. (2005). 'Second modernity as a research agenda: theoretical and empirical explorations in the meta-change of modern society', *The British Journal of Sociology*, 56(4), pp.525–557.

Beck, U. and Beck-Gernsheim, E. (2013). *Distant Love*. Cambridge: Polity Press.

Beck, U., Giddens, A. and Lash, S. (1994). *Reflexive Modernization. Politics, Tradition and Aesthetics in the Modern Social Order*. Cambridge: Polity Press.

Beck-Gernsheim, E. and Beck, U. (1995). *The Normal Chaos of Love*. Cambridge: Polity Press.

Beebe, J. (1992). *Integrity in Depth*. College Station: Texas A&M University Press.

Benjamin, J. (1977). 'The End of Internalization: Adorno's Social Psychology', *Thelos*, 32, pp.42–64.

Benjamin, J. (1988). *The Bonds of Love*. New York: Pantheon.

Benjamin, J. (1995). *Like Subjects, Love Objects: Essays on Recognition and Sexual Difference*. New Haven: Yale University Press.

Bernhard, T. (1970). *Gargoyles*. New York: Vintage International.

Bishop, P. (1995). *The Dionysian Self: C.G. Jung's Reception of Friedrich Nietzsche*. Berlin: De Gruyter.

Bishop, P. (2017). *On the Blissful Islands with Nietzsche & Jung: In the Shadow of the Superman*. London: Routledge.

Boyne, R. (2001). 'Cosmopolis and risk: A conversation with Ulrich Beck'. *Theory, Culture & Society*, 18(4), pp. 47–63.

Calvino, I. (1978). *Invisible Cities*. New York: Harcourt Brace Jovanovich.

Campbell, J. (1976). *The Portable Jung*. London: Penguin Classics.

Carpani, S. (2004). The Formation of Narratives of Self-identities. A Study of the Turkish Community in Berlin. Unpublished M.Phil. thesis. University of Cambridge.

Carpani, S. (2020). *Breakfast at Küsnacht: Conversations on C. G. Jung and Beyond*. Asheville: Chiron.

Casement, A. (2001). *Carl Gustav Jung*. London: Sage.

Casement, A. (2007). *Who Owns Jung?* London: Karnac.

Ceppa, L. (1994). 'Introduction', in A. Adorno (Ed.), *Minima Moralia*. Torino: Einaudi.

Clark, A. (1983). 'Sleeper in Metropolis', in *Changing Places*. London: Red Flame Music / Virgin Music Ltd. Retrieved from the internet on 11.1.2022. https://www.discogs.com/es/release/454520-Anne-Clark-Changing-Places.

Clark, A. (1984). 'Killing Time', in *Joined Up Writing*. London: Ink Records / Red Flame Music / Virgin Music Ltd. Retrieved from the internet on 11.1.2022. https://www.discogs.com/es/release/104637-Anne-Clark-Joined-Up-Writing.

Clark, A. (1987). 'This Be the Verse', in *Hopeless Cases*. London: 10 Records Ltd. / Virgin Records. Retrieved from the internet on 11.1.2022. https://www.discogs.com/release/191837-Anne-Clark-Hopeless-Cases.

Crespi, F., Jedlowski, P., and Rauty, R. (2000). *La sociologia: Contesti storici e modelli culturali*. Roma-Bari: Laterza.

Colacicchi, G. (2021). *Psychology as Ethics*. London: Routledge.

Del Lago, A. (1994), in Crespi, Jedlowski, and Rauty, 2000, (Del Lago, A. (1994), *Introduzione a D. Bloor*. Milano: Cortina.

Dieckmann, H. (1991). *Methods in Analytical Psychology*. Asheville: Chiron.

Dixon, P. (1999). *Nietzsche and Jung: Sailing a Deeper Night*. Frankfurt: Peter Lang.

Durkheim, E. (1982 [1895]). *The Rules of Sociological Method*. New York: The Free Press.

Durkheim, E. (2006 [1950]). *On Suicide*. London: Penguin Classics.

Encyclopædia Britannica Online. (2009). 'Frankfurt School'. http://www.britannica.com/EBchecked/topic/217277/Frankfurt-School (Retrieved 19 December 2009).

Erickson, E. H. (1995 [1950]). *Childhood and Society*. London: Vintage Books.

Eulert-Fuchs, D. (2020). 'The Other Between Fear and Desire', in E. Kiehl (Ed.), Vienna 2019. Encountering the Other: Within Us, between Us and in the World. Proceedings of the Twenty-First Congress of the International Association for Analytical psychology. Einsiedeln: Diamon Verlag.

Ferliga, P. (2005, unpublished). La marcia di Radetzky di Joseph Roth.

Finlayson, J. G. (2005). *Habermas a Very Short Introduction*. Oxford: Oxford UniversityPress.

Freud, S. (1969 [1915–1917])). *Introduzione alla psicoanalisi*. Torino: Boringhieri.

Freud, S. (1991 [1917]). *Introductory Lectures on Psychoanalysis*. London: Penguin.

Freud, S. (2002 [1930]). *Civilization and Its Discontents*. London: Penguin.

Frey-Rohn, L. (1974). *From Freud to Jung*. New York: Dell Publishing.

Fromm, E. (1941). *Escape from Freedom*. New York: Holt Paperbacks.

Fromm, E. (2020 [1947]). *Man for Himself*. London: Routledge.

Frosh, S. (2013). 'Transdisciplinary Tension and Psychosocial Studies', *Enquire*, 6(1), pp.1–15.

Frosh, S. (2014). 'The Nature of the Psychosocial: Debates from Studies in the Psychosocial', *Journal of Psycho-Social Studies*, 8(1).

Garavelli, B. (1993). 'Introduzione', in D. Alighieri (Ed.), *Divina Commedia: Inferno*. Milano: Bompiani.

Giaccardi, C. and Magatti, M. (2022). *Supersocietà. Ha ancora senso scommettere sulla libertà?* Milano: Il Mulino.

Giddens, A. (1990). *The Consequences of Modernity*. Cambridge: Polity Press.

Giddens, A. (1991). *Modernity and Self-identity. Self and Society in the Late Modern Age*. Cambridge: Polity.

Giddens, A. (1992). *The Transformation of Intimacy: Sexuality, Love and Eroticism in Modern Societies*. Cambridge: Polity.

Giddens, A. (1994). *Reflexive Modernization*. Cambridge: Polity.

Giddens, A. (1998). *The Third Way: The Renewal of Social Democracy*. Cambridge: Polity.

Giddens, A. (2015). Obituary for Ulrich Beck. In *Süddeutsche Zeitung*, 5/6 January, p.9.

Giddens, A. and Pierson, C. (1992). *Conversations with Anthony Giddens: Making Sense of Modernity*. Cambridge: Polity.

Giddens, A. and Pierson, C. (1997). *Sociology*. Cambridge: Polity.

Giegerich, W. (2010). *The Collected English Papers, Vol. 4: The Soul Always Thinks*. New Orleans: Spring Journal Books.

Giegerich, W. (2020). *What Are the Factors that Heal?* London and Ontario: Dusk Owl Books.

Gray, R. (1996). *Archetypal Explorations: Towards an Archetypal Sociology*. London: Routledge.

Gross, O. (2009). *Selected Work*. New York: Mindpiece.

Groys, B. (2012). *Antiphilosophy*. London and New York: Verso.

Grudin, R. (1999). *The Grace of Great Things*. New York: Ticknor & Fields.

Hannah, B. (2001 [1971]). *Striving Towards Wholeness*. Wilmette: Chiron.

Hargaden, H. and Schwartz, J. (2007). 'Editorial', *European Journal of Psychotherapy and Counselling*, 9(1), pp.3–5.

Havel, V. (1976). *Horský Hotel*. Venezia: Marsilio.

Held, D. (1980). *Introduction to Critical Theory: Horkheimer to Habermas*. Berkeley: University of California Press.

Heller, A. (2002). *The Time Is Out of Joint: Shakespeare as Philosopher of History*. Lanham: Rowman & Littlefield Publishers.

Hillman, J. (1975). *Revisioning Psychology*. New York: Harper & Row.

Hillman, J. (1983). *The Myth of Analysis: Three Essays in Archetypal Psychology*. New York: Harper Collins.

Hillman, J. (1997a). *Archetypal Psychology*. Woodstock: Spring Publications.

Hillman, J. (1997b). *The Soul's Code: In Search of Character and Calling*. New York: Ballantine Books.

Hillman, J. and Shamdasani, S. (2013). *Lament of the Dead: Psychology After Jung's Red Book*. New York: Norton & Company.

Horkheimer, M. (1979 [1972]). *La Società di Transizione*. Torino: Einaudi.

Huskinson, L. (2004). *Nietzsche and Jung: The Whole Self in the Union of Opposites*. London: Routledge.

Jacoby, J. (1973 [1942]). *The Psychology of C. G. Jung*. London: Routledge.

Jaffe, A. (1979). *C. G. Jung, Word and Image*. Princeton: Princeton University Press.

Jarrett, J. L. (1981). 'Schopenhauer and Jung', in Renos Papadopoulos (Ed.), *Carl Gustav Jung, Critical Assessments*. London and New York: Routledge, pp.83–93.

Jung, C. G. Except as below, references are to the *Collected Works* (CW) and by volume and paragraph number.

Jung, C. G. (1967 [1916b]). 'The Structure of the Unconscious', in H. Read, M. Fordham and G. Adler (Eds.). W. McGuire (Executive Ed.). R. F. C. Hull (Trans.), *The Collected Works of C. G. Jung*. Princeton: Princeton University Press. [Hereafter *Collected Works*]: *Volume 7: Two Essays on Analytical Psychology*, 2nd Edition.

Jung, C. G. (1969 [1916c]). 'The Transcendent Function', in *Collected Works, Volume 8: The Structure and Dynamics of the Psyche*, 2nd Edition.

Jung, C. G. (1966 [1946]). 'The Psychology of the Transference', in *Collected Works, Volume 16: The Practice of Psychotherapy*, 2nd Edition.

Jung, C. G. (1967 [1912]). *Collected Works, Volume 5: Symbols of Transformation*.

Jung, C. G. (1967). *Collected Works, Volume 7: Two Essays on Analytical Psychology*, 2nd Edition.

Jung, C. G. (1968). *Collected Works, Volume 12: Psychology and Alchemy*.

Jung, C. G. (1969 [1934]). 'A Study in the Process of Individuation', in *Collected Works, Volume 9i: The Archetypes and the Collective Unconscious*, 2nd Edition.

Jung, C. G. (1970). 'A Psychological View of Conscience', in *Collected Works, Volume 10: Civilization in Transition*, 2nd Edition.

Jung, C. G. (1970). *Collected Works, Volume 11: Psychology and Religion: West and East*.

Jung, C. G. (1971 [1921]). *Collected Works, Volume 6: Psychological Types*, 2nd Edition.

Jung, C. G. (1977). *Collected Works, Volume 18: The Symbolic Life: Miscellaneous Writings*.

Jung, C. G. (1979 [1955]). *Collected Works, Volume 14: Mysterium Coniunctionis*, 2nd Edition.

Jung, C. G. (1989 [1916a]). 'Septem Sermones ad Mortuos', in *Memories, Dreams, Reflections*. New York: Vintage Books.

Jung, C. G. ([1977]). *C. G. Jung Speaking: Interviews and Encounters* (W. McGuire and R. F. C. Hull, Eds.). London: Thames & Hudson.

Jung, C. G. (1978 [1964]). *Man and His Symbols*. London: Picador.

Jung, C. G. (1984). *Seminar on Dream Analysis*. Princeton: Princeton University Press.

Jung, C. G. (1989 [1961]). *Memories, Dreams, Reflections*. New York: Vintage Books.

Jung, C. G. (1990). *Analytical Psychology*. London: ARK Paperbacks.

Jung, C. G. (1990b [1976]). *C. G. Jung Letters: 1951–1961* (G. Adler and A. Jaffé, Eds., R. F. C. Hull, Trad., Vol. 2). Brighton: Routledge.

Jung, C. G. (1997 [1965]). *Jung's Seminar on Nietzsche's Zarathustra* (J. L. Jarrett, Ed.). Princeton: Princeton University Press.

Jung, C. G. (2009). *The Red Book*. New York: Norton & Company.

Jung, C. G. (2014 [1958]). *The Undiscovered Self: Present and Future*. London: Routledge.

Kalsched, D. (2020). 'Opening the Closed Heart: Affect-Focused Clinical Work with the Victims of Early Trauma', in E. Kiehl (Ed.), Vienna 2019. *Encountering the Other: Within Us, Between Us and in the World. Proceedings of the Twenty-First Congress of the International Association for Analytical psychology*. Einsiedeln: Diamon Verlag.

Kast, V. (1993). 'Animus and Anima: Spiritual Growth and Separation', *Harvest*, 39, pp.5–15.

Kaufmann, W. (1977). *The Portable Nietzsche*. London: Penguin.

Kaufmann, W. (1980). *Freud, Adler, and Jung*. London: Routledge.

Langwieler, G. (2018). 'Jung's Theory of Neurosis between Dissociation and Imagination', *Zeitschrift für Analytische Psychologie*, 190, 2/2018.

Larkin, P. (1971). 'This be The Verse', in *Collected Poems*. London: Faber and Faber. Retrieved from the internet on 11.1.2022. https://www.poetryfoundation.org/poems/48419/this-be-the-verse.

Lash, S. and Friedman, J. (1992). *Modernity and Identity*. Hoboken: Wiley-Blackwell.

Layton, L. (2013). 'Dialectical Constructivism in Historical Context: Expertise and the Subject of Late Modernity', *Psychoanalytic Dialogues*, 23, pp.126–149.

Loewenthal, D. (2014). 'The Magic of the Relational?', in D. Loewenthal and A. Samuels (Eds.), *Relational Psychotherapy, Psychoanalysis and Counselling: Appraisals and Reappraisals*. London: Routledge.

Lopez-Pedraza, R. (2018 [2000]). *Dionysus in Exile: On the Repression of the Body and Emotion*. Asheville: Chiron.

Lukes, S. (1982). 'Introduction', in E. Durkheim (Ed.), *The Rules of Sociological Method*. New York: The Free Press.

Lyotard, J.-F. (1984 [1957]). *The Postmodern Condition: A Report on Knowledge*. Minneapolis: University of Minnesota Press.

Magatti, M. (2018). 'Non può esserci libertà senza responsabilità', *Corriere della Sera*. Retrieved from the internet on 11.11.2018. https://www.corriere.it/opinioni/18_settembre_10/non-puo-esserci-liberta-007b4212-b450-11e8-8b0b-dff47915528b.shtml.

Magatti, M. and Giaccardi, C. (2014). *Generativi di tutto il mondo unitevi*. Milano: Feltrinelli.

Mandela, N. (1995). *Long Walk to Freedom: The Autobiography of Nelson Mandela*. New York: Back Bay Books.

Marcuse, H. (1969 [1957]). *Psicanalisi e Politica*. Bari: Laterza.

Marcuse, H. (1974 [1955]). *Eros and Civilization*. Boston: Beacon Press.

Marcuse, H. (1986 [1964]). *One-Dimensional Man*. London: Ark.

McFarland Solomon, H. (2007). 'The Transcendent Function and Hegel's Dialectical Vision', in A. Casement (Ed.), *Who Owns Jung?*

Merton, T. (1999). *The Seven Storey Mountain*. Boston: Mariner Books.

Mythen, G. (2020). 'Ulrich Beck: E-Special Introduction,' *Theory, Culture & Society*, 37(7–8), pp.383–409.

Moore, R. and Gillette, D. (1991). *King, Warrior, Magician, Lover*. San Francisco: Harper Collins.

Nagy, M. (1991). *Philosophical Issues in the Psychology of C. G. Jung*. New York: State University of New York Press.

Niebuhr, R. (1955). *The Self and the Dramas of History*. New York: Scribner's.Nietzsche, F. (1969 [1901]). *The Will to Power*. New York: Vintage Books.

Orbach, S. (1998). *Fat Is a Feminist Issue*. London: Arrow.

Orbach, S. (1999). *The Impossibility of Sex*. London: Penguin.

Orbach, S. (2014). 'Democratizing Psychoanalysis', in D. Loewenthal and A. Samuels (Eds.), *Relational Psychotherapy, Psychoanalysis and Counselling: Appraisals and Reappraisals*.

Orbach, S. (2020). 'How Are Women today? Feminism, Love and Revolution', in S. Carpani (Ed.), *Breakfast at Küsnacht: Conversations on C. G. Jung and Beyond*.

Peay, P. (2015). *America on the Couch: Psychological Perspectives on American Politics and Culture*. Brooklyn: Lanters Books.

Progoff, I. (1956). *The Death and Rebirth of Psychology: An Integrative Evaluation of Freud, Adler, Jung, and Rank and the Impact of their Culminating Insights on Modern Man*. London: Routledge.

Progoff, I. (2013 [1955]). *Jung's Psychology and its Social Meaning*. London: Routledge.

Rainwater, J. (1989). *Self-therapy: A Guide to Becoming Your Own Therapist*. New York: Harper Collins.

Ribi, A. (2020). 'C. G. Jung, von Franz and Alchemy', in S. Carpani (Ed.), *Breakfast at Küsnacht: Conversations on C.G. Jung and Beyond*.

Ricoeur, P. (1977). *Freud and Philosophy: An Essay on Interpretation*. New Haven: Yale University Press.

Rimbach, P. K. (2011). *Retirement: Life's Mt. Everest: Man's Journey Through Psychological Hell*. Self-Published (Xlibris.com).

Rocher, G. (1989). *Introduzione alla Sociologia Generale*. Milano: SugarCo Edizioni.

Rosen, D. H. (2005). 'Preface', in J. Beebe (Ed.), *Integrity in Depth*. College Station: Texas A&M University Press.

Roth, J. (1999 [1932]). *La marcia di Radetzky*. Milano: Adelphi.

Saban, M. (2019). *'Two Souls Alas...': Jung's Two Personalities and The Making of Analytical Psychology*. A thesis submitted for the degree of Doctor of Philosophy. University of Essex.

Sadock, B. J., Ahmad, S. and Sadock, V. A. (2001). *Kaplan and Sadock's Pocket Handbook of Clinical Psychiatry*. Philadelphia: Lippincott Williams and Wilkins.

Samuels, A. (1985). *Jung and the Post-Jungians*. London: Routledge.

Samuels, A. (1989). *The Plural Psyche*. London: Routledge.

Samuels, A. (1993). *The Political Psyche*. Oxford: Taylor & Francis.

Samuels, A. (2001). *Politics on the Couch*. London: Profile Books.

Samuels, A. (2012, unpublished). The Analyst is as Much "in the Analysis" as the Patient (1929): Jung as a Pioneer of Relational Psychoanalysis.

Samuels, A. (2014). 'Appraising the Role of the Individual in Political and Social Change Processes: Jung, Camus, and the Question of Personal Responsibility-Possibilities and Impossibilities of "'Making a Difference'", *Psychotherapy and Politics International*, 12(2), pp.99–110.

Samuels, A. (2015). *A New Therapy for Politics*. London: Karnac.

Shamdasani, S. (2003). *Jung and the Making of Modern Psychology: The Dream of a Science*. Cambridge: Cambridge University Press.

Singer, T. and Kimbles, S. L. (2004). *The Cultural Complex*. Essex and New York: Brunner-Routledge.

Sørensen, M.P. and Christiansen, A. (2013). *Ulrich Beck: An Introduction to The Theory Of Second Modernity And The Risk Society.* London: Routledge.

Spielrein, S. (1994). 'Destruction as the Cause of Coming into Being', *Journal of Analytical Psychology*, 39, pp.155–186.

Spinoza, B. (2021). *Ethica.* Kindle Edition.

Staude, J. R. (1976). 'From Depth Psychology to Depth Sociology: Freud, Jung, and Lévi-Strauss', *Theory and Society*, 3(3), pp.303–338.

Stein, M. (1998). *Jung's Map of the Soul.* Chicago: Open Court.

Stein, M. (2005). 'Individuation: Inner Work', *Journal of Jungian Theory and Practice*, 7(2), pp.1–13.

Stein, M. (2006). 'Individuation', in R. Papadopoulous (Ed.), *The Handbook of Jungian Psychology.* London: Routledge.

Tacey, D. (2012). *The Jung Reader.* London: Routledge.

Thompson, C. (1950). *Psychoanalysis: Evolution and Development.* New York: Hermitage House.

Umbach, M. and Huppauf, B. (2005). *Vernacular Modernism: Heimat, Globalisation, and the Built Environment.* Stanford: Stanford University Press.

von Franz, M.-L. (1964). 'The Process of Individuation', in C. G. Jung (Ed.), *Man and His Symbols.* Garden City: Doubleday.

van Krieken, R. (2002). 'The paradox of the "two sociologies": Hobbes, Latour and the constitution of modern social theory', *Journal of Sociology*, 38(3), pp.255–273.

Walker, G. (2017). *Jung and Sociological Theory: Readings and Appraisal.* London: Routledge.

Walker, G. (2012). 'Sociological Theory and Jungian Psychology', *History of the Human Sciences*, 25(1).

Watkins, M. (2003). 'Dialogue, Development, and Liberation', in I. Josephs (Ed.), *Dialogicality in Development.* Westport, CT: Greenwood. Retrieved from the internet: https://www.pacifica.edu/wp-content/uploads/2017/01/DialogueDevelopmentLiberatio.pdf

Watkins, M. (2013). *Accompaniment: Psychosocial, Environmental, Trans-Species, Earth.* Retrieved from the internet: http://mary-watkins.net/library/Accompaniment-Psychosocial-Environmental-Trans-Species-Earth.pdf.

Watkins, M. and Shulman, H. (2008). *Toward Psychologies of Liberation.* New York: Palgrave Macmillan.

Winnicott, D. W. (1989 [1965]). *The Family and Individual Development.* London: Routledge.

Winnicott, D. W. (1990 [1965]). *The Maturational Process and the Facilitating Environment.* London: Karnac.

Winnicott, D. W. (1991 [1953]). *Playing and Reality.* London: Routledge.

Woodman, D. (2009). 'The Mysterious Case of the Pervasive Choice Biography: Ulrich Beck, Structure/Agency, and the Middling State of Theory in the Sociology of Youth', *Journal of Youth Studies*, 12(3), pp.243–256.

Wollheim, R. (1971). *Freud.* New York: Harper Collins.

Wollheim, R. (1971). *Freud.* New York: Harper Collins.

Zoja, L. (1999). *Coltivare l'Anima.* Bergamo: Moretti & Vitali.

Zoja, L. (2009). *La Morte del Prossimo.* Torino: Einaudi.

Zweig, S. (2015 [1931]). *Freud.* Roma: Castelvecchi.

Afterword: Stefano Carpani and the Birth of Neo-Jungian Studies

I remember meeting Stefano Carpani for the first time (2016) and was struck by his energy and enthusiasm and the lasting impression he made upon me. There was an undeniable presence, and he exuded such momentum that I had no other choice but to come to one conclusion: Stefano would become a major voice and leading light in Jungian and Post-Jungian Studies (although he prefers to call them "neo-Jungian Studies").

That initial intuition was proven correct as Stefano completed publication after publication, delivered keynote addresses at prestigious conferences, organized international conferences (including the most recent 5th *Analysis and Activism* Conference in Ljubljana), and stood at the forefront of creative and ground-breaking projects, living the psychosocial ideas and values he sought to express throughout his writing, videos and research.

Stefano's tireless efforts to carve a space for *Jungian relational psychosocial studies* through the conceptualization of the 'I+I' culminates in the book you now hold in your hands. This book may be situated as the third part of what may be considered Stefano's 'freedom trilogy', which includes his paper titled *The Consequences of Freedom: Moving Beyond the Intermediate States of Broken Individualisation and Liquidity*[1], and his edited book titled *Individuation and Liberty in a Globalized World: Psychosocial Perspectives on Freedom After Freedom* (Routledge, 2022).

I will not repeat how the current book came to fruition and when the seeds of Stefano's ideas began to germinate, which he covers in his Introduction. What I would like to leave you with is what I appreciate most about Stefano – his unwavering commitment to living and shaping his ideas through his activism and actions in the world. He is a testament to the fact that theory cannot be divorced from the way we conduct ourselves, the relationships we maintain, break and/or repair, the battles we decide to fight, and the choices we make as we navigate an uncertain world that never ceases to challenge the core of our being. In other words, his attempt to find balance between inner and outer, thought and action, individual and collective *is* the challenge of cultivating individuation in an individualized society – the search for what it means to exist in a state of *absolute freedom*. Theory is not divorced from reality but can only be informed by it.

I once asked Stefano what he understood as 'activism'. He referred to the words and sentiments of Italian poet Giovanni Raboni. Activism does not mean to be merely active with your hands and body, but with your mind. Raboni writes, in his poem *Politica estera* (1996):

> The speaker has to say
> The thing he says and maybe not
> Or maybe others.
> But it is a fact that those who keep silent
> Let everything happen to them and what is worse
> Let what has been done to them
> Be done to someone else.

Raboni's words are those by which Stefano lives, a constant reminder of our responsibility to act and to speak truth to power.

With the onset of the pandemic, Stefano offered free counselling for those in need. The work gained momentum and became the initiative, *Accogliere le ferrite di chi cura*. Stefano and a group of colleagues provided free, online psychological support to doctors, nurses, and other health professionals engaged in the frontline battle to treat COVID-19 patients in Italy. Later in 2020, services were made available to include the wider Italian population, with 140 colleagues volunteering and offering four free counselling sessions to anyone in need. During the same period, Stefano joined forces with sociologist Mauro Magatti to develop *La prossima gerazione*, a think tank dedicated to the under 40s, encouraging them to creatively imagine a 'new' Italy post pandemic. This initiative was borne out of the urgent necessity of empowering younger generations to take responsibility for relaunching society and to counter the malaise that embedded itself due to successive lockdowns. Alongside this, Stefano curated a speaker series entitled *Lockdown Therapy*, which entailed conversations with Jungian analysts on a variety of topics related to, and emotions arising from, the pandemic. This became the foundation for part one of Stefano's edited volume (co-edited with Monica Luci), *Lockdown Therapy: Jungian Perspectives on How the Pandemic Changed Psychoanalysis* (Routledge, 2022). This period of isolation and distance – which gave rise to our desire to connect in novel ways and through largely digital means – compelled Stefano, alongside Bernhard von Guretzky and Paul Attinello, to launch a digital salon entitled *Psychosocial Wednesdays*. The series is now in its fifth season and continues to bring together authoritative voices from Jungian and Post and Neo-Jungian Studies to reflect upon the most urgent issues facing us today; it is another outlet through which Stefano has shown his commitment to thinking and acting psychosocially.

When Russia's invasion of Ukraine gave rise to a new humanitarian crisis, Stefano contacted two colleagues – Jakob Lusensky and Johanne Schwensen [2] – to suggest to take action and create (what few days later became)*Therapists for Ukraine*, based on the previous model Stefano devised for free counselling services during the pandemic. In less than a week of launching the project, 200 volunteers had signed up and each had no less than three individual cases. Sessions were open to anyone directly impacted by the war in Ukraine, which ensured that the initiative transcended perceived boundaries and enshrined inclusivity at its core. In parallel, Stefano launched a new web series entitled *War as Reset*, which reflects on the nature of war from multiple disciplinary angles while centring depth psychological approaches as the foundation and starting point for meaningful conversation. This became the foundation for part one of Stefano's forthcoming edited volume (co-edited with Ludmilla Ostermann), *War as Reset: Insights from Contemporary Analytical Psychology on the Age of Hypocrisy* (Routledge, 2025).

Stefano's membership of the Fondazione Arché (which he has held since 1996) is also noteworthy. Arché is a non-profit organization that actively responds to the plight of sick children and has since expanded its activities to speak to the most pressing humanitarian crises of our times. In June 2022, Stefano joined a humanitarian convoy from Milan to Lviv, driving 28 hours nonstop to deliver humanitarian aid to this region of western Ukraine devastated by relentless Russian bombings and attacks.

In focusing on Stefano's activism, it would be remiss of me to neglect his theoretical contributions that may be framed as *kulturkritik* broadly defined. His understanding of a *Neo-Jungian* approach complementing Andrew Samuels' Post-Jungian ethos has been both controversial and illuminating; his insistence on a specifically Essex School of Jungian Studies has aptly captured an approach in need of articulation. Yet his desire to bring structure to the new does not overshadow his deep respect for the roots of Jungian traditions. His illuminating interviews with Jungian analysts – captured in the web series and publication titled *Breakfast at Küsnacht* (Chiron, 2020) – will no doubt become a classic and is highly regarded as a key contribution to the oral history of our discipline. His *Anthology of Contemporary Theoretical/Clinical Classics in Analytical Psychology: The New Ancestors* (which granted him his first *Gradiva* nomination as "Best Edited Book in 2022"), collects seminal papers that have defined the field while providing unique reflections – from the authors – on the impact of their work. Crucially, the book includes Stefano's own manifesto for the future of Jungian Studies, blending both his intuition and thinking in producing a mission statement and agenda up to 2050 ("The Agenda 2050 for Analytical Psychology").

His profound commitment to the dissemination of influential texts while promoting the creativity of future scholars and practitioners finds expression in his project *Jungianeum: Initiatives for Contemporary Analytical Psychology and Neo-Jungian Studies*. Under this umbrella, since 2022, Stefano is developing a series of initiatives called: *JUNGIANEUM/Books: Re-Covered Classics in Analytical Psychology; JUNGIANEUM/Talks: Psychosocial Wednesday; JUNGIANEUM/Yearbook for Contemporary Neo-Jungian Studies; and JUNGIANEUM/Masterclasses* (in collaboration with Pacifica Graduate Institute, USA). As per his YouTube interviews and published books and papers, Stefano wishes these initiatives will continue to help Carl Gustav Jung's psychology become visible and audible, therefore, impactful for individuals and collectives, who benefit – respectively – from Jungian therapy and our knowledge in shaping policy and society.

The initiative ensures that future generations continue to benefit from the deep knowledge and foundation created by those who have come before.

Stefano's devotion to research extends to a research-led approach to educational initiatives.

This includes his partnership with Pacifica Graduate Institute in developing a series of online lectures delivered by senior figures in the field and his continued contribution as a lecturer at the C. G. Jung Institute (Zurich) and beyond (which includes engagements in Brazil, China, The United States, France, Spain and Italy).

This list of accomplishments is neither extensive nor is meant to be a record of Stefano's 'good deeds.' What I want to highlight is the real impact Stefano's work has had on diverse communities, and the mutually enriching relationship that he has cultivated between research and activism. In fact, Verena Kast took note of this and eloquently highlighted it in her preface to Stefano's debut book, Breakfast at Küsnacht (2020), that we should expect a rich contribution from him: "Breakfast at Küsnacht: this title is intended to link the various interviews. Why Breakfast at Küsnacht […]. Is it his "breakfast"—and can we expect other nourishing activities in the course of time?"

Stefano lives what he writes, and what he writes is informed by how he chooses to live. Above all else, I want to articulate what I saw in him initially and what has been reinforced time and again throughout the many years since our first encounter. There is an urgent necessity in him, something that calls and compels him to act, write and research, something that drives him to do what is necessary for the greater good.

Kevin Lu, PhD, Professor of Applied Psychoanalysis

Royal Central School of Speech and Drama,
University of London, UK

Notes

1 in E. Brodersen, and P. Amezaga (Eds.), 2020. *Jungian Perspectives on Indeterminate States: Betwixt and Between Borders*. London: Routledge.
2 Founders and owners of *It's complicated*, an online platform and community for psychologists, therapists, consultants and coaches who want to expand their practice and strengthen their professional identity online.

Index

Note: Page numbers followed by "n" denote endnotes.

For Product Safety Concerns and Information please contact our EU
representative GPSR@taylorandfrancis.com
Taylor & Francis Verlag GmbH, Kaufingerstraße 24, 80331 München, Germany

www.ingramcontent.com/pod-product-compliance
Lightning Source LLC
Chambersburg PA
CBHW050656280326
41932CB00015B/2934

9 781032 487847